The Antihero in American Television

"Combining an informative survey of salient research in psychology and philosophical aesthetics with careful conceptual analysis and close examinations of well-known television series, Margrethe Bruun Vaage's book offers a fresh perspective on the nature of contemporary American television drama and the ways it engages viewers. Exemplifying the virtues of the best interdisciplinary scholarship in the humanities, this book opens up new avenues of research for television studies scholars, cognitivist theorists, and philosophers of film, and will also appeal to any students or scholars with an interest in the question of what makes characters like Tony Soprano and Walter White so compelling."

—*Ted Nannicelli, University of Queensland, Australia*

The antihero prevails in recent American drama television series. Characters such as mobster kingpin Tony Soprano (*The Sopranos*), meth cook and gangster-in-the-making Walter White (*Breaking Bad*) and serial killer Dexter Morgan (*Dexter*) are not morally good, so how do these television series make us engage in these morally bad main characters? And what does this tell us about our moral psychological make-up, and more specifically, about the moral psychology of fiction?

Vaage argues that the fictional status of these series deactivates rational, deliberate moral evaluation, making the spectator rely on moral emotions and intuitions that are relatively easy to manipulate with narrative strategies. Nevertheless, she also argues that these series regularly encourage reactivation of deliberate, moral evaluation. In so doing, these fictional series can teach us something about ourselves as moral beings—what our moral intuitions and emotions are, and how these might differ from deliberate, moral evaluation.

Margrethe Bruun Vaage is Lecturer in Film at the University of Kent, UK. She explores the spectator's engagement with fictional film and television series. She has published in numerous anthologies and journals such as the *British Journal of Aesthetics, Midwest Studies in Philosophy* and *Screen*.

Routledge Advances in Television Studies

1 **Parody and Taste in Postwar American Television Culture**
Ethan Thompson

2 **Television and Postfeminist Housekeeping**
No Time for Mother
Elizabeth Nathanson

3 **The Antihero in American Television**
Margrethe Bruun Vaage

The Antihero in American Television

Margrethe Bruun Vaage

Routledge
Taylor & Francis Group
NEW YORK AND LONDON

First published 2016
by Routledge
711 Third Avenue, New York, NY 10017

and by Routledge
2 Park Square, Milton Park, Abingdon, Oxon OX14 4RN

Routledge is an imprint of the Taylor & Francis Group, an informa business

© 2016 Taylor & Francis

The right of Margrethe Bruun Vaage to be identified as author of this work
has been asserted by her in accordance with sections 77 and 78 of the
Copyright, Designs and Patents Act 1988.

All rights reserved. No part of this book may be reprinted or reproduced or
utilised in any form or by any electronic, mechanical, or other means, now
known or hereafter invented, including photocopying and recording, or in
any information storage or retrieval system, without permission in writing
from the publishers.

Trademark notice: Product or corporate names may be trademarks or
registered trademarks, and are used only for identification and explanation
without intent to infringe.

Library of Congress Cataloging-in-Publication Data

Vaage, Margrethe Bruun, 1975-
The antihero in American television / by Margrethe Bruun Vaage.
   pages cm. — (Routledge advances in television studies; 3)
Includes bibliographical references and index.
   1. Antiheroes on television. 2. Television—Social aspects—United
States. I. Title.
PN1992.8.A65V33 2015
791.45'652—dc23   2015022260

ISBN: 978-1-138-88597-4 (hbk)
ISBN: 978-1-315-71516-2 (ebk)

Typeset in Sabon
by codeMantra

Printed and bound in the United States of America by Publishers Graphics,
LLC on sustainably sourced paper.

To Steffen

Contents

List of Figures	ix
Preface: Quality and Moral Complexity	xi
Acknowledgments	xxi

1	**Morally Murky: On Navigating Fictional Worlds by Moral Emotions and Intuitions**	1
2	**Partiality: How Knowing Someone Well Influences Morality**	39
3	**Suspense and Moral Evaluation: How Morality Is Shaped by Suspense and Style**	64
4	**Why so Many Television Series with Antiheroes?: The Attraction of the Antihero's Very Immorality**	90
5	**Crossing the Line: On Moral Disgust and Proper Villains in the Antihero Series**	120
6	**The Antihero's Wife: On Hating Skyler White, and on the Rare Female Antihero**	150
7	**Conclusion**	182

References	187
Index	203

List of Figures

1.1	Dexter Morgan enjoys killing (*Dexter*, Showtime).	25
2.1	Tony Soprano threatens Dr Kennedy (*The Sopranos*, HBO).	46
2.2	Adriana La Cerva finds the FBI agents unsympathetic to her situation (*The Sopranos*, HBO).	51
2.3	Dr Melfi refuses to tell Tony Soprano about her rapist (*The Sopranos*, HBO).	54
3.1	Walter White is in a tight spot (*Breaking Bad*, AMC).	79
3.2	Jesse Pinkman faces the consequences (*Breaking Bad*, AMC).	84
4.1	Dr Hannibal Lecter is strangling a victim (*Hannibal*, NBC).	94
4.2	Nurse Jackie Peyton is defiant and powerful (*Nurse Jackie*, Showtime).	100
4.3	Giuseppe "Gyp" Rosetti appears in a spectacular sequence (*Boardwalk Empire*, HBO).	106
5.1	D'Angelo Barksdale finds Keisha raped and dead (*The Wire*, HBO).	125
5.2	The rape of Gemma Teller makes the Sons of Anarchy morally preferable (*Sons of Anarchy*, FX).	130
6.1	Skyler White has "the talking pillow" (*Breaking Bad*, AMC).	156
6.2	Abby Donovan asks her husband who he is (*Ray Donovan*, Showtime).	158
6.3	Carrie Hopewell needs funding to save her son (*Banshee*, Cinemax).	172
6.4	Patty Hewes is smiling sweetly at her target (*Damages*, FX).	177
7.1	Lorne Malvo dies spectacularly (*Fargo*, FX).	184

Preface
Quality and Moral Complexity

The Sopranos (HBO, 1999–2007) is one of many American drama television series in recent decades featuring a severely morally flawed main character that the spectator is generally encouraged to like. *Banshee* (Cinemax, 2013-present), *Boardwalk Empire* (HBO, 2010–2014), *Breaking Bad* (AMC, 2008–2013), *Dexter* (Showtime, 2006–2013), *Fargo* (FX, 2014-present), *Hannibal* (NBC, 2013-present), *House of Cards* (Netflix, 2013-present), *Ray Donovan* (Showtime, 2013-present), *Sons of Anarchy* (FX, 2008–2014), *The Shield* (FX, 2002–2008) and *The Wire* (HBO, 2002–2008) are some of the television series with main characters who commit serious crimes – murder is one of the crimes the main characters in these series have in common. These main characters are not just morally flawed in the humdrum sense that all of us, in some way or another, are morally flawed. It is not just the case that the main character in these series is no saint – he truly is immoral, in the sense that he is continually violating moral principles. This book is about the spectator's engagement with these morally flawed main characters – or antiheroes.

These series are part of a trend or cycle[1] of critically acclaimed television series discussed as *Quality TV, high-end TV* and *Complex TV* (see e.g., Akass and McCabe 2007; Dunleavy 2009; Nelson 2007; Mittell 2015).[2] Although seen as problematic by some, for example because these notions can be said to reproduce a hierarchy of taste by implying that regular TV somehow lacks quality and complexity (Newman & Levine 2012), Quality TV can also be seen not so much as an evaluative label, but as a genre denomination, as in Robert Thompson's by now classical discussion of the trend (Thompson 1997). In his influential account,

> the "quality" in "quality TV" has come to refer more to a generic style than to an aesthetic judgment.
>
> (Thompson 1997: 13)

> What emerges by the time we get to the 1990s is that "quality TV" has become a genre in itself, complete with its own set of formulaic characteristics. (...) By 1992, you could recognize a "quality show" long before you could tell if it was any good. Quality television came to refer to shows with a particular set of characteristics that we normally

xii *Preface*

> associate with "good," "artsy," and "classy." (...) "Quality TV" is simply television's version of the "art film" (Ibid., 16).

One could argue that art film is not so much a genre as a mode, yet nonetheless agree with Thompson's general observation, namely that Quality TV series share some traits with art film (cf. Bordwell 1979; see K. Thompson 2003). I will not discuss this further here, and I bring this up only to contextualise the antihero series in this historical development in American television. Quality TV can be said to be a response in the television industry to a particular challenge: how to catch – and keep – the attention of affluent, highly educated, urban viewers, viewers who have not traditionally (or were not, as this trend emerged in the 1980s) attracted to 'regular TV'. With more competition between cable and network channels from the 1980s onwards, the TV industry increasingly targeted specific segments of the audience; in particular, segments that were especially attractive to advertisers, or, in the case of a subscription channel such as HBO (see e.g., Anderson 2008 and De Fino 2014), segments of the audience who were willing and able to pay monthly subscription rates. One of the primary market strategies for American cable channels would thus be to make a product that appeared distinctly different from regular TV, intended to attract this profitable demographic. This process is known as segmentation, and it is an important backdrop for the wide range of antiheroes currently found on American television.

Many Quality TV series are morally complex and have antiheroes. When Thompson lists twelve points on which he claims viewers, critics and scholars typically agree when assessing a series as Quality TV, one of these points is that Quality TV has "grim and thought-provoking subject matter [that] clashed with the simple and happy world presented on most TV" (Thompson 1997: 35). Whereas regular TV would typically adhere to what has become known as the LOP paradigm (Least Objectionable Programming) in order to appeal to an undifferentiated mass audience, Quality TV took grim topics as its subject matter as part of the strategy to appear distinctly different. Robin Nelson sums this up by arguing that what he labels high-end TV is "risky, 'edgy' television which flouts the historic tendency for small-screen fictions to be conservative, particularly in the USA" (Nelson 2007: 3). As traditional fictional storytelling on American TV was dominated by Manichean moral structures – good cops and bad criminals – Quality TV goes for complex moral structures. One way to introduce such moral complexity is to rely on "anti-hero leads versus broadcast's more likeable protagonists" (Ryan and Holmes paraphrased in Newman and Levine 2012: 34). Amanda Lotz has explored these morally complex characters in a book descriptively entitled *Cable Guys* – as these characters are most typically male, and they proliferated first on American cable (Lotz 2014). Although she dismisses the notion of the antihero as imprecise, she observes that the main character in many drama series on cable is a flawed protagonist – clearly not a traditional hero, and more or less bad by dominant social and legal norms; he is typically a

Preface xiii

criminal (Ibid., 63, 83). Jason Mittell also notes that "[o]ne common trait shared by many complex television series is the narrative prominence of unsympathetic, morally questionable, or villainous figures, nearly always male" (Mittell 2015: 142). Thus, whereas Quality TV series surely need not have antiheroes, a fair amount of them do, and it is these series that will serve as case studies in this book.

However, this book project started not with the aim to describe the antihero series, but with the desire to explore the moral psychology of fiction. With what or whom are we as spectators of fiction willing to engage, and where do we draw the limit? How come we seem willingly to sympathize with characters in fiction we would hardly even like in real life? The fascinating nature of theoretical questions such as these brought me to the antihero series. These questions have been discussed in cognitive film theory, media psychology and philosophical aesthetics, and this study aims to introduce these debates into television studies, to create a dialogue between these fields, and finally to serve as a theoretical intervention in these debates. I will try to answer these questions by using drama antihero series in recent American television as case studies.

The rest of the book is thus dedicated to case studies and examples in order to tease out what we as spectators engage imaginatively with, and the narrative techniques used to make us engage. This book is not a corpus analysis *per se* – meaning that the primary aim is neither to cover all nooks and crannies in American television, nor to cover all antihero series, but to try to use a few of them to tease out what these series, and our engagement with them, can say about our morality. Whereas my starting point in this introduction is in television studies, it will become evident for the reader that I am, by training, not a television scholar, but a film theorist – and a cognitive film theorist at that. I will return to what cognitive film theory is, and what it can do, in the first chapter, but a few notes here already may be helpful for the reader who is unfamiliar with this theoretical approach.

Readers might expect a zeitgeist explanation as to why there are so many antihero series – pointing to various cultural trends, topics and themes that make the antihero series appeal to us (or perhaps even more specifically, to American spectators) right now. I will not offer any such cultural explanations. This is not because I do not think there are many cultural factors contributing to what spectators find appealing at any given time. Lotz, for example, analyses the same trend as do I in relation to hegemonic masculinity, and explores how these cable guys represent what is perceived as masculine in contemporary American society (Lotz 2014). I agree with Lotz that these series, with their overwhelming dominance of male antiheroes, do say something important about hegemonic masculinity in the U.S., and the antihero series trend can fruitfully be used to tease out these assumptions.

On the other hand, the antihero is not uniquely a new phenomenon. Morally complex characters are present in other genres as well – see for example Dan Flory's careful discussion of the sympathetic, but morally

xiv *Preface*

flawed characters in film noir and Spike Lee's films (Flory 2008). Also, the antihero is a gangster genre convention in film, and cultural explanations of the appeal of the antihero should thus include the very first classical gangster films in the 1930s (*Scarface, White Heat* and *Public Enemy*). Or, to track the notion back even further, the antihero in the gangster film has been seen as related to Shakespeare's notoriously bad main characters, such as Richard III (e.g., Loehlin 1997; see also Salamon 2000). For example, James Loehlin writes:

> Like the Elizabethan tragedies, *Richard III* among them, that focus on an overreaching Machiavellian anti-hero, the gangster film is built on a structure of identification and alienation. In violating the moral and political laws that constrain the viewer, the gangster, like Tamburlaine, the Jew of Malta or Richard III, provides a focus for audience identification and wish-fulfillment. Once the viewer's trangressive [sic] desire is vicariously satisfied – when the gangster reaches the "top of the world" – he may be safely rejected, and his fall and destruction assuage the viewer's guilty conscience.
>
> (Loehlin 1997: 74)

Notably, Loehlin uses the notion antihero with reference to Richard III. The movement between identification and alienation that he finds both in Shakespeare's play and the classic gangster film is arguably present in the antihero series as well, as we shall see. There is nothing distinctly televisual about antiheroes, and they are not restricted to the present historical epoch.[3] Cultural explanations for the appeal of the antihero series should take this into account.[4]

Furthermore, the conceptual apparatus that I am exploring points to some general tendencies based on the way we – as human beings – work psychologically. Building on empirical research on Western morality in moral psychology, we can, tentatively and cautiously, assume that most individuals in Western societies share some moral responses – or, minimally, that there are some general tendencies in the way we respond morally. When I make assumptions about what "we" do in this book, this is informed by research in moral psychology (the empirical study of (how we form) judgments of morally right or wrong). Furthermore, whereas our response as spectators varies culturally and depends on numerous factors, such as gender, class, age, political orientation and so on, I assume that an intended response to a film or a television series can be teased out through textual analysis of that film or television series.[5] When making such assumptions through textual analysis, I write about *the spectator*, singular. This abstract, theoretical construct is a methodological assumption shared by various strands of film theory, from Screen theory to cognitive film theory. There may be methodological problems with assuming such an abstracted spectator, but this is not the place to sort them out. It is an established methodological approach in

Preface xv

film theory, based on the idea – which is sound – that there is such a thing as an intended response to a film or television series.[6] Some television scholars share this view; Nelson, for example, argues that TV series invite dispositions of viewers without determining their response (Nelson 2007: 10). The spectator response I write about should be read as claims about intended responses and, linked to the psychological research I build on, about general tendencies due to our moral psychological and emotional makeup.

The only factor contributing to the trend of antihero series that I will explore here is the attraction antihero series offer the spectator emotionally and cognitively. The television industry capitalizes on a trend that has proved successful. And the antihero series offer some specific attractions that are appealing, and arguably became a trend for this very reason, as I will argue in chapter 4. Furthermore, I concentrate on the attractions that come with the antihero series' basic invitation, namely to like its antihero. Surely a spectator may decline this invitation and find the antihero despicable.[7] One likely result may be that the antihero series appears unattractive, and that the spectator gives up on the series altogether. One may also root for other characters in the ensemble casts found in antihero series instead of the antihero. This can be a valuable and enjoyable experience, too. However, this is not the experience I investigate in this book. I explore the intended response of liking the antihero, at least initially. In other words, mostly I take for granted that there is uptake of this intended response. Empirical research is needed to uncover variation among various audience groups, depending for example on cultural context, gender, class, age, and so on, and I welcome more such research. However, I remain focused only on a textually embedded intended response.

To complicate matters, I will argue that the intended response is not only to like the antihero, but also, at least ultimately, to dislike him too. Indeed, I argue that the design of the antihero series typically includes a normative element (one should also recognize the antihero as morally bad), and the intended response is aimed at appreciation of this very element. There is thus a "right" way to respond to these series as an appreciator. This response is arguably to be read out of the series' construction. I will return to this in chapter 4, problematizing the idea of intended response in a discussion of so-called bad fans who arguably watch *Breaking Bad* (and other antihero series) wrongly because they reduce the morally complex antihero to a heroic figure, whom they only like and never come to see as morally problematic. I argue that the bad fan gets the actual design of these series wrong. Spectatorial response is not determined, but the design of a series (narratively and stylistically) can be said to invite, warrant or authorize one type of response more than others.

Finally, a reader might expect a detailed investigation of the notion antihero *per se*, and its history in literary theory and film theory. I will not offer such a history – again, not because I do not think that would be worthwhile and interesting, but simply out of practical concerns. It would make the topics

xvi *Preface*

covered in this book too vast. It has become common in the critical reception of these series, in the press and the media, to describe these morally flawed main characters as antiheroes, and so will I. I have concentrated on the phenomenon I am trying to describe by use of this notion rather than to track how this notion might or might not deviate from earlier usage. However, briefly, the notion has been used differently than I use it here, for example by Murray Smith, who uses the notion to refer to a main character with which we are aligned but who remains unsympathetic (Smith 1995: 188).[8] In this book, when I use the notion antihero, I take it to mean a clearly – or even, severely – morally flawed main character whom the spectator is nonetheless encouraged to feel with, like and root for. The moral complexity of the antihero series entails that the spectator is intended to like the antihero – but through a challenging narrative also come to dislike him. The antihero series typically encourages sympathy for the antihero initially, but increasingly also questions this positive orientation with the antihero. So the spectator is intended to feel conflicted about the antihero at the end of the antihero series.

Again, this could be seen in relation to the ways Quality TV is intended to appear distinctly different from regular TV: Nelson, for example, contrasts (what he labels) high-end TV with regular TV in that whereas the latter basically offers pleasures tied to security, a sense of familiarity and ritual, the former operates at the "frisson of risk": indeed, that "to those who seek it, there is a pleasure even in the anticipation of the transgression of social codes" (Nelson 2007: 19). High-end TV should be surprising and edgy. He discusses how there is often a form of defamiliarization or Brechtian alienation effect to be found in these TV series' genre hybridity (Ibid., 21–22). Thus, in relation to a series such as *The Sopranos*, for example, he argues that "though it is possible for a macho male viewer to have his values reaffirmed through watching *Sopranos*, it is equally likely – or even more likely – that the security of that position will be dislocated" (Ibid., 181). It is this insecurity and thought-provoking complexity in our responses to the antihero that I wish to explore.

The first chapter lays out the theoretical background for this study, which is cognitive film theory and media psychology. Murray Smith and Noël Carroll postulate that moral evaluation of the characters is fundamental to the spectator's engagement with fiction film. Antihero series pose a challenge to this assumption: is our liking of the morally bad main characters in series such as *Breaking Bad*, *The Sopranos* and *Dexter* grounded in a moral evaluation? Carl Plantinga has argued, against Smith, that we often like and sympathize with characters on other grounds than moral ones, and in media psychology, Arthur Raney has explored what he labels *moral disengagement for the sake of enjoyment*: in order to enjoy a narrative as entertainment, we disengage morally. I support these critical revisions and explore further what moral disengagement is. I argue that it means that when we engage with fiction we rely on moral emotions, and circumvent rational, deliberate moral evaluation. In order to understand how this is so, I turn to moral

Preface xvii

psychology. I draw on Jonathan Haidt and Joshua Greene's related work on the so-called dual-process model of morality. Moral evaluation is a dual process – one way goes through deliberate, rational evaluation, and the other way is a quick-and-dirty shortcut through our intuitions.

When engaged in a prototypical fiction, I argue that we typically bracket rational, moral evaluation such as considering implications or consequences, and allow ourselves to rely on the intuitive route to moral evaluation. I label this attitude *fictional relief*. We do not feel that we must evaluate characters and events in a fiction rationally and objectively. The fictional context teases out what our moral emotions and intuitions are and how they work. The narrative can easily manipulate the spectator's response to a fiction by activating some particular moral intuitions and emotions.

Fiction does not, however, solely engage this one route to a moral evaluation. On the contrary, a main thesis in this book is that the antihero series deliberately encourage re-activation of the other route – deliberate, rational evaluation – at certain points in the narrative. By manipulating narrative strategies, fiction can deactivate and reactive rational deliberate moral evaluation in a controlled manner. I label this re-activation of a rational moral evaluation *reality check*.

The starting point in chapter 2, entitled "Partiality: how knowing someone well shapes our morality", is how the spectator becomes partial to well-known characters in *The Sopranos* and *Breaking Bad* – most notably the antiheroes Tony Soprano and Walter White. And these antihero series, too, rely on the moral intuition that loyalty with those we already know – partiality towards members of our own in-group – is morally good. The antihero typically embarks on his criminal trajectory in order to care for his family, and this is central to seeing him as basically adhering to a moral code. Personal relations make us partial: knowing someone well makes us more likely to explain away their moral trespasses. Television series activate some of the same mental mechanisms as personal relations do in real life, and due to their long duration, do so more prominently than the relatively short fiction film (Blanchet and Vaage 2012). We become stubborn sympathizers with the antiheroes – blinded by familiarity. The moral compass we use to navigate these series is flawed when judged from an impartial, strictly rational perspective, but makes sense in the dual-process model of morality, in which our moral intuitions and emotions evolved first and foremost to secure cooperation in a small group.

In chapter 3, "Moral inversion of suspense: how our engagement is shaped by suspense and style", we will see that Noël Carroll argues that suspense is generated when the spectator wishes for one outcome – the moral one where the hero conquers the villain – but fears an immoral outcome. However, Alfred Hitchcock encouraged the spectator to feel suspense for villainous characters in his films. Richard Allen discusses this as moral inversion of suspense. *Breaking Bad* and other American antihero television series carry this legacy forward. I use the notion empathy in order to suggest xviii *Preface*

that we have a 'natural instinct' (in Hitchcock's terms) to simulate the action alternatives of characters we see. We tend to replace a cognitively demanding task, such as deliberate moral evaluation, with a less demanding, intuitive response. Simulating the character's action alternatives suppresses the cognitively taxing operation of moral evaluation. Adding to this effect is the spectator's narrative desire that a story should be maximally engaging. Time and again the antiheroes Walter White and Jesse Pinkman find themselves in a tight spot: how can they possibly make it this time? This question easily suppresses the question the spectator should perhaps be asking herself: why should she want Walter and Jesse to make it in the first place?

Chapter 4, "Why so many television series with antiheroes? The attraction of the antihero's very immorality", hypothesizes that one main attraction of American antihero series is in empathizing with the antihero. The experience he offers is an assertive and powerful one, and pleasant even if – or perhaps even because – the antihero is immoral. Immoral elements in a story make the story more engaging, and the spectator has narrative desires that the story is just that. The spectator appreciates the antihero aesthetically. One type of aesthetic admiration enhanced by these series is related to the spectator finding her own liking of and loyalty with the antihero puzzling. What we feel is morally right when relying on moral intuitions and emotions is not the same as what we think is morally right on reflection. The two routes to a moral evaluation are in conflict when it comes to the antihero series. The recent cycle of series with antiheroes capitalizes on this effect, and is regarded with great esteem by both the audience and critics partly because of this thought-provoking effect. One explanation for the cycle of antiheroes is thus that the spectator both enjoys the narrative and appreciates the way these series invite her to reflect on her own engagement.

I turn to the line that separates between antihero and proper villains in chapter 5, "Crossing the line: on moral disgust and proper villains in the antihero series". Rape marks one limit to what moral transgressions are portrayed in a sympathetic light in antihero series in American television. Rape evokes antipathy, stirs up desire for revenge, and has a polarizing effect morally in series such as *The Wire* and *Sons of Anarchy*. But why do we as spectators seem willing to engage imaginatively with murderers but not rapists, when murder is considered a graver moral trespass than is rape in real life (at least as reflected in real life laws in Western societies)? The notion *moral disgust* can explain. Although gory murders can also be found morally disgusting, sex crimes most prominently evoke feelings of moral disgust. Disgust reactions are less flexible than feelings of anger, which are more open to justification. We are willing and able to justify a murder in a fictional setting, but rape evokes moral disgust, and this excludes rape from the crimes we are willing to allow a transgressive protagonist. The asymmetry between our reluctance to sympathize with rapists yet willingness to do so with murderers in fiction, corroborates the argument in this book that we primarily rely on moral emotions and intuitions when engaging in fiction.

Preface xix

Whereas antipathy towards raping psychopaths might be easier to explain, it is arguably harder to see how the antihero is morally preferable to his wife. Nonetheless, some spectators hate the antihero's wife, such as Skyler White and Carmela Soprano. Contrary to what they argue in online discussions, rationally speaking the antihero's wife is in fact morally preferable to her husband. In the final chapter, "The antihero's wife: on hating Skyler White, and on the rare female antihero", I explain the antipathy some spectators feel for her by exploring how easily a narrative can manipulate moral emotions. Several factors enhance antipathy towards the antihero's wife: she is tied to a home that is typically presented as unhappy and restricting, and her resistance to her husband's illegal escapades can make her appear as a drag, a kill-joy and an obstacle to everything fun – not least of all to the entertaining suspense sequences that in many ways can be said to offer the spectator the enjoyable transgressions at the heart of the antihero series. Compared to the male antihero and his wife, the female antihero's transgressions, such as those of Jackie Peyton (*Nurse Jackie*), Anastasia/Carrie Hopewell (*Banshee*), Nancy Botwin (*Weeds*) and Patty Hewes (*Damages*), are often less grave than those of the male antihero. And although resembling the (male) antihero's wife, the (female) antihero's husband is not portrayed as negatively.

Finally, the audience has learned to expect certain things from the antihero series. This book ends by briefly exploring *Fargo* in order to sum up the conventions of the antihero series and the pleasures it offers its spectator.

Notes

1. As Peter Stanfield points out, a theory of cycles is underdeveloped in Film Studies; the standard view is that the commercial success of a film encourages repetition of key elements, leading to a cycle or trend of similar films – but whereas this view enables the scholar to escape the view of genres as fixed, somewhat ideal types outside of history, he argues that a more careful study of Hollywood cycles is needed in order to track the nuanced shifts in innovation and repetition, situating film production and reception in culture (Stanfield 2015). My study of the moral psychology of the antihero series will not provide a fully fledged study of the cycle of antihero series in American television in this sense. However, I will refer to the trend of antihero series as a cycle in the simple sense that the trend is cross-generic: antihero series in American television are found across a number of genres, such as gangster (*The Sopranos*), political drama (*House of Cards*), thriller/horror (*Hannibal*), etc. Complex or Quality TV is indeed typically seen as mixing genres and thus characterized by genre hybridity, see e.g., (Nelson 2007: 20; Mittell 2015: 233ff; Polan 2009; Thompson 1997: 15).
2. Various authors discuss what I take to be the very same trend by use of different labels. There may be essential differences between these terms, but for my purposes I will assume they can be used interchangeably. However, I will stick to the notion Quality TV when referring to this trend, unless specifically citing authors who use other labels.
3. See also e.g., Victor Brombert's discussion of antiheroes in European literature from 1830–1980 (Brombert 1999).

xx *Preface*

4. This counterargument does not, as I see it, pose a problem for Lotz's specific conclusions about the portrayal of masculinity in these series.
5. The notion of intended response can be seen as related to David Bordwell's 'cued response', e.g., the way the *syuzhet* in a film (the form the plot takes as the spectator encounters it in the film, or the patterning of the story in the film) cues the spectator to construct the *fabula* (the imaginary construct the spectator creates based on the syuzhet, e.g., the story as a chronological, cause-and-effect chain). In this model, the syuzhet *cues* the spectator to construct the fabula in certain ways (Bordwell 1985: 48ff). However, Bordwell primarily discusses story construction, whereas in philosophical aesthetics the notion 'intended response' includes a larger array of spectator responses, such as consideration of authorial argument and appreciation (cf. Livingston 2005, 2009). I want to explore the spectator's response to the antihero series in this latter, more inclusive sense, and use 'intended response' instead of 'cued response'.
6. An informative, classical paper about this theoretical construct – the "spectator in the text" – is Brown (1975–6). See also Plantinga (2009: 11ff) for an informative account of intended responses.
7. Thanks to both Sarah Cardwell and Elke Weissmann for pressing me on this point.
8. However, in more recent discussions he uses the notion akin to the way I use it in this book. See e.g., Smith (2014).

Acknowledgments

This book project started as my postdoctoral research project at the Norwegian University of Science and Technology, generously funded by the Norwegian Research Council from 2010 to 2013.

While working on this project I have benefited from feedback from audiences at a number of talks. Parts of this material have been presented at the Annual Conference of the British Society of Aesthetics in Cambridge, 2013; the Society for Cinema and Media Studies Conference in Chicago in 2013; the Society for Cognitive Studies of the Moving Image Conferences in New York (2012), Budapest (2011), and Copenhagen (2009); the Network for European Cinema Studies Conference in London, 2011; the Nordic Society for Aesthetics Conference in Trondheim, 2009; the Symposium of the Moral Psychology of Fiction in Trondheim, 2012; the Serial Forms Conference in Zürich in 2009; at research seminars at the University of Kent in 2010, 2011 and 2014, as well as at the Norwegian University of Science and Technology in Trondheim in 2009 and 2010; and finally at the London Aesthetics Forum in 2014. I thank each and every one present on these occasions.

Furthermore, I have had many good readers and discussion partners. In particular I am grateful to and would like to thank Richard Allen, Robert Blanchet, Dan Flory, Roger Giner-Sorolla, Anne Gjelsvik, Dan Hassler-Forest, Tanya Horeck, Jason Mittell, Carl Plantinga, Paul Taberham, Aaron Taylor, Francis X. Shen, Rikke Schubart and Lisa Zunshine. They have all read earlier drafts for either whole or parts of individual chapters, or made comments that turned out to be particularly valuable – indeed, formative.

I am especially indebted to Paisley Livingston and Ted Nannicelli, both of whom read a draft of the full manuscript. In its final phases this book project thus benefited greatly from their many helpful comments and suggestions.

My colleagues in the Film Department and Aesthetics Research Centre at the University of Kent have provided a fertile and stimulating environment in which to finish this book. First and foremost I would like to thank Murray Smith. Parts of this book are a polemic, critical discussion of his work, but there is in fact a lot more on which we agree than that on which we disagree. Nevertheless, as academic discourse goes, the disagreements make the most interesting material. Murray is a generous colleague and friend, and I thank him for our many discussions and also for opening up this burgeoning field of study in the first place.

xxii *Acknowledgments*

I have had the privilege of designing and teaching a module on the spectator's engagement with television series, both in my time as a postdoctoral research fellow at the Norwegian University of Science and Technology, and at the University of Kent. I want to thank all the students for the wonderful discussions we have had – this study would not have been as much fun without these, and I have learned a lot from your input.

Parts of chapter 5 have previously been published as "The Repulsive Rapist: On the Difference Between Morality in Fiction and Real Life" in Lisa Zunshine (ed.). (2015). *The Oxford Handbook of Cognitive Literary Studies,* New York: Oxford University Press, pp. 421–439; and parts of chapter 2 have previously appeared as "Blinded by Familiarity: Partiality, Morality and Engagement in Television Series" in Ted Nannicelli and Paul Taberham (eds.), (2014). *Cognitive Media Theory,* New York: Routledge, pp. 268–284. I thank the publishers for permission to reprint this material.

Finally, I want to thank my husband Steffen Borge for his invaluable support and continual feedback on this project. Your various suggestions and comments are too numerous to acknowledge individually, so suffice it to say that we have discussed this project from its very conception to the end result. It has at times been a bumpy ride, and your confidence in my project and me truly helped me through it.

1 Morally Murky
On Navigating Fictional Worlds by Moral Emotions and Intuitions

Whenever Dexter Morgan has hunted down one of his carefully chosen victims, strapped him onto a table covered in plastic, and woken him up from the tranquilized sleep he induced until he is ready to kill, Dexter's facial expression communicates the pleasure he finds in taking someone's life. Furthermore, Dexter is the television series *Dexter*'s main character, and the spectator is encouraged to like and sympathize with him. And Dexter is not alone; the antihero prevails in recent American drama television series. Characters such as mobster kingpin Tony Soprano (*The Sopranos*), meth cook and gangster-in-the-making Walter White (*Breaking Bad*), and serial killer Dexter are not morally good. How do these television series make us like and sympathize with their morally bad main characters? And what does this tell us about our moral psychological makeup, and more specifically about the moral psychology of fiction?

This first chapter lays out the theoretical background for this book, which is cognitive film theory and media psychology. I explain the dominate theories of our engagement with fiction and the role morality plays in these. Moral evaluation has been seen as foundational to our engagement with fiction – it is postulated that the spectator works as an untiring moral monitor throughout her engagement with a story. These theories have recently come under critical scrutiny: the antihero trend challenges the assumption that the spectator continually evaluates the characters and events morally. Does watching *Dexter* entail that the spectator morally evaluates its serial killer protagonist? Who of us would actually defend vigilante killings, such as he routinely commits in this fiction? Current research in moral psychology, and most notably Jonathan Haidt's and Joshua Greene's work on the so-called dual-process model of (real life) morality, can shed light on this debate. With a clearer picture of how a moral evaluation functions, the question of which role such assessment plays when we engage with fiction will be easier to answer. According to this model, one way to a make a moral judgment is to go through deliberate, reflective thinking – a rational evaluation. Another way to moral judgment is quick-and-dirty and pre-reflective, going through our moral intuitions and emotions. My main hypothesis about our engagement in fiction is that we primarily rely on moral emotions, and circumvent rational, deliberate moral evaluation. The fictional status of these series deactivates rational, deliberate moral evaluation, making the spectator

2 Morally Murky

rely on moral emotions and intuitions that are relatively easy to manipulate with narrative strategies. In the final part of this first chapter I turn to one possible counterargument to my theory. I postulate that there is a relevant difference between the way we engage with works of fiction and non-fiction respectively. In the last part of the chapter I elaborate on this claim.

To avoid misunderstanding in relation to my use of the notions intuition and rational, a few preliminary remarks are in order. A critic could argue that it is far from clear what terms such as rational deliberation and intuition mean philosophically. Indeed, there is a huge literature on either notion.[1] Michael Johnson and Jennifer Nado, for example, point out that

> [t]he nature of intuition itself is notoriously difficult to pin down (...) we will just stipulate that by 'intuition' we mean to refer at the very least to spontaneous, not-obviously-inferential judgments.
>
> (Johnson and Nado 2014: 69)

Johnson and Nado's understanding of intuition is mirrored in Jonathan Haidt's, who writes that moral intuitions are

> the sudden appearance in consciousness of a moral judgment, including an affective valence (good-bad, like-dislike) without any conscious awareness of having gone through steps of searching, weighing evidence, or inferring a conclusion.
>
> (Haidt 2001: 818)

By presenting moral judgment as either rational or intuitive, I do not suggest that the latter is irrational, in the sense that the two must contradict one another. It can be perfectly rational of us sometimes to rely on moral intuitions. However, neither should intuitions be seen as the most reliable way to track what is morally right – as the appeal to intuitions in philosophical thought experiments has sometimes suggested. Indeed, the role of intuitions in philosophical methodology has become controversial, primarily because intuitions can be manipulated easily through various means (e.g., they are highly sensitive to order of presentation, for example Swain et al. 2008). To say that the spectator's reaction of disgust toward a character is intuitive does not mean that her reaction is, therefore, justified. The antihero stories are indeed effectively designed to give rise to some intuitive moral responses that are, as a matter of fact, erroneous from a rational point of view. Moral intuitions and emotions are easily manipulated narratively, dependent as they are on narrative context. Deliberate moral reasoning would typically be more principled in nature.

Furthermore, saying that some moral judgments are intuitive does not mean that they are only "hardwired" – independent of social context and learning. Making an intuitive moral judgment simply means that an action in a situation strikes one as right or wrong, good or bad, and that this is a gut reaction, i.e., that one is not necessarily aware of having evaluated the situation with regard to right or wrong. It is a pre-reflective judgment, arrived at without reflective reasoning. Some intuitions may be hardwired – intuitions we are disposed to due to human nature – whereas others are socially learned. Some intuitions may be the result of prior rational deliberation: I may have taken a stand to be vegetarian, for example, because I have read up on industrialized meat production and found plenty of reasons not to support it. Over time, I have developed a gut reaction against eating meat, and need not reflect deliberately about questions relating to eating meat every time I encounter them.

My contribution is to show what the dual-process model can do in film and television theory, or more specifically how it can shed light on the spectator's engagement with the antihero. One prominent line of critique against this model is that the dual-process model of morality – and especially in Jonathan Haidt's formulation of it – is wrong in dismissing deliberate moral reasoning: the critic would thus point out that deliberate moral reasoning is more important than what the theory allows for (see e.g., Bloom 2010; Monin et al. 2007; Pizarro and Bloom 2003). For example, rational deliberation can be seen as of central importance in order to explain how our morality may change. However, I also rely on Joshua Greene's dual-process model of morality, which is similar to Haidt's, but which does grant rational, deliberate reasoning a more important role (as in the vegetarian example above). In my theory about the antihero series rational reasoning plays an important role, too. So this specific line of critique of the dual-process model of morality is less relevant for my use of it. Furthermore, if it turns out that the very idea that we rely most heavily on moral intuitions in real life is wrong, one could still potentially argue that moral intuitions play an instrumental role in our engagement with fiction. A critical discussion of the dual-process model of morality *per se* has, however, realistically been beyond the scope of the present study.

Finally, my use of the distinction between rational versus intuitive moral judgment is not normative. As I will reiterate later in this chapter, the dominate Western moral philosophies are all normative, and they prescribe rational moral deliberation. However, turning to moral psychology and its emphasis on moral intuition also entails or is at least compatible with a change from a prescriptive to a descriptive point of view: the dual-process model does not in itself prescribe what we should or should not do when we try to be morally good people.[2] It merely describes how we typically judge a situation morally. So, with the aim to uncover the realities of our morality (how our morality actually works rather than how we think it ought to work), let us start with theories of spectatorship in cognitive film theory and moral psychology.

Traditional Theories of Spectator Engagement: Moral Evaluation is Foundational

Rather than surveying all theories of spectator engagement in cognitive film theory and moral psychology, I will concentrate on a few influential views.[3] Indeed, these accounts can be said to represent the dominant views

4 *Morally Murky*

of character engagement in these two fields. The gist of these accounts is that a moral evaluation is foundational to our engagement with fiction.[4] An early articulation of this idea is to be found in Noël Carroll's essay on suspense (Carroll 1996a [1984]: 94ff), in which he argues that what generates suspense in film is a combination of morality and probability: if I desire a sequence to have a morally good outcome, but an evil outcome seems most likely, feelings of suspense can be expected to occur.[5] With this observation, the idea that morality plays an essential part for our engagement in films is planted. This idea is further corroborated in Murray Smith's *Engaging Characters* (Smith 1995), a pivotal study instrumental in establishing character engagement as one of the central questions on which cognitive film theory is focused. In the writings of Carroll and Smith, the spectator engages most prominently with those she sees as morally good. In his seminal essay on suspense, for example, Carroll uses the notion allegiance, and defines this as when "we can agree with and root for a character in a film on the basis of shared moral commitments with that character" (Carroll 1996a: 116n.22).

From the 1980s onward, cognitive film theorists have criticized the psychoanalytic concept of identification for entailing an illusionistic fusion between the spectator and a character or film, and for insufficiently specifying what kind of engagement the term picks out (e.g., Bordwell 1996: 15ff; Carroll 1998: 311ff; Currie 1995: xvff, 165ff; Grodal 1997: 81ff; Tan 1996: 189–90; Smith 1995: 1ff, 93–4, 1996).[6] In the view of the cognitive film theorists, the notion of identification entails that the spectator is under a kind of illusion where she loses herself in the character and mistakes the character's experiences for her own (see e.g., Baudry 1974–5). Thus, temporarily, the division between the self and other is abolished. The spectator is fully immersed in the character and experiences this as a fusion with her: the spectator's responses are determined by the responses of the character.

As part of this move away from the psychoanalytical fusion view, Carroll and Smith hold that the spectator's engagement with the characters on-screen is grounded in an assessment of the moral structure of the film. Carroll argues that the spectator does not unwillingly and unwittingly 'fuse' with the characters on-screen by mere use of point of view shots, for example, as psychoanalytic theorists such as Stephen Heath suggest, but "on the basis of holding similar values to the characters in question" forms an allegiance with them (Carroll 1996a: 166n.22). A central assumption in cognitive film theory is that the spectator actively makes sense of films, and that her response to film is rationally motivated: it is an informed attempt to make sense (cf. Carroll 1988, see also Currie 2004: 155). Emphasising the spectator's moral evaluation of the characters can be seen as one facet of this claim.

Smith recasts the terminology used to describe the spectator's engagement with films in psychoanalytic film theory, moving away from notions of identification entirely. Instead, any given film has a *structure of sympathy*, according to which a spectator is oriented (Smith 1995). The structure of sympathy has three tenets: first, the film establishes stable agents that the

Morally Murky 5

spectator identifies through a process of *recognition*. Also, the film narration filters the events of the story through one or several characters' experience in a process of *alignment*: the narration can be more or less aligned spatiotemporally with any given character, and give more or less access to the experiences of any given character (e.g., giving us information about how the character feels and what she is thinking). Finally, through alignment the narration gives the spectator clues that she uses in order to evaluate the narrative, its characters and events morally in a process of *allegiance*.

> Allegiance denotes that level of engagement at which spectators respond sympathetically or antipathetically towards a character or group of characters. It rests upon an evaluation of the character as representing a desirable (or at least, preferable) set of traits, when compared with other characters within the fiction. This basic evaluation is combined with a tendency to arousal in response to the character. That is, the level of intensity of the arousal may vary, and the type of emotion experienced will shift depending on the situation in which the character is placed, but both these factors are *determined by an underlying evaluation of the character's moral status within the moral system* of the text.
>
> (Smith 1995: 62, my emphasis)

Allegiance thus has both a cognitive and an emotional component – it is a moral evaluation and an emotional output. If I evaluate a character as morally good, I will form a sympathetic allegiance with that character, and if I see her as evil, the feelings triggered will be antipathetic. One important caveat to note is that the spectator's moral evaluation is seen as intrinsic to the fiction – all it takes is that she sees the character as morally preferable to other characters in the narrative. Portraying someone as morally worse than the antihero is indeed common in the antihero series (see chapter 5 and 6).

Nevertheless, there are problems with this understanding of character engagement. The spectator's response is seen as *determined* by her evaluation of the character's moral status within the moral system of the film. Notably, Smith does not explain in greater detail what a moral evaluation is. In order to tease out what he means by it, it is important to take note of the relation between alignment and allegiance. A film's moral structure or system of value is revealed to the spectator through alignment in a process Smith labels *moral orientation* (Smith 1995: 189). However, being aligned with a character does not mean that the spectator is encouraged to form a sympathetic allegiance with this character:

> The most we can say is that the conventional association of alignment and allegiance – most narratives in practice do elicit sympathy for those characters with whom they align us – primes us to be sympathetic to character with whom we are aligned. If this relationship were

6   *Morally Murky*

necessary, however, it would be impossible to conceive of anti-heroes –
protagonists around which the alignment structure of the film is built,
but who remain unsympathetic.

(Smith 1995: 188)[7]

Conventionally, the spectator is thus said to be aligned with those she is
also encouraged to form a sympathetic allegiance with, according to Smith.
However, Smith also holds that being aligned with a character does not
necessarily lead to a sympathetic allegiance.[8] Smith denies a systematic
relation between alignment and allegiance. This makes moral evaluation
sound like an independent, perhaps even rational deliberation in Smith's
theory – otherwise, one ought to acknowledge that who the spectator is
aligned with in a story, and who she gets access to, systematically influences how she evaluates that story and its characters morally, as I argue in
chapter 2. There are anti-heroes in a Smithian sense to be found in film and
television – characters with which the spectator is firmly aligned but whom
she is never encouraged to like. The antiheroes of recent American television series, however, are not of this kind, and in order to explain how the
spectator is encouraged to like such morally flawed characters, one needs to
acknowledge the systematic way alignment influences one's moral judgment
of characters. However, the more systematic this relation is, the less rational
is our moral evaluation of the characters.

Indeed, when discussing allegiance Smith suggests that iconography, music
and the star system are among the factors that influence our moral evaluation of a character (Smith 1995: 190ff). If beautiful music and associations
triggered by star personae can be said to influence our moral evaluation, is
it a rational evaluation? Smith also briefly comments that "a suspension of
values must occur" for us to engage in gangster films, for example (Smith
1995: 189). What is a suspension of values? It is not clear what a moral
evaluation is in Smith's account. It seems to be assumed that it is a deliberate evaluation of some kind, as it does not follow automatically from being
aligned with a character; nonetheless, it is also influenced by non-moral
factors, and our values when engaging with fiction are admittedly to some
degree different from our real-life values.

One counterargument to Smith's theory is this: sympathetic or antipathetic
allegiance is not always the product of a fully fledged moral evaluation of
the character. Smith tackles this counterargument in two later papers (Smith
1999, 2011a). When Smith writes that "moral evaluations and judgments
frequently underlie our emotional reactions (...) [m]any of our emotional
responses to both actual and fictional events are in this sense morally
saturated" (Smith 1999: 218), one could see this as a modification of his
initial theory, moving from a moral evaluation *determining* our response
to a moral evaluation *frequently* underlying our responses. However, as we
have seen, non-moral factors have always played a role in Smith's theory –
albeit an ambiguous one. In these later papers, Smith discusses several cases

Morally Murky 7

where the spectator forms a sympathetic allegiance with characters who are less than morally good, and that could be seen as counterexamples to his theory. I return to this discussion in chapter 4. Suffice for now to note that despite these nuances, Smith defends his overall claim that a moral evaluation is a vital part of the process of allegiance, and states that truly perverse allegiance (forming a sympathetic allegiance with a character who deviates from what is right, good and proper) is "actually rather rare (...) most fictions that elicit perverse allegiances do so only temporarily or strategically, ultimately eliciting morally approbatory emotional responses" (Smith 1999: 222). And although Smith later elaborates on how allures of the transgressive are also important in order to explain our sympathy with the gangster Tony Soprano, he holds that "our allegiance with Soprano (...) has a strong moral dimension" (Smith 2011a: 75–6); he "is at least as moral as all other major characters in the world of the show (and considerably more moral than many of them)" (Ibid., 77). This view is also mirrored in Carroll's writings on *The Sopranos*: "[o]f most of the relevant characters in this fictional universe, they are worse or no better than Tony Soprano (...) this provides us with our ground for our willingness to ally ourselves with Tony" (Carroll 2004: 132). Smith sums up his view as follows:

> The degree to which we find a character sympathetic or antipathetic is probably not *wholly* a matter of moral evaluation; we might be inclined to find a character sympathetic – likeable, attractive – because he or she is droll, or charming, or lively, or clever. Yet I maintain that moral evaluation lies at the core of allegiance.
> (Smith 2011a: 84, emphasis original)

In a more recent paper Carroll explores how the spectator's moral appraisal is perhaps less reliant on moral reasoning, but depends on moral emotions – a view I very much share and to which I will return (Carroll 2010). Nevertheless, one can argue that even in this more recent account the moral emotions are still seen as a reliable compass by which the spectator can navigate through the fictional world –

> what bonds us to the protagonists affectively is sympathy which emotional attachment is secured primarily by moral considerations and that, contrariwise, what engenders antipathy toward the villains is their discernible moral failings (Ibid., 15).
>
> The protagonists uphold justice, do not harm unavoidably, show respect and friendliness toward one and all. They are pro-family, courteous, and mostly pro-social (deep down this is even true of apparent anti-heroes ...) (Ibid., 17).

However, our moral emotions are much more susceptible to manipulation through narrative and stylistic means than what Carroll's description of

8 *Morally Murky*

them here allows for. Although Smith and Carroll both emphasize that the spectator's moral evaluation is relative to fiction, they do arguably still see this morality as on the right track – basically aligned with the morality we would also want to defend rationally or see as desirable in real life.

The general thrust of Carroll's and Smith's theories of character engagement is reflected in the dominate theory in media psychology about the spectator's engagement in stories, namely Dolf Zillmann's *Affective Disposition Theory* (ADT) (e.g., Zillmann and Bryant 1975; Zillmann and Cantor 1977; Zillmann 2000, 2003, 2006, 2013). In Zillmann' own words in a recent overview of the model,

> [t]he model emphasizes respondents' continual moral monitoring of others' behavior, its implications for the formation of dispositions of liking based on approval and disliking based on condemnation (...).
> (Zillmann 2013: 132)

Again, Zillmann does not elaborate on what he takes the notion of moral monitoring or moral evaluation to mean other than pointing to how we discern a pattern out of character-defining clues given by witnessing a character's interactions (Ibid., 133). This resembles the point Smith makes about the relation between alignment and allegiance. There are formulations that indicate that Zillmann primarily thinks of a moral evaluation as a rational deliberation, for example when he writes that "[d]istinguishing between friend and foe is *not an entirely cognitive, deliberate effort*" (Ibid., my emphasis). Even though Zillmann also points to evidence suggesting that emotional reactions can precede a (rational) moral assessment, he does then assume that a moral evaluation is dominantly a cognitive, deliberate effort.

The main idea in ADT is that a moral evaluation or assessment fosters dispositions toward the characters – after evaluating a character morally, the spectator becomes more or less favourably disposed; she likes or dislikes the characters. Liking or disliking the characters then predicts the spectator's emotional reactions and desires in relation to the story. She hopes that the characters she likes will make it, and fears that disliked characters will win. She empathizes with those she likes, and feels discordant affect or counter-empathy when witnessing those she does not like. One important prediction of ADT is that a moral evaluation precedes and determines the spectator's empathic responses.[9] The spectators act as "untiring moral monitors" (Zillmann 2000: 54).

The final part of ADT predicts that the spectator's dispositions toward the characters also influence the spectator's enjoyment of the story: the spectator is disappointed with the story if liked characters suffer and ultimately fail, and is likewise disappointed and enjoys the story less if disliked characters who are judged undeserving succeed. The spectator enjoys a story the most if liked characters succeed, and disliked characters are given a proportionate punishment. This is illustrated by some of the first empirical investigations of ADT. In one key study, Zillmann and Jennings Bryant showed four-year-old and seven- and eight-year-old American children a fairy-tale programme about one good and one evil prince (Zillmann and Bryant 1975). Upon conquering the kingdom the evil prince sends his brother to lifetime imprisonment in the dungeons, but a turn of events brings the good prince back to power. Shall he retaliate? The story is shown with three different endings: a fair retribution (convicting the evil prince to a life in the dungeons), an excessive punishment (physical abuse) and a forgiving ending (the good prince offers to share his kingdom with his evil brother). The seven- and eight-year-old children enjoyed the tale with a fair retribution more.[10] In a related study, Zillmann and Joanne Cantor showed that children's empathic activity was also related to their moral evaluation of a story (Zillmann and Cantor 1977). Two brothers are portrayed in a film. One is hostile and vindictive in one condition, and kind and supportive in the other. This brother is then shown as either receiving a bicycle as a gift from his parents and jumping for joy, or as being in an accident and cringing in pain. The children empathized with the kind brother when he was happy, as well as when he was in pain. They did not, however, empathize with the mean brother in either condition; they were disappointed when he was rewarded at the end, and displayed sheer delight when watching the version where he is punished – a reaction typically labelled counter-empathy.

These findings have been replicated by many studies, also studying adults (e.g., in Arthur A. Raney's work to which I shall soon turn). This supports the hypothesis that when it comes to stories with Manichean moralities, i.e., a polarized moral structure with good vs. evil characters (Smith 1995: 205ff), it is safe to say that the spectator typically comes to like the hero and dislike the villain; she empathizes with the hero and feels counter-empathy toward the villain; and finally, she wants to see the hero succeed and the villain punished, and enjoys the story less if these desires are not met. The problem, however, is how this works when the morality of a story is not as black and white. The morally murky waters of antihero series show that these theories exaggerate how rationally founded our moral evaluation of stories is. Our intuitive responses to these series often fly in the face of the moral principles we would defend rationally.

Challenging the Orthodox View: Our Liking Is Influenced by Many Non-Moral Factors

I will now focus on two accounts that highlight some for my purposes pertinent problems with these dominate theories of spectator engagement in cognitive film theory and media psychology. Carl Plantinga's critique of Smith's position, and Raney's critical amendment of Zillmann's ADT are related. Drawing on recent developments in moral psychology, both Plantinga and Raney question how central a rational moral evaluation is to our engagement with fiction.

10 *Morally Murky*

Plantinga agrees that one type of spectator response is what Smith labels allegiance, and that such a response is determined by moral judgment. However, *pace* Smith, he argues that it is important to acknowledge how "humans have a tendency to confuse moral and nonmoral judgments, a tendency that films (like other forms of discourse) exploit" (Plantinga 2010: 35). Plantinga's critique could be said to target the grey area in Smith theory's about the role played by non-moral factors: as mentioned, Smith opens up for non-moral factors such as iconography, music and star personae playing a role in the spectator's evaluative process resulting in allegiance, but does not address how these factors interact, and holds that although non-moral factors can influence our moral evaluation, they cannot replace it altogether. Plantinga calls for a more nuanced differentiation between the various pro-attitudes the spectator can come to take toward the protagonist (and con-attitudes toward the antagonist), pointing out that "Smith asks the concept of allegiance to do a lot of work" (Ibid., 38). He accepts and agrees with Smith's account of allegiance only on the condition that we distinguish allegiance from sympathy and liking. Sympathy, as feeling concern for a character, is not the same as a fully fledged sympathetic allegiance.[11] Sympathetic fellow-feeling "is not granted for moral good behavior, but rather to those who need care and concern" (Ibid., 41). Plantinga sums it up this way:

> At least much of the time, moral disapproval or approval does the heavy lifting in determining viewer allegiances. But perhaps viewer sympathy for characters must be distinguished from allegiance for a character or characters. As an emotional reaction of concern accompanied by congruent emotions, we might consider sympathy to be more flexible and protean than allegiance, and its causality more diffuse and unpredictable. We might consider allegiance – our allying ourselves with, focusing on, rooting for a character – to be a relationship established only after appropriate narrative and character development. Thus, we might say that allegiance is long term, relatively speaking, and more centrally depends on the viewer's moral evaluation of a character, while sympathies may be short term and more likely to be independent of moral evaluation.
>
> (Plantinga 2010: 41)

Plantinga differentiates between liking, sympathy and allegiance. The spectator likes a character because she is attractive, witty and graceful, for example, or because the character belongs to her own in-group in terms of ethnicity, religion or nationality. She sympathizes with characters whom she thinks are subject to unfair treatment, or who is in need of protection. And she forms a sympathetic allegiance with characters depending "fundamentally on the spectator's moral intuitions elicited over the course of the narrative" (Ibid., 42). This latter attitude is "closer to a benevolence than to sympathy, because the spectator's benevolent disposition toward a character might survive a moment-to-moment loss of sympathy or anger toward the character" (Ibid.). This latter formulation is interesting and evokes the line of reasoning in ADT: the spectator basically forms stable dispositions toward characters when responding to a narrative.

This differentiation between a sympathetic allegiance strictly speaking, and the more fleeting and fickle feelings of sympathy and liking makes good sense. Furthermore, Plantinga's choice of wording – that a sympathetic allegiance depends fundamentally on the spectator's moral *intuitions* – gives us a further clue to the way to approach this question. Plantinga argues that

> [t]he word "evaluation" suggests a kind of conscious measuring, and for this reason, I would prefer the words "approval" or "disapproval," which captures the often automatic and unconscious nature of this process. Thus, moral approval of a character might be considered to be something like an emotion or an intuition rather than a conscious and deliberate evaluation. This fits, of course, with the moral intuitionism that has recently been winning a great deal of attention in both philosophy and psychology.
>
> (Plantinga 2010: 46)

He points to current research in moral psychology to which I will turn shortly, and writes that

> our moral judgments of people and others tend to stem from many factors that have little to do with moral character *per se*. It would seem to me to be surprising, given this element of human nature, that our allegiance for fictional characters would be strictly rooted in moral criteria (Ibid., 47).

Plantinga concludes that our sympathies toward characters are easily manipulated through various narrative means, and that the rhetorical power of narratives depends on this in particular because audiences "tend to interpret their judgments as having legitimate moral force" (Ibid., 48). In essence, the spectator comes to see someone as morally good, but her evaluation of the character is influenced by many non-moral factors. This is the basic idea on which this book builds, too.

Most of us would not hold that what the antihero does is morally praiseworthy in principle. Indeed, I will argue that the antihero is not actually morally preferable, rationally speaking. The fact that the spectator may perceive the antihero as preferable to his peers in the story world is a different matter. Low-level, automatic responses, such as empathic responses,[12] and relatively simple feelings of liking and sympathy in a Plantingian sense, greatly influence even our long-term sympathetic allegiances. This is the correct causal relation between these various types of spectator responses. The spectator's moral evaluation of the characters in a fiction is not fully

12   *Morally Murky*

rational – it is rather a-rational, in the sense that a rational, deliberate evaluation is often simply not central to our approval or disapproval of a character.

This point ties in with Raney's critical discussion of Zillmann's ADT. Raney takes ADT as his starting point as support for this theory is widespread. Raney has also conducted several empirical studies providing some evidential support for ADT (e.g., Raney 2002, 2005; Raney and Bryant 2002). However, lately Raney has also questioned its validity. Sophie H. Janicke and Raney argue that

> the ADT formula explains well the enjoyment of classic Hollywood stories in which brave heroes fight for the forces of good against evil villains.
>
> (Raney and Janicke 2013: 153)

Nevertheless,

> ADT would be hard-pressed to explain the role of morality in the enjoyment of narratives containing (...) morally complex characters (Ibid., 155).

In another paper, Raney and Daniel M. Shafer point out that

> strictly following the ADT formula, it is reasonable to expect that Zillmann's moral-monitoring viewers would disapprove of an anti-hero's actions and motivations, thus hindering liking and ultimately decreasing enjoyment. But, there is no doubt that viewers *do enjoy* these characters and the narratives they inhabit.
>
> (Shafer and Raney 2012: 1030, emphasis original)

They point to empirical investigations confirming that viewers enjoy anti-hero narratives (Krakowiak and Tsay 2011; Raney and Janicke 2013).

However, instead of discarding ADT, Raney suggests a careful revision of it. In an earlier paper, before starting to explore antiheroes and morally complex protagonists specifically, he had already questioned whether the spectator's dispositions really are the result of constant moral monitoring. He pointed out that it

> seems at times that out affective dispositions toward characters are actually formed rather quickly, without much moral monitoring at all. Extensive evidence suggests that we are generally cognitive misers, that we expend as little cognitive energy or devote as few cognitive resources as necessary in most situations unless we are highly motivated to do otherwise (...). In some cases, especially no doubt with extremely complex narratives or documentaries, viewers dedicate tremendous

Morally Murky 13

amounts of cognitive resources to enjoyable media. Furthermore, most media researchers generally consider audience members to be relatively active during viewing. Nonetheless, it seems at times that our liking and disliking of characters, or at least our propensity to do so, is almost automatic to their introduction into the narrative. At times, it seems that our liking precedes our moral judgment.

(Raney 2004: 352–3)

Raney makes several important points in this paragraph, insights that I will build on in this book. One of them is that our dispositions toward characters in a story are formed very quickly and automatically, and that it seems wrong to say that they are the result of a careful and deliberate moral consideration of the characters and events. Indeed, as Raney also continues by pointing out, the ADT literature "does not seem to actually address how dispositional valence is initially determined" (Ibid., 353).

Another pertinent counterargument against ADT introduced by Raney in the quote above is that we tend to want to use as little cognitive energy as we can – if we can rely on automated, habitual processes, we do so to as great an extent as possible. We restrict deliberate, conscious reasoning to issues that truly demand our reflective attention (such as when we feel conflicted about an issue). I will return to some of the research backing up this claim in the next section. The question would then be how likely it is that we deliberately reflect rationally on moral issues when engaging with fiction, as long as fictional stories are used most prominently by most people for entertainment and enjoyment (cf. Vorderer, Klimmt and Ritterfeld 2004).

Raney concludes that "viewers experience *moral feelings* about characters, which dictate to whom favour is granted or withheld" (Raney 2011: 19, emphasis original). The original idea in ADT that the viewer morally monitors the story is thus adjusted. The viewer does form dispositions toward the characters that predict emotional reactions to and enjoyment of the story events. But notably, these dispositions are typically not the result of conscious moral deliberation; rather, they are formed quickly and automatically by use of moral intuitions and feelings. However, in line with ADT, our affective dispositions toward the characters are seen as of major importance to an enjoyment of the narrative. Raney does not see his own revisions of ADT as a break with the general theory, but rather an important amending of it – specifying what it would mean to morally monitor the narrative. The spectator allows moral intuitions to lead the way.

Raney adjusts other parts of ADT, too. He argues that the spectator goes to fairly great lengths to secure enjoyment of a narrative, often labelled escapism:

it seems that the motivation to escape enables the viewers to look beyond the moral quandaries inherent in the content. It is as if they have switched off the moral lens through which one can view the world.

(Raney 2011: 21)

14 Morally Murky

Raney explores this phenomenon under the label *moral disengagement for the sake of enjoyment* (see also Raney 2006). Moral disengagement is a notion taken from the work of Albert Bandura. He uses the term to explain how people are able to commit monstrous acts, for example during wartime (e.g., Bandura 2002). Bandura argues that even generally good people can be guilty of hideous acts as a result of moral disengagement. Examples of mechanisms of moral disengagement are justification (e.g., reconstructing one's acts, such as killing others, as moral, heroic and necessary); advantageous comparisons (e.g., comparing one's own acts with some even more reprehensible acts); disregarding or distortion of consequences (e.g., not seeing the effects of mass-destruction, as when preventing those giving the order from being present when the orders are carried out); and dehumanisation (stripping the victims of human qualities). It is especially interesting for the present purposes that many of these techniques are at work in antihero series: for example, the antiheroes typically justify what they do ("it is for my family"). Furthermore, they are typically portrayed as morally preferable to some other characters. Finally, the proper villains in the antihero series are dehumanized: in chapter 5 I explore how rape is used to portray the antagonist as subhuman and truly evil, thus fully deserving the antihero's wrath. One can thus say that antihero series use many of these techniques in order to secure the spectator's sympathy with the antihero.

Raney argues that the spectator also uses these techniques when she engages with fiction in order to secure engagement with characters she likes, and enjoyment of the narrative. Raney sums it up this way:

> [moral disengagement for the sake of enjoyment] happens, returning to the ADT formulation, because viewers like characters, know from past media experiences that enjoyment comes from seeing them prosper, and interpret their actions – even some that may be morally questionable, as in the case of so-called antiheroes – in a way that helps them view these characters as virtuous, morally appropriate, and motivated. (...)
>
> Embracing the cognitive-miser urge, viewers trade moral scrutiny for partiality and favoritism. Their desire to enjoy themselves is of utmost importance: thus, they freely give protagonists great moral license to ensure that enjoyment is experienced.
>
> (Raney 2011: 21)

Partiality with the characters we know the best influences our moral compass when we engage with stories – as I will explore further in the next chapter.[13] The spectator tends to bracket a rational evaluation in order to ensure that she enjoys the violence and transgressions found in many stories – not least of all in antihero series.

In line with this, I will also argue that when we engage with fiction, we rely heavily on moral intuitions and emotions rather than rational, moral deliberation – a process I will label *fictional relief*, to which I will return shortly. In order to conclude the present section, we are now better equipped to clarify how my position relates to Smith's and Carroll's related positions, as presented above: just as Raney adjusts ADT, and specifies what moral monitoring should rightly be taken to mean when we engage with fiction, I suggest that the process of forming a sympathetic allegiance with (or, conversely, antipathetic feelings toward) a character rests on moral intuitions and emotions, and not usually strictly speaking rational moral evaluation. When the spectator sees the antihero as morally preferable, she relies on pre-reflective gut reactions – moral intuitions. If amended accordingly, I think the basic insights in Smith's and Carroll's theories are right. My suggestion meshes with and corroborates Smith's idea that our morality does seem to be flexible and somehow partially suspended when we watch fiction, a point with which Plantinga also agrees. To flesh out this suggestion, however, I need to elaborate on what exactly moral intuitions and emotions are, and just how they stand in relation to more reflective moral judgments based on rational deliberation.

What a Moral Evaluation Is: the Dual-Process Model of Morality

Before the now-burgeoning field of moral psychology was established in its own right, but merely categorized under developmental psychology, the view on moral evaluation was one which Jonathan Haidt labels *rationalist* (Haidt 2012: 4ff).[14] Psychologists Jean Piaget and Lawrence Kohlberg saw morality as a type of reasoning: as children play together, slowly they construct moral rules as their knowledge base grows, and as their cognitive abilities mature (e.g., Kohlberg 1968, 1969; Piaget 1932). Children's moral reasoning progresses in stages given by increased cognitive sophistication. A moral evaluation was seen as a rational assessment according to a set of moral rules one had constructed from childhood on. This is the theoretical backdrop to the dominant theories of spectator engagement in cognitive film theory and media psychology that I have delineated.

For example, when investigating how children reasoned about morality, Elliot Turiel found that children differentiated between conventional rules (rules about clothing, food, etc.), and moral rules that relate to harm (Turiel 1983). In one setup, children were asked whether it was OK for a child to wear ordinary clothes to school instead of the required school uniform if the teacher said it was OK. Five-year old children typically say that this is OK; this is a conventional rule, and is not perceived as absolute. Then the children were asked if it was OK for a child to push a boy off a swing because she wants to use it if the teacher said it was OK – but the children say no: they recognize this as a moral rule, and understand such rules as being unalterable and universal. The problem, however, as Haidt sees it, is that with this kind of case studies the theorist narrowed down moral rules (as compared to mere

16 *Morally Murky*

conventional, social rules) to questions of harm. This is indeed what differentiated conventional rules from moral rules for these (American) children. The reason this is problematic is that in many cultures – indeed, in most non-Western cultures – there are many moral rules that have nothing to do with harm (Haidt 2012: 13). So one problem driving the critique of rationalist theories of morality was variation of morality across cultures.

In one classic study, Haidt and his colleagues wrote a series of harmless taboo violations in order to test this (Haidt, Koller and Dias 1993). In these short stories a taboo is violated but no one is hurt or harmed. Two of these stories go as follows:

> *Flag:* A woman is cleaning out her closet, and she finds her old [American or Brazilian] flag. She doesn't want the flag anymore, so she cuts it up into pieces and uses the rags to clean her bathroom.
> (…)
> *Dog:* A family's dog was killed by a car in front of their house. They had heard that dog meat was delicious, so they cut up the dog's body and cooked it and ate it for dinner.
> (Haidt, Koller and Dias 1993: 617)

So, in the flag story, for example, why not use an old flag as a rag? I will return to this line of research in more detail in chapter 5, so suffice it here to state that Haidt finds cultural variation: whereas educated Westerners (more specifically, Americans) tend to say that it is not morally wrong to do so because no-one is hurt, in Brazil – as indeed in most other cultures – they would be more prone to hold that taboo violations are unalterably and universally morally wrong.

Building on prior research conducted by Richard Shweder and his colleagues on the so-called CAD model, Haidt takes this finding to support the idea that our morality rests on several different moral foundations. The CAD model postulates that there are at least three moral domains: respect for hierarchies is in many societies seen as a moral matter in an ethics of community, violations to which elicit contempt (C); violation of personal autonomy triggers anger in an ethics of autonomy (A); and degrading what is holy or pure is a violation of an ethics of divinity eliciting disgust (D) (Shweder 1990; Shweder et al. 1997; see also Haidt 2012: 99). Shweder's main point with the CAD theory was to argue that whereas individualistic Western societies restrict questions of morality to violations of autonomy, most other known cultures have a wider understanding of what is considered a moral violation. In all cultures, issues relating to harm and fairness count as moral questions. However, in Western cultures we tend to narrow down what counts as moral questions to those matters that relate to harm and fairness only. And Haidt argues that nowhere is this more evident than in the rationalist theory of morality. In many non-Western cultures, however, issues relating to loyalty to the group also count as moral questions, as do respect for authorities and hierarchies, and questions relating

Morally Murky   17

to purity and degradation. The rationalist theories of morality have had less to say about these latter types of moral questions.

The Moral Foundations Theory that Haidt and his colleagues developed breaks with the rationalist view (Haidt and Graham 2007; Haidt and Joseph 2004, 2007; see also Haidt 2012: 124ff). In contrast to the rationalist focus on rational, cognitive reasoning about moral rules, Haidt argues that our moral judgments are first and foremost intuitive and emotional. Through evolution, several moral foundations have evolved akin to taste buds, making us perceive something as a moral violation intuitively and react emotionally to this before and without the need of a rational evaluation proper. Haidt takes the CAD model as his starting point, but develops this into a more complex theory with at least six different moral foundations. A basic assumption in the Moral Foundations Theory is thus that human evolution has yielded a set of moral foundations that are activated by moral issues.[15] These moral foundations are pre-reflective reactions, or moral gut reactions. How they are activated varies culturally – moral intuitions are thus shaped socially in the Moral Foundations Theory.

According to this view, morality is a mental mechanism that evolved as a solution to a problem facing humans as they evolved in small groups. According to this evolutionary account, morality is a feature of our mental make-up with a very specific function for mankind – namely to secure cooperation in a group (Greene 2013: 23; Haidt 2012: xiii, 190). This is one of the basic and most important assumptions in current moral psychology. Morality is not primarily seen as a truth-seeking, rational enterprise, but rather as a "set of psychological adaptations that allow otherwise selfish individuals to reap the benefits of cooperation" (Greene 2013: 23).[16] According to Joshua Greene, we have developed moral intuitions and emotions to make sure that we put 'us' ahead of 'me' – moral intuitions and emotions secure in-group cooperation. We need not reason about the logic or function of cooperation in order to cooperate with those in our group; rather, we have feelings such as various empathic responses, loyalty and care that make this natural for us. In order to prevent freeloaders and cheaters, we have developed moral emotions such as anger, disgust, righteous indignation, shame, guilt and vengefulness. These are all pieces in the emotional moral machinery that makes cooperation intuitive (Greene 2013: 49ff). Pre-reflective feelings aid cooperation. It is thus particularly our *social* judgments that are intuitive (Haidt 2012: 57). Haidt argues that morality "binds and blinds" – it makes us biased and partial to the views of the group to which we belong (Ibid., 28), and Greene, too, postulates that our moral intuitions and emotions first and foremost make us tribal. In the next chapter I explore the effects of partiality with those we know well in fictional stories – indeed, according to this view, being aligned with someone and knowing them well will have a strong effect on our moral judgment.

Another important basic assumption in these theories is that moral judgments are often – indeed, typically – intuitive and emotional, and on this

18 *Morally Murky*

Haidt and Greene also agree. Because of this emphasis on the role played by intuitions and emotions this model of morality is often categorized as an *embodied approach to morality*. Embodied cognition is a research paradigm most easily grasped if seen as a contrast to classical cognitivism: classical cognitivism, also known by the label Haidt gives it, namely rationalism, postulates that reason is ultimately what guides the decisions we make, or in morality, our moral judgments. [17] Cognitive film theory is labelled as such exactly because it grew out of classical cognitivism, and postulated that the spectator is actively making sense when watching a film – thus objecting to the illusionist psychoanalytic model that had up until then dominated contemporary film theory. However, nothing in cognitive film theory requires a cognitive film theorist to adhere to rationalism. Gregory Currie points out that there are few, if any, specific theoretical standpoints that all cognitive film theorists will agree on, and that this is a sign that cognitive film theory is "a programme rather than a specific theory" (Currie 2004: 154). Indeed, I am a cognitive film theorist, but what I do could just as well be labelled embodied film theory, as the models on which I draw most heavily in cognitive psychology are those found in the research tradition of embodied cognition. According to this view, our cognition fundamentally depends on and draws from other parts of our cognitive abilities than mere conscious, higher-order cognition strictly speaking, such as our affective and bodily feelings.

As we will see, however, what separates Greene and Haidt's accounts, and is controversial in moral psychology, is what role a proper rational moral evaluation can and should play. Although both emphasize the moral intuitions and emotions that have evolved in humans, neither Haidt nor Greene dismisses the idea that a moral evaluation can also be a fully rational assessment. Indeed, the model of morality that they support can be labelled a *dual-process model of morality*.[18] A moral judgment can rely on two different kinds of cognition, one intuitive, pre-reflective, low-level kind (through the intuitive moral machinery evolved to secure cooperation), and the other a reflective, deliberate kind going through higher-order conscious reasoning.

Another important predecessor to this model, in addition to the ones already mentioned, is the heuristics and biases approach developed by Daniel Kahneman and Amos Tversky. Over several decades of influential research they demonstrate that our thinking can take – as you will now predict – two routes; one fast, through our intuitions, and the other slow, through rational, conscious deliberation.[19] Kahneman and Tversky's main point is that although we tend to think that we typically rely on rational deliberation, the judgments we make (not just morally, but when engaged in any kind of thinking) tend to be reached through fast thinking of the intuitive kind. Our fast thinking is characterized by a number of biases and heuristics (rules of thumb) that we apply daily without much awareness that we do. These biases and heuristics are functional for us in that they alleviate us of the taxing burden of having to evaluate everything, always, strictly rationally – which would be next to impossible for any human being. We need to simplify things and delegate large parts of on-going cognitive processing to lower cognitive processes. This is what our intuitions do for us: they are pre-reflective, automated, low-level thinking, a process called intuitive with an end result called intuitions. Intuitive thinking helps us cope in the world. However, as Kahneman and Tversky also carefully point out, there are many situations where we should be sceptical of intuitive judgments, and turn to slow thinking, as our fast thinking is prone to a series of errors and mistakes.

The question of whether our intuitions are reliable or not is a hotly contested issue in moral psychology. Haidt and Greene disagree on the importance of rational moral judgment. This is evident in the metaphors they use in their respective popular accounts of the dual-process model of morality. Haidt evokes the metaphor of a rider with his elephant in order to explain the role of moral intuitions and reasoning. The elephant represents automatic, intuitive judgment – the way we easily come to see something as morally right or wrong without reflection (Haidt 2012: 45ff). It is the elephant that does all the walking and moving about – the main bulk of moral assessments. The rider, however, sitting on top of this great animal, has the delusion that he is fully in control. He is the metaphor for controlled reasoning, which Haidt concurs is relatively rare: our "*[i]ntuitions come first, strategic reasoning second*" (Ibid., 52, emphasis original). According to Haidt our moral reasoning typically works more like a politician, lawyer and PR relation manager justifying after the fact the moral judgments we have already made intuitively (Ibid., 46, 76). Moral reasoning is a "servant of moral emotions" (Ibid., 25). We think we assess something rationally, but in fact we seldom do – this is the *rationalist delusion* (Ibid., 28). Indeed, when faced with harmless taboo violations, as the one introduced above about eating one's dead pet dog, Westerners typically try to come up with post-hoc fabrications in order to justify their intuitive feelings of condemnation. In line with Western moral theories, they try to find reasons for why eating one's pet dog is harmful in one way or another. If no such harm can be found, they become what Haidt discusses as *morally dumbfounded*: they know what they feel, but are unable to explain why. This is the elephant at work, passing moral judgments, with a perplexed rider on top being unable to explain why the elephant that she supposedly controls is making one move instead of another.

Greene, however, disagrees with this view, and gives a more prominent role to moral reasoning. He uses the metaphor of a camera with two settings in order to explain the dual-process model of morality. The moral intuitive machinery is like a camera's automatic settings – quick-and-dirty, automated processes that are inflexible but have proven to work well in familiar settings as mankind evolved. It is point and shoot, morally speaking. However, Greene emphasises that the camera also has a manual mode, where one can switch to deliberate, moral reasoning in order to make a moral judgment.

20   *Morally Murky*

This manual mode is part of our evolutionary adaptation, too, as it was useful for mankind to be cognitively flexible upon facing unfamiliar situations (Greene 2013: 133ff). The description that Haidt gives of moral reasoning – as post-hoc fabrications given after the fact, like a lawyer defending her client – is not moral reasoning proper, according to Greene. Rather, what Haidt describes is *rationalization*. When you are morally dumbfounded, you are rationalizing – finding rational reasons for a moral judgment that you actually reached quickly through moral intuitions and emotions (Greene 2013: 301).

So if this is not moral reasoning proper, what then does it mean to reason about moral issues? The manual mode (in Greene's metaphor) typically works as a *conflict monitor* (Ibid., 295). If our intuitions about a moral issue are conflicted, we have the ability to switch to the manual mode. When reasoning morally, we are consciously aware of the moral rules we are applying – we know what we are doing and why (Ibid., 136). Reflecting the more important role Greene gives moral reasoning, he also gives a fuller definition of what reasoning is. For example, in one paper he and a colleague write that moral reasoning is

> [c]onscious mental activity through which one evaluates a moral judgment for its (in)consistency with other moral commitments, where these commitments are to one or more moral principles and (in some cases) particular moral judgments.
>
> (Paxton and Greene 2010: 516)

Greene emphasises to a much greater extent than does Haidt what moral reasoning can do. One reason for this difference between the two might be that the problem driving Greene's investigation of the dual-process model of morality was different from the problem that fuelled Haidt's research on this. As we saw, the blind spot that Haidt pinpointed was that of cultural variability. As a philosopher and cognitive neurologist, Greene approached moral psychology from a different angle. He was working on the so-called trolley problem in moral psychology – a thought experiment that has led to so much philosophical debate and empirical research that it is often referred to as a field of its own – as *trolleyology*.[20] The basic set-up is that a runaway train is heading your way. The train will crash into a group of people – let us say 30 people – unless you do something. You can pull a switch that will make the train change its course onto a sidetrack. However, there is one man working on the sidetrack, and the train will kill him. Will you nonetheless pull the switch in order to save 30? Empirical research shows that most people say yes to the switch case (O'Neill and Petrinovich 1998; Hauser et al. 2007; see also Greene 2013: 116). However, by changing the set-up slightly, the results change. Again, a train is heading your way and will kill 30 people. You are standing on a footbridge with another person. If you push that person onto the tracks, this will stop the train from killing the

Morally Murky 21

group of people. Will you push the one person? Most people say no to the footbridge case (Greene et al. 2001; Mikhail 2011; Petrinovich et al. 1993; Thomson 1985; see also Greene 2013: 114). Why do our responses differ between the two cases when the result – killing one person and saving 30 – is the same in both cases?

The reason Greene is interested in this problem in particular is because as a moral philosopher he is a utilitarian or consequentialist. According to this philosophical position, originally developed by Jeremy Bentham (1781) and John Stuart Mill (1865), what is morally right to do is what maximizes happiness or well-being in the world impartially (Greene 2013: 203). The utilitarian position postulates that we should very much switch to the manual mode of our morality in order to do the right thing (as do the other dominant Western moral theories, such as virtue ethics and deontology). When it comes to morality, less is more: we should indeed narrow down what counts as moral questions to harm and fairness, for example (Ibid., 173, 338–9). In essence, this is what the utilitarian position did when it postulated that impartiality is the essence of morality (Ibid., 173). As will be rehearsed throughout this book, this stands in stark contrast to the general thrust of our moral intuitions and emotions, where partiality with those in our own group drives our moral response. Greene and Haidt thus agree that historically in Western societies we have narrowed down what counts as moral questions, and that our dominant moral philosophies postulate impartiality and focus merely on questions of harm and fairness.[21] However, where Haidt sees this as a problem, Greene thinks this is the solution to a series of moral difficulties. Be that as it may, Haidt and Greene's respective normative evaluations of what morality should be are not my focus here. Let us instead return to the trolley problem, and the difference between the switch case and the footbridge case.

Greene assumed that our differing responses to these two scenarios touch upon the two routes a moral evaluation can take:

> The tension between fast and slow thinking is highlighted by moral dilemmas, such as the *footbridge* case, in which gut reactions ("Don't push the man!") compete with conscious, rule-based moral reasoning ("But it will save more lives!").
>
> (Greene 2013: 148, emphasis original)

On further empirical investigations and closer scrutiny, what became evident was that the footbridge case evokes a stronger emotional response than does the switch case: imagining pushing someone triggers emotional warnings that pulling a switch just does not.[22] Because the switch case does not evoke as much of an emotional reaction, we give utilitarian answers: it is better to save 30 people by sacrificing only one. The footbridge case, however, is more upfront and personal about the sacrifice one is making, and the emotional reaction this triggers prevents people from giving utilitarian responses.

22 *Morally Murky*

Furthermore, people whose emotional system is impaired (such as patients suffering from specific brain damage, and psychopaths) tend to give more utilitarian responses to the footbridge case as well: their emotional warning signals are not felt at all, or not as deeply felt, so they still reason that it is morally better to save the 30 and sacrifice one, even in the footbridge case (see Greene 2013: 124).

Greene and his colleagues tested responses to various trolley dilemmas while scanning the respondents' brains in order to map the neurological activity. What emerges from this research is that when we are making utilitarian judgments, a specific part of our brains (DLPFC) is activated. This area is associated with conflict monitoring and conscious decision between conflicted responses. Whereas the areas in the brain that are activated by emotional reactions (VMPFC) are variable and diverse, the areas for conscious reasoning show a high degree of unity to neural substrates (Greene 2013: 136). According to Greene, empirically speaking it should thus be relatively easy to know when someone is deliberately, rationally reasoning about a dilemma. The DLPFC is one area in the brain specifically tied to cognitive control.

Furthermore, what is interesting about the DLPFC as an area for cognitive control is that it has a limited capacity. If the respondents are put under a cognitive load (typically by being asked to memorize and keep in mind a fairly long sequence of numbers, for example, which is doable but difficult for most adults), the DLPFC is so preoccupied with this task that its ability to keep control with other tasks is impaired. Thus, if asking people to evaluate trolley dilemmas morally while under cognitive load, they tend to respond along less utilitarian lines. The cognitive load slows down the utilitarian response as the DLPFC is too busy remembering numbers (Greene 2013: 127ff). One then relies more heavily on intuitive moral judgments instead. Utilitarian responses are cognitively demanding. It is less cognitively demanding to rely on intuitive moral responses. This is the important take-home message from Greene's trolleyology studies.

Fictional Reliefs and Reality Checks

Turning our attention again toward our engagement with fiction, a basic question is what kind of moral judgments we typically make when engaging in a fictional story. As mentioned, in media psychology, an important assumption is that first and foremost we consume fiction in order to be entertained. We generally want fiction to be enjoyable, relaxing, entertaining and pleasurable.[23] With moral reasoning being cognitively taxing, how likely is it that this is the morality on which we typically rely when engaging in a story? Why should I be deliberately trying to do the right thing, and continually consciously monitor my own moral responses when engaging? The main argument in this book is that this is unlikely. It is not that the spectator cannot reason deliberately about moral issues when engaging with

Morally Murky 23

fiction; on the contrary, antihero series regularly and deliberately trigger conflicted moral responses precisely in order to enhance deliberate moral reasoning. However, as I will show, there would not be much of a conflicted response to monitor consciously if it had not been for the fact that when we engage with fiction, we allow ourselves to rely most heavily on moral intuitions and emotions. Rationally speaking, cheering for murderous drug dealers and mobsters would be a non-starter, as the antihero is clearly not morally good; however, our liking these antiheroes is less puzzling when we know which intuitive buttons are pressed narratively in order to make us engage in this way. As Raney argues, the fact that we want to be entertained makes this more likely. The very core of his ideas about moral disengagement for the sake of entertainment is that we morally disengage because we want to be entertained.

In an earlier paper I gave this circumvention of rational, moral judgment the label *fictional relief*, and defined it as follows:

> A fictional relief can be defined as the relief from fully considering the moral and political consequences of one's engagement with fiction, from considering whatever relevance the fiction film may have for the real world, and from whatever realistic basis the narrative has.
>
> (Vaage 2013: 235)

With this I suggested that engaging with fiction typically enhances a specific form of moral evaluation, namely merely an intuitive one. Thinking back to Greene's investigations of the neural correlates of a rational vs. an intuitive moral evaluation, my theory predicts specific neural patterns when engaging with fiction. When engaging with fiction one should typically find the VMPFC areas to be activated, as we evaluate the characters intuitively. The spectator allows herself not to fully consider what moral and political consequences a liked character's actions would have, and which consequences it would have for her to approve what this character does. For example, Dexter's vigilante killings would have as a possible consequence the deaths of innocent people. It is an important principle in our legal system that a person is presumed innocent until proven otherwise. The 'proof' that Dexter sources before he kills would not hold up in court. He is a menace to our legal system. While crucial, this is only one reason why the consequences of Dexter's actions would make them wrong. Another would be the irredeemable nature of killing someone as punishment – if one later were to discover that this person was innocent after all, one can do nothing to amend. This is only one of several reasons why I am against capital punishment. There are a number of reasons why the consequences of Dexter's killings are unacceptable to me on principle. However, in order to enjoy the story about Dexter, I grant myself a fictional relief and turn a blind eye to all of these principles.

Against my account here about the fictional relief in relation to Dexter, one could argue that the narration in this series in fact builds up the series'

24   Morally Murky

premises as a consequentialist justification of Dexter's killings: Dexter cannot resist his killer instincts, so his only choice is putting these instincts to work in detecting and eliminating other serial killers. And as fans of *Dexter* will know, he adheres strictly to this moral code: he only kills serial killers. By doing so, he performs useful vigilante prevention of further crimes – both potential crimes done by other serial killers and by himself, as a compulsive serial killer. If one accepts this narrative setup, it is thus the morally best solution that Dexter acts as a vigilante executioner. However, again, who would defend such a thing in real life? Should real life serial killers be trained to act as vigilante revengers, and given a free pass to kill others so long as they only kill other killers? Would we defend anyone in the police force acting like this? Impartially and rationally, the best thing for Dexter to do would be to hand himself over to the police. Dexter's crimes are not truly justifiable. Rather, what is remarkable is how unimportant and irrelevant these concerns seem when I engage with this series. I, and many others with me, seem ever so easily to allow ourselves not to think about these kinds of consequences when engaging. This is a fictional relief. Through fictional relief, the spectator allows herself to enjoy a vigilante avenger like Dexter, because she does not consider the consequences of police forensics taking the law into their own hands in this way: Dexter's victims simply get what they deserve.

Insisting on a critical evaluation of Dexter's actions almost seems silly – you are not willing to play the game of *Dexter* if you keep insisting that its main character ought to be found out and put behind prison bars. Kendall Walton's notion of silly questions is relevant here. The notion points to things that one should not dwell on if one intends to play the appropriate game with a work of fiction: silly questions are pointless, inappropriate and "irrelevant to appreciation" of the work (Walton 1990: 174). Engaging in the series *Dexter* and persistently questioning the righteousness of its anti-hero seems like such a silly question, or relatedly, a silly response to the series. Rather, if one sympathizes with Dexter, at least in the sense that one wants Dexter to catch the villain instead of continually wanting Dexter to be found out, one cashes in on the suspense and humour in *Dexter* to a much greater degree (see chapter 3). It is more entertaining. Rooting for him is the intended spectator response, and it is what makes the series work. Again, many non-moral factors may contribute to the spectator's sympathy for Dexter – such as admiring his skill, wit, and so on. Furthermore, Dexter appears morally preferable to the other serial killers (justification through advantageous comparison), by making us know him better than the other characters and by pleas for excuses; e.g., Dexter was traumatized as a child (see the next chapter). Through these and other narrative techniques, instead of deliberating on Dexter's right to kill other criminals, the spectator is encouraged to allow intuitive moral responses such as partiality with those she knows the best and enjoyment of punishment of wrongdoers (see chapter 4 and 6) to take centre stage.

However, it seems unreasonable to suggest that an intuitive response is all there is to our engagement with fiction. Do we deliberately turn off our capacity for rational moral evaluation only to rediscover this capacity for higher cognition after viewing? Although I do suggest that we typically allow ourselves to circumvent deliberate, rational evaluation when engaging with fiction – and with the antihero series in particular – I do not think this is the full explanation for the spectator's enjoyment of these series. Indeed, I think part of the attraction of these series is that at regular intervals they confront us as spectators. For example, the moment when Dexter kills may leave the spectator conflicted.

Figure 1.1 In spite of rooting for Dexter, the moment he kills another human being, and enjoys doing so, is arguably intended to make the spectator feel conflicted (*Dexter*, Showtime).

Punishing a wrongdoer may be intuitively pleasurable to watch, but there is something repulsive about serial killers, too (see chapter 5). As I will show in later chapters, many antihero series seem deliberately to try to induce such a conflicted state at specific moments in the narrative. I have labelled this response a *reality check* (Vaage 2013). In an earlier paper I defined it as

> that which occurs when something in a fiction reminds the spectator of the moral and political consequences his or her emotional engagement would have, were the fictional events real (Ibid., 220).

The spectator feels conflicted because she has been disregarding a rational moral evaluation of what the antihero does, but the reality check confronts her with and reminds her of the consequences of his actions, had they been actions in the real world, not just a fictional one. In reality, Dexter is not

26 *Morally Murky*

someone with whom she wants to be associated. Intuitively the spectator finds Dexter's suspenseful chase of other serial killers entertaining and pleasurable, and she does want to see those horrible criminals punished. She has supported his vigilante quest. Rationally speaking, however, few of us support vigilante killings in principle – and intuitively, too, it is unpleasant to see the antihero kill with glee. Antihero series trigger such reflections deliberately, often leaving the spectator sufficient time at moments of reality checks in order to secure such a conflicted response. Again, Greene's findings predict a specific (testable) neural activation if my theory is accurate: the DLPFC area should be activated by reality checks. The DLPFC is activated when we are feeling conflicted, and this is exactly what the reality check intends to do.

Furthermore, if the DLPFC is activated by reality checks, the effects of the latter should be prevented or at least lessened if one were put under cognitive load – as will be remembered, the DLPFC can only tend to so much at any given time. So, if trying to keep in mind a memorized series of numbers while watching a suspenseful episode of Dexter, when the moment comes that he kills the spectator should feel less distanced from him than if she is left to her own devices, fully able to process the conflicted response the killing sequences usually give rise to. Furthermore, as I will also appreciate the series' narration, the actors' performances and other responses that take as their object the series as an object made by someone, my capacity for higher-order thinking can perhaps already be seen as under cognitive load. In chapter 4 I discuss how aesthetic appreciation too may circumvent moral evaluation, and part of the reason might be that the DLPFC's control mechanism function is temporarily impaired by the deliberate attention I am paying to a series' aesthetic features.

During the course of this book I will elaborate on the structuring of antihero series through fictional reliefs and reality checks. However, in order to complete the theoretical overview of the present chapter it is necessary to say a few words about the difference between fiction and non-fiction. I argue that it makes a difference for our engagement in a story whether it is taken to be fiction or non-fiction. Not everyone agrees with this, and in the next, final section I discuss why my claim can be seen as problematic. Readers who are less interested in this philosophical discussion can skip this part and turn to chapter 2.

Does a Story Being Fictional Really Make an Essential Difference for Our Engagement?

Several of the theories I have explored so far do not differentiate between fiction and non-fiction. For example, according to Zillmann, ADT applies to all stories – not just to fictional stories, but to news stories, too. Although ADT has been investigated most prominently in relation to fiction, empirical studies on responses to news (Knobloch-Westerwick and

Morally Murky   27

Keplinger 2007; Zillmann and Knobloch 2001), to sports (e.g., Bryant, Raney and Zillmann 2002) and reality programmes (e.g., Dalakas and Langenderfer 2007) are all in line with ADT. Furthermore, Bandura's notion of moral disengagement is intended to explain how people can commit horrible acts in real life; his theory is not about fiction. Furthermore, when I use dual-process theories about moral evaluation in order to argue what we do when we engage with fiction specifically, it is important to keep in mind that these theories have little or nothing to say about fiction – on the contrary, the dual-process theories developed by Haidt and Greene are very much about real life. If these dual-process theories of morality are right, it is thus obviously true that depending on moral intuitions is not specific only to engagement with fiction.

Turning to cognitive film theory, however, it is usually assumed that it makes an important – perhaps even essential – difference for our engagement in a story whether it is fiction or non-fiction. An intention-response communicative approach is the orthodox way of differentiating fiction from non-fiction film in cognitive film theory and analytical aesthetics.[24] According to this view, non-fiction films do not necessarily differ from fiction films stylistically or by any textual feature. The difference between fiction and non-fiction is anchored in communicative practices. While the director's intention with a fictional film is that the spectator should *imagine* its content, the intention of a non-fiction film is that the spectator should *believe* its content. In presenting a non-fiction film, the director can be seen as asserting something about what is presented as true. The non-fiction filmmaker is committed to the truth of what is presented, beholden to standards of evidence and reasoning appropriate to truth. However, typically the fiction filmmaker knows that the spectator knows that he knows that this is fiction, and thus merely intended to be a prop for imagining, and not to be taken as assertions. The difference in the director's intentions with non-fiction versus fiction film is mirrored in the reception of the film: whereas the spectator assesses what is true in the fiction while watching fiction film, when watching non-fiction film the spectator assesses what is true in the actual world.[25]

Related to this basic theory is the idea that there is a difference between the fundamentally truth-seeking rationale behind watching works of non-fiction (e.g. news, documentaries) and the gratification of entertainment offered by works of fiction. Admittedly, this is a simplification, as there are many reasons the spectator may use fiction, not all of them restricted to merely being entertained. However, keeping in mind that I write about ordinary spectators who, conceivably, after a long day at work snugly curl up on the sofa to watch a piece of fiction, I do defend the claim that relaxation-and-entertainment is the most central gratification that the spectator seeks from a work of fiction, and that other uses of fiction (to learn, to educate oneself, etc.) are secondary to this main function.

The theories I have discussed can be adjusted according to this theory about what differentiates the spectator's experience of fiction from

28 *Morally Murky*

non-fiction. For example, in relation to Bandura's notion of moral disengagement, one could be tempted to say that moral disengagement works in exactly the same way in real life and in relation to fiction. One difference, however, is that we do not seem to truly hold the attitudes we can sometime take on when engaging with fiction: I for one do not truly believe that Dexter's killings are justified, although in the context of fiction I root for him catching the antagonists and finishing them off. One would assume that if moral disengagement were to fulfil its function in real life – that is, the function of allowing people to cross boundaries and perform actions that they would normally see as wrong – the individual who disengages must probably truly believe that what she is doing is right (the victim deserves it; others are worse; I'm fighting for a noble cause, etc.). When we morally disengage in relation to fiction this does seem to be contained to our engagement with fiction to a greater degree. Otherwise, applauding organized crime should perhaps be all the more common, as the gangster genre has made us sympathize with mobsters since the 1930s, thus long before we engaged with Tony Soprano; and if we had not kept our sympathy for the vigilante revenger in fiction contained, one should perhaps have expected the formation of vigilante revenge groups to beat up criminals after seeing *Dirty Harry* (Don Siegel, 1971) or any other vigilante narrative long before *Dexter*. This is not to say that some spectators cannot be influenced in immoral ways by fiction; nor is it to claim that in real life we only root for, or behave as, moral saints. Nevertheless, it seems hard to deny to there is a gap between the ease with which many of us root for serial killers on-screen and what most would find even remotely acceptable in reality. Moral disengagement in relation to fiction seems thus – at least partly – to be cognitively quarantined or compartmentalized. This makes sense in the orthodox view in cognitive film theory, where one assumes that when engaging with fiction the spectator does not fully believe what she sees; she is only invited to imagine. Her responses to the story are thus quarantined. For example, as discussed in the vast literature on the paradox of fiction, the spectator reacts emotionally as if what she sees is happening without truly believing that this is the case.[26]

Nevertheless, although there is not a lot of empirical research to be found on the topic, there are a few pertinent studies which complicate this picture. Indeed, they show that people's real world beliefs and attitudes are influenced by fiction. A careful discussion of these studies is needed in order to say why I nonetheless think it is correct to say that there is a difference between belief-formation while engaging with non-fiction as compared to fiction. This discussion is necessary in order to defend the notion 'fiction' in 'fictional relief'.

Before moving on to this empirical research, however, note that the orthodox view that ties fiction to imagining and non-fiction to belief has recently come under critical scrutiny from a philosophical point of view also. Both Derek Matravers and Stacie Friend, for example, reject the view that a text's fictionality is defined by its encouraging imagining (Matravers 2010, 2014; Friend 2011, 2012). One line of critique has thus

Morally Murky 29

been that belief formation is involved when one engages with fiction, as is imagining when reading or watching non-fiction. This is seen as going against the communicative intention-response view on the division between fiction and non-fiction, defining as one does fiction as something that triggers imagining, and non-fiction as triggering beliefs. Friend, for example, argues that instead of trying to define what fiction and non-fiction are through necessary and sufficient conditions (such as by proposing that prescribing imagining is necessary and/or sufficient for labelling a work as fiction), we should see fiction and non-fiction as genres.[27] Many factors typically discussed in theories of fiction – such as stories being made up and evoking imagining instead of beliefs – are indeed standard features of the fiction genre, according to Friend. Nonetheless, use of the imagination is not exclusive to fiction, or belief to non-fiction.

One problem with Friend's Genre Theory is that it does not offer a good explanation for why there are two (supra-) genres – fiction and non-fiction – to be found in the first place. The intention-response communicative theory easily explains why this is so; stories are either categorized as fiction or as non-fiction because we expect different things from each. The authors' intentions behind the two kinds of stories differ, as audience's engagement with them also differs. If all there is to this differentiation is convention, one can wonder why there is such a seemingly arbitrary separation between these two types of stories. After all, other genre categorizations point to different viewing experiences: a comedy promises a different experience from that of a drama, a thriller or a horror (see e.g., Grodal 1997).

Furthermore, Friend argues that use of the imagination is not exclusive to fiction. For example, she explores how readers of literary texts construct mental situation models while reading to facilitate comprehension of the texts. Briefly put, a situation model is a mental map that we construct in order to understand the story: we continually construct mental models of the space we are reading about (or seeing on-screen), and also about the characters' mental state (simulation as mind-reading in the traditional sense). Friend argues that this is use of the imagination. Importantly, she also points out that there is good reason to think that we construct situation models, and also that we use our imaginations to empathize with characters to the very same degree when reading (or watching) a work of non-fiction as when we engage with a work of fiction. This is an important observation. The spectator orients herself spatiotemporally and emotionally with the characters she sees or reads about.

Nevertheless, it begs the question whether this means that imagination cannot define what is commonly called a fictive stance or fictional attitude. In Gregory Currie's theory of fiction, for example, empathizing with characters onscreen, or simulation in the traditional sense of mind-reading,[28] is given a role in Currie's theory as well, but only a secondary role: he labels it *secondary imagining*. He might fully agree that secondary imagining is just as important for engagement in non-fiction. The term he uses to explain what

30   *Morally Murky*

I label a fictional attitude, however, is *primary imagining*. When engaged in primary imagining, the spectator does not first and foremost simulate someone else (i.e., engage in mind-reading). Her activity should be seen as more closely related to hypothetical thinking. Indeed, when we engage with fiction, more primary than simulating other minds (or, one could add, simulating the space they are in through situation models), is the attitude we take toward the events in the story overall: the spectator simulates that the events of the story are taking place, as in hypothetical thinking. The spectator simulates the process of acquiring beliefs when engaged in a fiction film "the beliefs I would acquire if I took the work I am engaged with for fact rather than fiction. Here I imagine myself acquiring factual knowledge" (Currie 1995: 148).

Or put differently, "readers of fiction simulate the state of a hypothetical reader of fact" (Currie 1997: 68). Thus, the spectator imagines being in a situation where he sees depictions of actual events. She simulates believing that the depictions are factual.[29] Primary imagining in Currie's theory is on a level of our story engagement beyond understanding a character (empathy) in a space (situation models). It denotes an attitude or stance taken toward the work: is it to be believed, or am I merely invited to simulate it (e.g., think that hypothetically this is the case)? Primary imagining has to do with the attitude one takes toward the work overall. I understand that this very idea is what Friend wants to undermine. However, her exploration of the use of imagination in real life and in relation to non-fiction merely shows that secondary imagining is just as relevant for non-fiction. She has not demonstrated that primary imagining is.

Empirical research might help settle this dispute. In one investigation of the neurocognitive effects of reading short stories either labelled 'real' or 'invented', Ulrike Altmann and her colleagues found that

> both contexts, the factual and the fictional one, activate processes of imagination but both reflect different levels of simulation (...). One the one hand, the term *simulation* is used in a broader sense for the representation of inner imitation of actions. Thus, in our study, factual reading would refer to this broader concept of simulation. Fictional reading, on the other hand, seems to represent simulation in the narrower sense of 'imaginative constructions of hypothetical events or scenarios.'
> (Altmann et al. 2014: 28, emphasis original)

Thus, Friend's assumption that we construct situation models when reading non-fiction, and that this is a kind of imagination or simulation, is supported. On the other hand, this empirical research also points to a narrower sense of imagination or simulation being activated by fiction only – that of hypothetical thinking. This latter finding supports Currie's idea that the imagination is activated by fiction in a way it is not by reading non-fiction, thus supporting the intention-response communicative theory of fiction and

Morally Murky 31

non-fiction. The categorization of the work we are watching as either fiction or non-fiction makes a difference for our engagement.

Furthermore, this is also in line with similar research findings in an earlier text comprehension study conducted by Rolf Zwann. He found that readers processed (the same) stories differently according to whether the subjects were told the stories were literary stories or news stories (Zwann 1994). When reading news stories readers allocate more resources to constructing situation models than when reading literary stories. Zwann suggests that readers construct weaker situation models when reading literary stories because they want their interpretation of literary stories to remain more open as they often have twists and unexpected turns that news stories seldom have, so unimportant information can turn out to be more important in a literary story than in a news story. It is interesting that readers of news stories construct stronger situation models than readers of fictional stories – in a sense, then, the imagination is important for reading non-fiction, even more so than when reading fiction! Nevertheless, there are relevant differences between reading non-fiction and fiction when it comes to constructing such mental maps: readers of news stories construct more solid situation models, and disregard unimportant information to a greater degree than readers of fiction, because they are quicker to integrate information about the story they are reading with information about real-world issues.[30] This can also be said to be in line with the intention-response communicative theory of fiction and non-fiction: we expect to believe news stories, so it makes sense that we integrate this information quicker than we integrate information from fiction.

Zwann also points out that readers pay more attention to what he labels surface-level comprehension (focusing on the verbal code itself while reading; being attentive to the text's aesthetics features) when reading a literary story. This also makes sense, as fiction is an object made by someone deliberately for our entertainment, appreciation and enjoyment. News stories are not primarily made for our entertainment and enjoyment.

This brings us back to the central question here: if we form beliefs, too, when engaging with fiction, and not merely imagine (say, in the way described by Currie as primary imagining), do we form beliefs in exactly the same way as when we engage with non-fiction? There is one more relevant study I want to discuss in some detail here because it suggests that we do not. Deborah A. Prentice and Richard J. Gerrig conducted three experiments to tease out how we process information in fictional and non-fictional stories. They suspected that the general idea I have labelled an intention-response communicative approach is flawed: they were sceptical toward the idea that we process fiction using some special cognitive capabilities (one can add: such as the imagination). They thus postulate that "there is nothing unique about the experience of fiction, and no need to invoke special mental processes to account for it" (Prentice and Gerrig 1999: 530). Without postulating any special cognitive capabilities used for fiction only, they do actually find some fine-tuned differences between reception of fiction and non-fiction. Let us see what they are.

32   *Morally Murky*

The first thing they point to is that there are many studies showing that people's attitudes have changed resulting from exposure to fiction – from attitudes about sex roles to ethnic stereotypes (see Prentice and Gerrig 1999: 531). Prentice and Gerrig write that this shows that readers of fiction, too, assume that the information given in the story applies to the real world. However, notably, not all the information in the story is treated as relevant for the real world: they point out that it is only the general assertions about the world that people tend to believe – we assume that the author wants to say something that is indeed generally true about the world when producing a work of fiction. We may come to believe general assertions in a work of fiction – such as a moral in the story and general attitudes – but not everything in it.

Prentice and Gerrig proceed by exploring more carefully how exactly information in stories is processed. The model they find most likely is the dual-process model that will be familiar from my presentation of information processing in relation to moral issues. They point out that what they label *systematic processing* (deliberate, rational evaluation) requires effort: one must be highly motivated to engage this cognitively demanding information processing system. And they then argue that "fictional information is not processed systematically" – among other things because the spectator will not be sufficiently motivated to do so (Prentice and Gerrig 1999: 533). The spectator does not "approach works of fiction concerned about being misled by their content" (Ibid.). This mirrors Raney's assumptions, and my claims about fictional relief, too. Although Prentice and Gerrig do not point to the spectator primarily wanting to be entertained, this may be part of the logic behind this assumption.

Drawing on the dual-process model of information processing, Prentice and Gerrig point out that if information is processed non-systematically (they label this low-level processing as *experiential processing*), one can predict that the influence from fiction is "greatest when readers are responding in the experiential rather than the rational mode", and that fiction can "exert a greater influence on intuitive than on rational beliefs" (Ibid., 535). If this holds true, there is then a difference to be found between belief formation resulting from exposure to fiction and non-fiction respectively. If fiction is processed less systematically/rationally than is non-fiction, we can be more easily influenced by fiction than non-fiction – and paradoxically so, exactly because we do not expect to be influenced by fiction. Nothing in this theory contradicts the intention-response communicative theory. It is true that we engage with fiction and non-fiction differently in that we analyse the claims of non-fiction more deliberately. However, the question of effects is complicated. We sometimes come to believe things in fiction even more easily than we believe things in non-fiction exactly because we have our cognitive guards down, so to say: as we are only engaging with fiction, we are not motivated to critically scrutinize all of the story's claims, attitudes and assertions, and, therefore, we may be influenced by these, unreflectively.

Most relevant for my discussion here, Prentice and Gerrig tested this assumption by manipulating some factors intended to influence the

Morally Murky 33

respondents' motivation to process the information systematically. They assumed that labelling the story the respondents read as either fact or fiction would have such an effect. Even though they started out assuming there was not an essential difference between fiction and non-fiction, Prentice and Gerrig end up making a clear distinction between fiction and non-fiction after all, as summed up in the following quote:

> Fictional information is taken to be motivated by aesthetic considerations, low in persuasive intent, and of indirect relevance to real-world concerns; factual information is taken to be motivated by a desire to inform, or perhaps even to persuade, and of direct relevance to real-world concerns. Therefore, everything else being equal, readers should feel more strongly encouraged to engage in systematic processing of factual than of fictional information.
>
> (Prentice and Gerrig 1999: 539)

This is fully in line with the main thesis in this book, as captured by the notion fictional relief. When testing this empirically, Prentice and Gerrig's prediction was supported. Students at Yale and Princeton read stories from the unfamiliar university setting (i.e., not from the university at which they were students), and told either that they were reading a description written by a journalist (fact condition) or a fictional short story (fiction condition). As expected, the assertions made in the story influenced the respondents' real-world beliefs in the fiction condition, but not in the fact condition. Thus, seemingly paradoxically, the respondents believed the (context-free, i.e., general) assertions in the fictional story, but not the very same assertions when presented as factual! Again, this should not be taken to show that we expect fiction to be true. On the contrary, these effects are found exactly because we do not. As Prentice and Gerrig sum up, "[b]ecause participants processed story information less systematically when it was labeled as fiction than when it was labeled as fact, they were more vulnerable to influence from its weak and unsupported assertions" (Ibid., 540). The take-home message, I suggest, is that there is a difference between how we process fiction and non-fiction, and exactly because we process fiction less systematically or deliberately, it can actually influence us more. Or in Prentice and Gerrig's words: "fictional information is persuasive because it is processed via some nonsystematic route" (Ibid., 542). We do not believe all contextual details in fiction, but we can unreflectively come to believe its general assertions.

In relation to the antihero series, one can see why, from a normative perspective, reality checks are important. What the reality checks do is to trigger systematic, deliberate processing of the information in the story. It is highly likely these checks will make the spectator much more critical toward whatever general assertions can be said to be found in these stories. When engaging in *Dexter*, for example, the reality checks remind the spectator of the atrocity of Dexter's vigilante killings. If the spectator were to become prone

34 *Morally Murky*

to unreflectively succumb to the tempting idea that what Dexter is doing is legitimate, during the stretches of fictional relief offered by the suspense sequences in the series, for example (see chapter 3), these reality checks ought to give her a rude awakening and leave her conflicted.[31] As Greene points out, conflicted states trigger conscious, deliberate reasoning – the manual mode. In spite of their morally bad main characters, antihero series are in fact fairly conscientious. They seldom allow the spectator to rejoice in the antihero's moral transgressions for long, undisturbed by ethical considerations.[32]

If we now turn to the very final question I want to address in this first chapter, this discussion leaves us with a complex yet discernible picture of what it means to engage with fiction in dual-process theories. Reading a story that we know is fictional makes a difference, as compared to reading a story labelled as fact. First and foremost, it makes us rely heavily on low-level, automatic information processing (what Prentice and Gerrig discuss as the experiential information processing system); more so than when we engage with non-fiction. The idea that this is because we do not primarily expect fictional stories to authorize or warrant beliefs, found in the intention-response communicative approach, is basically vindicated. After reviewing some relevant empirical studies in this chapter, it still rings true to say that we process fiction and non-fiction differently, and hold only the latter to standards of evidence. There seems to be a recognizable attitude that we may call a fictional attitude, and that this is different from the attitude we take toward non-fiction stories. For one thing, when adopting this attitude, we do not believe contextual details in the stories (about specific characters or events), but merely some general assertions. Our real-world beliefs can be influenced by fiction, but perhaps first and foremost because we merely expect to engage imaginatively, and thus lower our cognitive guard.

Over time some kind of schemas or heuristics must develop (as Raney has also suggested; see the next chapter), allowing us to recognize something as fiction and aiding us in tuning into such a mode of reception. I label it as fictional relief. Fundamentally, what drives this mode of reception is our desire to be entertained. We morally disengage in order to secure enjoyment. This is also tied up with narrative desires toward the story: we want the story to be maximally engaging, and therefore, for example, we crave suspenseful sequences (again, see chapter 3 and 4).

Finally, it is important to note that we also probably keep some kind of awareness that what we are watching is only fictional in order to maintain this mode of reception. For example, as evident in Zwann's research, we pay more attention to aesthetic features when reading fictional stories than when reading fact. Entering the fictional mode does not leave us unprotected and unreflectively unaware of what we are doing. One concern for me, as a cognitive film theorist, is that the dual-process model may make it tempting to say that when relying on low-level processes, we have no higher-order awareness of the fictional nature of what it is we are engaging with. Presenting the spectator as actively making sense of the information in the fiction she is engaging with has been one of the most central ideas in cognitive film theory.

Arguing that our engagement with fiction consists of automated, low-level responses may seem as a setback to older illusionistic theories with a passive spectator merely taking it all in and possibly being influenced in bad ways. And it is indeed the case that when dual-process theories have been used in media psychology, these theories sometimes sound like illusion theories. For example, in the words of Tilo Hartmann writing about computer games, players "temporarily tend to feel that the things they see and hear are real" (Hartmann 2013: 110). Mirroring the findings already discussed, Hartmann also argues that while playing, the players "primarily process the game in an experiential mode rather than a rational mode" (Ibid., 112), and it is when experiencing the game in this experiential mode that it appears as real. However, Hartmann also want to argue that in spite of coming to *feel* that the portrayed violence in computer games is real when playing because one is processing the information through low-level, experiential processing systems, the players also process the information rationally – thus *knowing* the violence they see is not real. In order to explain why players are not repelled by the violence in the games, he suggests that they "always keep in mind that the ongoing action is, in fact, not really happening" (Ibid., 116). This, however, ends up in a contradiction: if the players always keep in mind that the ongoing action is not really happening, they do not experience it as real.

At the end of the day it is difficult to explain our engagement with fiction without granting the spectator some sort of awareness of the mediated, fictional nature of what she is engaging with. Returning to the paradox of fiction, had we truly believed what we see and hear, we ought to have reacted radically differently. Low-level processing can explain the relief we grant ourselves while engaging, ensuring that the entertainment experience is relaxing and enjoyable, all the while keeping a certain awareness of what it is we see. Indeed, had we not been aware of the fictional nature of the programme, we would probably not have allowed ourselves to rely so heavily on low-level processing. A fictional relief is an attitude or mode we deliberately choose to enter, and that we can snap out off either willingly or because the story calls for more systematic, rational processing. The spectator is never under any illusion that what she sees and hears is actually happening, and using dual-process models do not set us back to illusion theories of fiction.

It is time to investigate the specific effects of the dual-process information processing that is at work when we engage with antihero series. In the next chapter I will turn to the effect of partiality – the tendency we have to show favouritism toward those we know well.

Notes

1. The essays collected in DePaul and Ramsey (1998) and also in Booth and Rowbottom (2014) provide some starting points, and Pust (2012) gives a good overview. Thanks to Jussi Haukioja.
2. Although some of its main proponents also develop a normative theory; see later in this chapter.

36 *Morally Murky*

3. For comprehensive accounts, see e.g., Eder (2006, 2010) and the essays collected in Eder, Jannidis and Schneider (2010).

4. This idea is also shared by many philosophers discussing so-called imaginative resistance, see e.g., Gendler (2000, 2006), Walton (1994), and more recently and in relation to fiction film Flory (2013, 2015). I will not discuss these theories here, but the basic idea is that whereas we are willing to imagine many things we do not hold to be true when engaging with fiction, we seem unwilling or unable to imagine alien moralities. It is thus suggested that story world and real world differentiation seems to break down when it comes to morality. However, our engagement with the antihero series can be seen as a counterexample to this observation, as most of us would – at least rationally – hold that what the antihero does is indeed irredeemably morally wrong. On the other hand, my suggestions about the antihero series can also be said to be in line with the literature on imaginative resistance, as I basically argue that the antihero's moral code is not entirely alien to us; see the next chapter.

5. I discuss Carroll's theory of suspense in greater detail in chapter 3.

6. For an excellent introduction to cognitive film theory, see Nannicelli and Taberhamn (2014); see also Allen and Smith (1997); Currie (2004: 153ff); Nannicelli (2014).

7. See also Smith (1999: 220). And note that Smith uses the notion anti-hero differently here from how I do; in Smith's terminology, an anti-hero is a character with which we are aligned but not encouraged to form a sympathetic allegiance. In my terminology, an antihero is someone who is seriously morally flawed, but whom we are nonetheless encouraged to sympathize with. See my discussion of this in the preface.

8. I discuss the POV shot's function in relation to allegiance in Smith's theory more specifically in Vaage (2014).

9. Again a parallel is found in Smith's theory. He writes about empathy, which he subdivides into emotional simulation and affective mimicry, that they typically "function *within the structure of sympathy* (...) are subordinate to [it]" (Smith 1995: 103, emphasis original). I return to this discussion in chapter 3, as Smith does discuss the effects of affective mimicry as potentially "running against the grains of the [response] invited by the structure of sympathy" (Ibid., 104).

10. The younger children enjoyed the story more the more severe the retaliation – this result is taken to confirm Piaget's theory about the maturation of moral reasoning. I return to Piaget's theory later in this chapter.

11. Plantinga also includes the notion of empathy, as feeling congruent emotions with a character, in the notion sympathy, as he points out that the two responses (feeling for and feeling with) typically accompany each other. I agree that this is the case – they typically travel in pairs (see Vaage 2010). However, as I will argue in chapter 3, keeping them separate is useful in order to tease out the causal relations between low-level character engagement stemming from mere emphatic mirroring effects and a moral evaluation proper.

12. See Vaage (2010). I will have the most to say about what I label *embodied empathy* in this book (see chapter 3), but *imaginative empathy* will also sometimes be central to my argument, for example in my thought experiment about seeing *Breaking Bad* from Skyler's point of view (see chapter 6).

Morally Murky 37

13. Another important part of Raney's solution is *schema theory*: viewers develop schemas that provide them "with the cognitive pegs upon which to hang their initial intepretations and expectations of characters" (Raney 2004: 354, see also Raney 2011 and Raney and Jackie 2013). I will not explore this furher here, but will return to this in the next chapter.
14. This view can also be tied to classical cognitivism. I will return to this.
15. Others, such as Jesse Prinz, have explored similar theoretical ideas. See chapter 5.
16. As Greene points out, this idea originates in Darwin (1871). For further references, see Greene (2013: 362n.23).
17. See e.g., Wilson and Foglia (2011).
18. In chapter 3 and 4 I also explore a related dual-process model of empathy. The theoretical thrust of this book can thus in more than one way be seen as belonging to the tradition of embodied cognitition.
19. For an excellent overview, see Kahneman (2011), and for example also the essays in Gilovich, Griffin and Kahneman (2002).
20. The trolley problem was first introduced by Philippa Foot in 1967, and has since given rise to a large amount of literature in ethics. See Greene (2013: 367, unnumbered note on "The Trolley Problem").
21. For Haidt's account of this, see Haidt (2012: 114ff), and for Greene's quite different assessment, see Greene (2013: 338ff).
22. For Greene's detailed explanation for why we experience the two scenarios so differently, see Greene (2013: 105ff).
23. Notable counterarguments to this general statement are easy to find, as in the much discussed paradox of tragedy or the related paradox of horror, where it is rightly pointed out that we seem to seek out these genres in order to feel negative emotions. Nonetheless, the main point is that spectators do seem to enjoy being sad or frightened, and this is what makes this phenomenon appear paradoxical. For a good overview of both paradoxes, discussed as the paradox of negative emotions, see Plantinga (2009: 169ff). See also Paisley Livingston's analysis of Du Bos' early take on the paradox, oft-ignored in the literature (Livingston 2013). Indeed, in line with my analysis here, Du Bos argues that we use fiction primarily to find some relief from boredom.
24. See e.g., Carroll (2003: 193–224); Currie (1990); and Plantinga (1987; 1996; 1997). See also Lamarque and Haugom Olsen (1994) for a related view in relation to literature.
25. I restrict my analysis here to cases of accurate or correct uptake of the director's intention, and do not consider cases where people get it wrong (e.g., think that a work is fiction whereas it is actually non-fiction, and *vice versa*).
26. See e.g., Carroll (1990), for a disucssion more specifically tied to fiction film, and the essays collected in Hjort and Laver (1997).
27. See also Stock (2011) for an overview of the debate and a defence of an imagination-based theory of fiction.
28. On simulation theory, see e.g., Goldman (2006).
29. See also my analysis of Currie's account in Vaage (2009). Although in this paper I criticize Currie for not giving empathy a more important role in his theory about engagement with fiction, I do see how primarily imagining is more important in order to explain what characterizes engagement with fiction specifically.
30. Zwann also suggests that reading news stories entails a more radical integration process, but the latter seems merely to denote integrating textbase

38 *Morally Murky*

assumptions into a coherent representation on his account (drawing on Kintsch's construction-integration model), see Zwann (1994: 930).

31. As Lerner and Goldman point out in their discussion of dual-process models in another context, rational, systematic processing is indeed more normatively based (Lerner and Goldman 1999: 632). When processing rationally, we pay greater attention to what we think ought to be the case in a more principled deliberation.

32. See chapter 4.

2 Partiality

How Knowing Someone Well Influences Morality

Among the many brute killers in the New Jersey Mafia portrayed in *The Sopranos* – including the antihero Tony Soprano – Tony's mother Livia acts as the first season's antagonist in the dramatic season finale. Livia conspires with Tony's uncle Junior to have her own son killed. This is indeed an immoral act – but in many ways not objectively worse than the many other murders in the series. Nevertheless, for the spectator, I contend that Livia's betrayal of her own son stands out as nothing short of a monstrous act. The spectator will typically perceive Tony's mother as a despicable human being. By what moral standard is Livia an antagonist?

In this chapter I propose that the moral code that *The Sopranos* and other antihero series both exploit and explore, and that Livia violates, is loyalty with those in one's own group. The antihero is not amoral; he is loyal toward his own and can thus be seen as following a moral code. Furthermore, these series capitalize on this basic morality in another sense as well: the spectator tends to become partial to the antihero's perspective through alignment. Partiality with one's own is both explored thematically in *The Sopranos* and is an effect on which these series rely in order to make the spectator grow increasingly fond of the morally flawed antihero. The thematic exploration of the moral code of partiality and the intended effect of partiality on the spectator are probably linked: it might be easier for the spectator to allow herself to become biased by Tony's and other antiheroes' perspective when the series presents partiality as morally good, basically.

I concentrate on the morality of *The Sopranos* through investigating four examples. First, I delineate how this series induces sympathy with its antihero Tony. Second, I analyse why Livia is the antagonist in the first season; third, I argue that the FBI agents pressuring Adriana La Cerva to "rat" on her mobster boyfriend Christopher Moltisanti also come off as antagonistic. Finally, I point to Dr Jennifer Melfi's function as a meta-perspective on Tony throughout the series, and I argue that through this character, the series engages in a self-aware commentary on the engagement it entails. At the end of the chapter I also look at the spectator's sympathy with Walter White in *Breaking Bad* to illustrate how other antihero series after *The Sopranos* carry forward the heritage from this ground-breaking study of sympathy with its morally dubious main character; once she has sided with someone, the spectator is a stubborn sympathizer.

40 *Partiality*

As Amanda Lotz points out in her study of what she labels *cable guys* – the flawed protagonists in so many contemporary American television series on cable television – they typically do what they do for their families (Lotz 2014). These protagonists "are mostly driven by motivations related to families – a need either to provide for or to reconstitute them. (...) [T]he motivation of family need [is presented as] a noble cause in the narratives" (Lotz 2014: 63). A commonly found trope in these series is thus the antihero's claim that he does it all for his family. As Tony Soprano puts it in one of his sessions with Dr Melfi: "I'm a good guy, basically. I love my family".[1] As Walter White works his way up in the Albuquerque drug underworld, he reassures his wife Skyler that "how matter how it may look, I only had you in my heart", and that "I've done a terrible thing. But I've done it for a good reason. I did it for us."[2] And the biker Jackson Teller in *Sons of Anarchy* uses the very same excuse: "I love this club, but I love my family more".[3] This dedication and loyalty to his family contributes to making the antihero appear to the spectator as morally preferable to any character who violates this norm – it is an intuitively attractive character trait to care about one's family. Later, in chapter 6, I will return to Lotz' analysis and explore further her observation that in spite of these good intentions, "the burdens he takes on in provision consistently end poorly for him and his family" (Ibid., 73). However, here I will investigate how the antihero's devotion to his family is important in order to enhance sympathy with him in the first place.

That loyalty toward one's own enhances sympathy with a character is confirmed in an empirical study conducted by Allison Eden and colleagues (Eden et al. 2015). They asked their respondents to name heroes and villains in film and television and rate them using the domains of morality (loyalty, care, fairness, purity and authority) found in the Moral Foundations Theory (as mentioned in the previous chapter). Not surprisingly, they found that villains violate all domains more than do heroes. However, heroes may also violate some domains – most notably authority (e.g., the superhero can defy what the mayor of his crime-ridden city says in order to save people). However, for heroes, upholding the loyalty domain (not betraying his own group) is of the utmost importance. Furthermore, although the researchers did not initially plan to compare pure heroes to antiheroes (and then to villains), many respondents named heroes that the researchers would label as antiheroes (e.g., Dr Gregory House, Don Draper). Although cautioning against the *ad hoc* nature of these results, the researchers did also run a comparison of antiheroes vs. heroes vs. villains, and – again not surprisingly – found that the antihero fell somewhere in between heroes and villains (Eden et al. 2015: 204n.5). Interestingly, they also found that the antiheroes would violate several domains more than a pure hero would (e.g., harm, fairness, authority) – but there were no significant differences for loyalty. This points to the importance of group loyalty even for antiheroes. Let us then start by exploring the function of loyalty in our moral minds.

Friendship, Morality and Television Series

Kwame Anthony Appiah argues that whereas according to the dominate moral theories in Western philosophy, we should apply the same criteria impartially in all judgments of the same kind, we do in fact apply different criteria in different situations (Appiah 2008: 108).

> We know, too, how easily an engaging story can defeat our allegiance to this or that dictum. Should cars parked in front of fire hydrants, such as one belonging to Bob the accountant, be towed? Sure. Now tell me a story about Joanna, a good woman who's having a bad day, with details about her hopes and dreams, her kindness to an ailing friend, her preoccupation with a troubled child. I don't want *her* car to be towed. In the abstract, we're opposed to theft. But any competent screen-writer could concoct a story about a cool, big-hearted car thief, shadowed by a Javert-like detective as he prepares to pull off one last heist – and get you to switch sides, at least until the credits roll (Ibid., 104, emphasis original).[4]

Learning about someone's background and her reasons for doing whatever she does influences our moral evaluation of that person to a great extent. And the people we know the most about are typically our family and friends. Furthermore, we also tend to see loyalty to family and friends as morally good; I feel a special obligation toward my husband, my mother or my long-time friend, and it seems morally right to favour these individuals over complete strangers – to a certain extent.[5] Personal relations make us biased and partial. We tend to show favouritism toward the ones we know well and love, and we feel morally warranted in doing so. Arthur Raney has proposed an explanation for why this is so (Raney 2004). Evaluating something rationally from an impartial perspective is cognitively taxing, and on the whole, we are cognitive misers. On an everyday basis we try to use as little cognitive energy as we can – unless something definitely calls for deliberate, rational evaluation, we generally rely on low-level responses, rules of thumb and cognitive schema as long as we can. Hence, if we like and love certain people, it is by far more comfortable for us to go on loving and liking them instead of truly evaluating, and continually re-evaluating, them from an impartial perspective. Thus we see everything they say and do through a lens of favouritism, explaining away or turning a blind eye to things they may do that we would not normally approve of. This avoids cognitive dissonance and conflict, and allows us to go on loving and liking them.

As will be remembered from the previous chapter, in the dual-process model of morality the basic idea is that our moral intuitions and emotions evolved to secure co-operation in a small group. We are fundamentally tribal, as Greene labels it for example – we favour those close to us (Greene 2013: 48ff, see also Haidt 2012: 234ff). This phenomenon is often discussed as *parochial altruism* (cf. Choi and Bowles 2007). It is universal: despite

42 *Partiality*

cultural differences, all humans show in-group bias (Brown 1991). Greene and Haidt point to several different kinds of studies that demonstrate how easily group membership favouritism is awakened in us. For example, even six-month-old infants prefer looking at speakers without foreign accents (Kinzler et al. 2007), and most whites – even children as young as six years – have an implicit preference for whites over blacks (Baron and Banaji 2006; Greenwald et al. 1998).

One line of research tests how people behave when given nasal spray with oxytocin, a hormone naturally released in maternal care and associated with empathy and trust. In one experimental setting with respondents linked in teams playing economic games, researchers found that in-group favouritism increases with higher oxytocin levels – the players given oxytocin made less selfish decisions and cared more about helping their own group (De Dreu et al. 2010). In a follow-up study, they found that oxytocin made Dutch people favour Dutch names more (De Dreu et al. 2011). As Haidt points out, oxytocin is often described as the love-hormone in popularized accounts, but notably, it does not make us love humanity in general – merely those we perceive as part of our own in-group (Haidt 2012: 234). Greene concludes that "our brains are wired for tribalism. We intuitively divide the world into Us and Them, and favor Us over Them" (Greene 2013: 54). Indeed, as Heidi L. Maibom points out, empathy is parochial – "we feel more empathy for those close to us spatially, temporally, and affectionately" (Maibom 2014: 28).

While (in Western societies) our collective sense of morality is now also shaped by the transition to large societies (wherein our laws build on impartial, universalistic reasoning), emotionally we are still easily manipulated into favouritism and partiality. This tendency was an evolutionary advantage to our forebears living in small groups, and it is not something we have left behind. Indeed, Robert Blanchet and I have argued that "[e]ngagement in long-term narratives activates some of the same mental mechanisms as friendship does in real life" (Blanchet and Vaage 2012: 28). Through narrative mechanisms of alignment, i.e., following a character spatio-temporally and being allowed access to what he is thinking and feeling, the spectator gets to know fictional characters intimately. There is much work in film theory and media psychology to explain the fact that the spectator comes to care for the characters we get to know.[6] Moreover, Blanchet and I argue hat television series activate these mental mechanisms of partiality more prominently than the, relatively speaking, short and self-contained fiction film.

Blanchet and I point to a variety of empirical research in support of this idea. For example, Roger Zajonc is an early proponent of dual-process models of cognition, and he established the research tradition on what has been known as *the familiarity principle* or *exposure effect* (see e.g., Zajonc 1968). Through a series of experiments, Zajonc showed that mere exposure to an object tends to increase liking of it. Later this finding was also replicated in relation to exposure to people (see e.g., Bornstein 1989; Moreland and Beach 1992; Saegert et al. 1973; Zajonc 1968). Blanchet and I argue that television

Partiality 43

series capitalize on the effects of familiarity. Being exposed to characters (and the series in its own right) over months and years is bound to create a warm feeling of familiarity when snuggling up in the sofa to watch a new episode – indeed, as when catching up with old friends. Blanchet and I sum this up in the following way:

> Spectators tend to like what they have been exposed to more, and the feeling of familiarity is pleasurable. Familiar characters are powerful tools to get the spectator hooked. Furthermore, by generating an impression of a shared history, television series activate mental mechanisms similar to those activated by friendship in real life. These factors, and several others, create a bond with characters in television series that tends to be described in everyday language as a sort of friendship.
>
> (Blanchet and Vaage 2012: 18)

Television series can probably to a much greater extent than fiction film rely on the mere familiarity principle to maintain a sympathetic attitude toward characters once these have been established.

Zajonc used his findings on the familiarity principle to argue that before we process information rationally, there is a flash of affect that prepares us affectively for an encounter with someone or something – a basic mechanism to signal to us instantly whether we should approach or be cautious. As Haidt shows, the idea is an old one in psychology, although it lost ground in the early days of cognitivism that focused on rational processes. Wilhelm Wundt had already argued for the doctrine of affective primacy in the 1890s (see Haidt 2012: 55). Haidt sums up affective primacy as follows:

> we find ourselves liking or disliking something the instant we notice it, sometimes even before we know what it is. These flashes occur so rapidly that they precede all other thoughts about the thing we're looking at. You can feel affective primacy in action the next time you run into someone you haven't seen in many years. You'll usually know within a second or two whether you liked or disliked the person, but it can take much longer to remember who the person is or how you know each other.
>
> (Haidt 2012: 55)

Adding to the effects Blanchet and I discuss, one can thus predict that our affective recognition of the characters in television series precedes our rational, conscious recognition of who they are. Before remembering reflectively exactly who all supporting characters are in the often huge ensemble casts of Quality TV series, one probably instantly feels whether this is a sympathetic or unsympathetic character. I may not remember what exactly this character has done to be liked or disliked – but my basic sympathetic orientation is usually in place even after months (or sometimes years) of hiatus between seasons.

44 *Partiality*

Long-term narration is facilitated by the familiarity principle in more than one way: by creating a strong bond with the characters, drawing on our tendency to like what and whom we know the best; and also by relieving the series creators of the need to constantly remind the spectators of who the characters are and what they have done – we may not remember all preceding narrative events reflectively, but our basic affective memories are better equipped to separate between friend and foe.

Quality TV series have less explicit exposition (e.g., dialogue reminding the spectator of previous events to make up for the memory loss that naturally occurs between episodes) than other kinds of long-term narration on television, such as soap operas, traditionally have. Part of the reason for this might very well be the massive growth of extra-textual sources of information, such as the Internet – nowadays one can rapidly Google in order to refresh one's memory about a supporting character in a TV series, whereas just a few decades ago long-term narration had to make sure the spectator got all this information through the narrative.[7] *Game of Thrones* (HBO, 2011-present) is a good example here – this series has a huge ensemble cast and exceptionally little traditional exposition. However, when engaging in this series, too, Wundt's old insight about affective primacy makes good sense: although I often find myself not remembering exactly what narrative turn put any character x in situation y, I know whom I like and dislike in the series. And these feelings are remarkably stubborn.[8]

How does all of this mesh with existing theories about spectatorship in cognitive film theory? Returning to my discussion of the role played by moral evaluation in Murray Smith's theories, he holds that the distinction between alignment and allegiance (introduced in chapter 1) is important. While earlier film theorists such as Wayne Booth, Mieke Bal, and Seymour Chatman have "all argued or implied that alignment with a character necessarily creates a basic sympathy for that character," Smith holds that "[i]t is particularly important that we grasp the distinction between alignment and allegiance" (Smith 1995: 187). Although fiction film typically aligns the spectator with the character(s) she is also supposed to see as morally preferable and feel sympathy toward, this is not necessarily the case, according to Smith. To be fair, he does suggest that alignment can perhaps "exonerate actions" that would otherwise be "easier to condemn" (Smith 1995: 223). And he asks:

> Am I not inclined to forgive, or at least overlook, the immoral actions of someone whom I like or love rather more than in the case of someone I dislike or detest? Surely our judgments of particular traits and actions continually contaminate or inflect one another. This might not reflect our moral ideals, but it is surely a reality of our moral existence.
> (Smith 1999: 228)

What Smith points to here is that understanding the background someone has for doing something wrong may indeed make the deed seem less of a

Partiality   45

moral trespass. Moral evaluation of the characters should not be seen as an objective and impartial evaluation of all characters, independently of whether or not we know them well. Nevertheless, as discussed in the first chapter, Smith maintains that "[m]oral assessment of characters (...) constitutes a kind of center-of-gravity that amoral factors may inflect, but not displace" (Smith 2011a: 84).

There is good reason to argue that the relation between alignment and allegiance is more systematic than Smith acknowledges. Whom the spectator gets to know through alignment makes a systematic difference for her moral evaluation; we typically evaluate those we know well more favourably than those we do not know at all. Thus, when engaging in a television series, narrative alignment activates some of the mental mechanisms that make us as spectators take sides, show favouritism and evaluate the narrative events with the biases given by the well-known character's point of view. The spectator is blinded by familiarity – meaning that she will turn a blind eye to the liked character's moral flaws. In this way, the literature on partiality and morality potentially explains the relation between narrative alignment and moral allegiance with a fictional character.[9]

For example, the episode "Second Opinion" in *The Sopranos* offers a pleasurable depiction of vengeance.[10] Tony Soprano is the boss of the New Jersey Mafia and his uncle Junior has cancer. Junior is worried about the treatment he has been given, but his oncologist, Dr Kennedy, does not return his calls. This infuriates Tony. He approaches Dr Kennedy on the golf course and scares him into taking better care of his patient. Smith writes of this scene: "If we isolate the miniature drama that unfolds between Soprano and Kennedy during 'Second Opinion', there's no doubt that Soprano comes across as the more sympathetic character, largely on moral grounds" (Smith 2011a: 78). I agree with Smith that the spectator perceives Tony as the most sympathetic character. I would assume that a typical reaction is to enjoy the humiliation of Dr Kennedy, and cheer for Tony. But is the spectator's perception of Tony as most sympathetic really made on moral grounds? The doctor may be arrogant, but as long as Junior is given the proper treatment, this is no crime; however, intimidating people with threats of violence is. On the one hand one could say that the spectator enjoys this sequence even though she knows that what Tony is doing is not morally right, and I will return to the question of enjoying the antihero's very immorality in chapter 4. Here, however, I would like to stress the point that it is easy to perceive Tony as being, in some sense or another, morally right in this sequence, although arguably on reflection the doctor is morally preferable to Tony. Notably, stepping up to Dr Kennedy adheres to the morality of partiality, which also influences the spectator's evaluation of this sequence: it corroborates on Tony as a man who loves his family and who is a good man, basically, because of this. He threatens Dr Kennedy for what appears to be a good reason, namely to take care of his poorly, old uncle.

46 Partiality

Alignment with and access to Tony have profound effects on the spectator's judgment of him. The spectator has followed Tony through his anxiety attacks, learned about his psychopathic mother, his troubled conscience, and about how much he cares for a little family of ducks that has lived in his pool for the summer. The spectator does not learn much about Dr Kennedy, besides his arrogance as a doctor. All these pleas for making excuses on Tony's behalf, and none on behalf of Dr Kennedy! What if Dr Kennedy is somehow inattentive toward his patient because he is going through a divorce? Or what if being forced to take better care of Junior means that some other poor cancer patient, like the ageing charity worker Eva, who has no relatives to fight for her interests, gets less attention? Would this not entirely change our perception of Tony when he threatens Dr Kennedy on the golf course? However, the spectator is not invited to imagine in this way in relation to the doctor. It is only Tony's reasons for intimidating Dr Kennedy that she learns about. It is Tony's point of view she is invited to share, and Tony perceives Dr Kennedy as arrogant. No wonder the spectator perceives Tony as morally right. But from an impartial point of view he is not. Threatening whomever one perceives as arrogant is not morally right. The spectator's evaluation of Tony's behaviour is not grounded in general moral laws and principles. One thus needs to recognize the systematic way in which alignment influences allegiance. Knowing someone well makes us evaluate his or her behaviour more favourably.

Figure 2.1 The spectator sees Tony as in the right threatening Dr Kennedy due to the way alignment systematically influences allegiance (*The Sopranos*, HBO).

Smith and Carroll suggest that one way of making a character morally preferable is to present other characters as morally worse (Carroll 1996a, 2004, 2010; Smith 1995, 1999, 2011a). A character can be portrayed as morally preferable, relatively speaking in the fictional universe, and this is

Partiality 47

sufficient to make the spectator sympathize with this character. I will call characters who serve the function of making the main character morally preferable *contrast characters*. *Pace* Carroll and Smith, I argue that what makes the spectator perceive these contrast characters as morally worse is often merely the fact that the spectator is aligned narratively with the anti-hero. Sometimes these contrast characters are actually morally worse, but often they are only perceived this way: the antihero is after all typically the leader of whatever criminal enterprise in which he takes part, and as such would, rationally speaking, carry the full responsibility for many of its consequences. Tony is not just any old gangster, but a gangster boss. Although some of his subordinates may appear as complete psychopaths – such as Ralph Cifaretto, whom I also discuss in chapter 4 – were we to imagine a court case against Tony and Ralph, Tony would probably get the most severe punishment, as the Mafia leader. So the effect of mere partiality on moral judgment does arguably appear to be strong. The spectator's evaluation of Dr Kennedy is one clear-cut case, as this doctor is not by far as immoral as any of these mobster killers, but as a spectator to the sequence where Tony humiliates Dr Kennedy, it is probably difficult not to feel that Tony is in the right.

An important part of the explanation for our sympathy with the antihero is that through alignment with him he is portrayed as a complex human being with positive sides in addition to his negative sides. Smith argues that the spectator may like the character for these positive or at least deeply human sides, in spite of the character's morally bad sides (Smith 1999). It is indeed true that the spectator learns to know Tony through his human weaknesses, i.e., his depression and panic attacks, and also through his positive sides such as his being a loving father and a family man. Tony cares both for his biological and extended gangster family. Giving the spectator access to Tony's inner demons – his anxiety, his worries, his conscience, his troubled family background – generates understanding and sympathy for Tony. As Adam Morton argues, making someone familiar in one way or another may even enable empathy with someone doing something evil: a "basic function of empathy is to transfer understanding from the familiar to the unfamiliar" (Morton 2011: 328). However, again the effect of partiality plays an important role: beyond the question of liking Tony because of or in spite of his morally bad sides, the spectator's mere perception of Tony changes because she gets to know him so well. I will refer to this as the narrative making *pleas for excuses* one the character's behalf: as Appiah points out, learning to know someone's background makes us treat her case as an exception (see also Austin 1956/7). It may be that generally, what Tony does as a gangster is morally wrong, but *in this case* perhaps it is less wrong because he had such a terrible childhood/he does it for his family, etc. Or so the spectator may think. Making pleas for excuses on the character's behalf is a prominent way through which alignment systematically influences allegiance.

48   *Partiality*

We have seen that alignment with a character, getting to know him well, influences the spectator's moral evaluation of that character to a great degree. Interestingly, *The Sopranos* not only relies on the spectator becoming partial, but explores the morality of partiality thematically as well, in the mobster obsession with loyalty. It is in this light that Livia makes sense as an antagonist. So before exploring our relation with Tony further, let us look at the portrayal of three female characters in this series that further illustrate the morality of partiality at work.

In the Ninth Circle of Hell: Livia and Betrayal

Livia is introduced in the very first episode of *The Sopranos*. We have learned about Tony's depression and anxiety attacks through his sessions with psychiatrist Dr Melfi. Through flashbacks, we are introduced to Tony's way of life as Tony describes it to Dr Melfi. Despite the dramatic material, or probably more precisely, due to the not just dramatic but also grim material of the series (Tony's depression, his brutal way of life), this pilot episode seems to want to ease the spectator into engagement through emphasizing its comical aspect. The episode is narrated in a light-hearted fashion, with non-diegetic doo-wop music. When Tony enters his mother's home, however, the tone in the narration changes. Tony has brought her a CD player, but Livia is gloomy. Tony puts on a classic Crooner to cheer her up. Our first impression of her is repeated in every encounter: she is a negative, angry, resentful, guilt-inducing martyr mother, always complaining, always blaming Tony (for not calling; for not caring; for wanting to put her into a retirement community; for not taking her into his own home, etc.). In a later episode, when Dr Melfi asks Tony to think of a happy childhood memory with his mother, Tony struggles to find such a memory.[11] Through therapy, Tony slowly realizes that his mother never properly cared for him and that he should resist feeling the guilt that she is constantly trying to induce. This background information is of great importance for the construction of sympathy with him in this first season. Livia is everything a good mother is not supposed to be – selfish and ungenerous. This invites the spectator to understand why Tony has turned out to be the aggressive brute he is, and to feel sorry for him – in other words, to sympathize.

There are many other mobsters, such as Richie Aprile and Ralph Cifaretto, that serve as unsympathetic contrast characters in later seasons in the series. However, in the first season sympathy for Tony is primarily constructed by making him recognizably human. The most important contrast character to ensure sympathy for Tony in the first season, is Livia. However, Livia's role as antagonist in the first season goes beyond merely being a tyrant mother. Tony and his wife Carmela finally succeed in convincing her to move into a retirement community (in Livia's view, a nursing home to which she is sent to die). Livia cannot forgive Tony for this, and when she learns that Tony is seeing a psychiatrist, she drops a comment about this to Tony's

Uncle Junior – newly made North New Jersey gangster boss.[12] She is well aware of the damage this may do Tony in the gangster world, as he cannot show any sign of weakness. One suspects she does this with the purpose of harming her son. These sinister suspicions are confirmed later in the season. Ultimately, she even conspires with Uncle Junior to have someone take Tony out. Toward the end of the first season, the major conflict building up toward the season finale is Livia's conspiring with Tony's Uncle Junior to kill Tony.

In his essay on *The Sopranos*, Peter J. Vernezze points out that if we were to judge the different characters according to medieval author Dante Aligheri's description of Hell, Livia would in fact be guilty of committing the greatest crime in the series: fraud against an individual with whom one has a special relationship (Vernezze 2004). Betraying a relative is perceived as among the ultimate crimes against humanity and sentenced to the Ninth circle of Hell, where the sinners are devoured by the Devil himself. Thus, while we would find many of the mobsters in *The Sopranos* in rivers of boiling blood as punishment for violence to others, this is merely in the Seventh circle of Hell and not by far as grave a sin as the one Livia is guilty of committing. To be fair, Livia would not be alone in the Ninth circle; Junior Soprano would be there with her, as he also conspires to kill his own nephew Tony.[13] Nevertheless, Livia's betrayal of her own son is the reason that, among brutes and killers, Livia serves as the antagonist in the first season of *The Sopranos*.

On reflection, the contemporary spectator may perhaps find it strange that Livia's betrayal should be conceived of as morally so much worse in such a violent series. One could argue that it is inconsistent of the series' creators to seem to want us as spectators to judge her so harshly, as the mobsters do scheme to have each other killed on a regular basis – despite them all being 'family'. Perhaps there is a gendered aspect to this, in the sense that the spectator is cued to judge a woman more harshly for doing nothing worse than mobsters typically do.[14] Livia could be seen as a woman who is resentful of her lack of power and influence, scheming in her personal relationships in the restricted way that she can. Tony also voices this view. In an outburst of anger, he hisses to his mother: "I got to hand it to you. If you had been born after those feminists, you would have been the real gangster".[15]

On the other hand, one could argue that when a mother is plotting to have her own son killed this is monstrous, even in this context. Notably, despite some power struggles within the Mafia family, the mobsters mostly kill those from competing families, or they kill one of their own as punishment for having been disloyal to the group (e.g., for having talked to the police). Betraying the Mafia family is the mobster's ultimate deadly sin. Livia turns on her own offspring, apparently for no other reason than her own resentment toward him. Betraying one's own kin in this way is portrayed as a truly immoral act, from which there is no redemption, in this series. The morality of *The Sopranos* can be said to be quite consistent in this regard: be loyal toward those in your own group.

50 *Partiality*

"Is Your Name Even Danielle?" Adriana in a Tight Spot and Antipathy with the FBI

It has been duly noted that the FBI do not make a good impression in *The Sopranos*. As Douglas L. Howard suggests, "we never really identify with the FBI, a rather odd occurrence considering that they are (...) 'the good guys'" (Howard 2006: 174). Howard is right to point out that the supremacy of the law is no longer a given in this show, as the FBI seem more like rival businessmen or rival family members, using many of the same methods to accomplish their goals as do the Mafia – for example, they work through intimidation, pressuring mobsters and associates to become informants despite the potential informant's well-founded fear for his or her own life (as most of the FBI informants on the show are indeed killed by the Mafia in retribution). Furthermore, to stay with Howard's analysis, the FBI never succeed in their strenuous efforts to catch the leading Mafia figures. For example, some fairly comical sequences in season 3 depict them struggling to plant a wiretap in Tony's basement, only to gain access to some trivial information like Tony's choice of dental floss, before Meadow decides to take the lamp in which the wiretap is planted to her college dorm. The FBI agents come across as caricature figures. They are ineffective and cynical, and appear far from morally preferable to the mobsters they are supposed to catch. Furthermore, the spectator never gets to know them beyond their role as officers – they are dehumanized. In parallel to the way sympathy is constructed with the gangsters, the very opposite methods are used to prevent sympathy with, or even encourage antipathy toward, the FBI.

Adriana is one of the characters pressured by the FBI to become an informant, in a storyline that spans from the end of season 3 to the end of season 5. Adriana is the girlfriend and later fiancée of Christopher Moltisanti, Tony's distant cousin. An undercover FBI agent, Deborah Ciccerone, approaches her disguised as the tacky Danielle and befriends Adriana.[16] The FBI later brings her in on the charge of heroin distribution in the nightclub she runs, and uses this charge to pressure her into becoming an informant. Her contact is now mostly with Agent Robyn Sanseverino. However, Adriana meticulously avoids giving the FBI important information. When the FBI learns that she had covered up a murder in her nightclub, they decide to use this knowledge to pressure her to make Christopher "flip", offering Adriana and Christopher immunity as witnesses if he does. When Adriana approaches Christopher with this offer, revealing her ties to the FBI, Christopher almost kills her in a fit of rage. He then turns to Tony for advice, who orders her killed (although we never actually hear him give this order – perhaps to maintain sympathy with him). Adriana is shot screamingly off-screen by Silvio Dante.[17]

Adriana is slowly crumbling under the pressure of the situation, and her desperate efforts not to reveal any important information to the FBI while still making them think she is doing her best, leaves an impression of unfairness: the FBI are ruthlessly using her to get to Tony and his associates, although she is not their target. She confides in Danielle the undercover agent and tells her about her inability to have children, something she has never shared with anyone else. When it is revealed to Adriana in the FBI office that Danielle only pretended to be her friend, Adriana's trust has been violated in the most cynical way.[18] "Is your name even Danielle?" Adriana asks distrustfully, to emphasize the sense of betrayal of what she thought was a real friendship. Agent Ciccerone, however, seems unmoved by Adriana's frustration, as do the other FBI agents.

Figure 2.2 The FBI agents remain unmoved by the difficult position into which their informant Adriana has been forced; dehumanizing the FBI is one technique used to undermine the fact that they are 'the good guys' (*The Sopranos*, HBO).

When Adriana later regularly meets Agent Sanseverino, Sanseverino is typically cold and distant, with an expressionless face and seemingly without any concern for her informant's mental and physical state. On the contrary, they laugh behind her back, as when jokingly commenting "maybe Darwin was right. Nature really does weed out the nimrods" when Agent Ciccerone reveals at a FBI meeting that Adriana cannot have children.[19] The FBI uses Adriana instrumentally to get to Christopher, and ultimately also Tony. They discuss whether it would be useful for them if Adriana married Christopher, and decide that they should support this union because it might make his well-being even more important to her – thus making it easier to pressure her for information. Severino agrees that Tony is attractive in conversation with Adriana, obviously hoping to get her closer to him, while mocking her attraction to Tony in a later meeting with the other FBI agents.[20] At one point, Adriana begs Sanseverino to tell her something about herself, as friends do, as Adriana is revealing so much about her life. The one-sidedness

52 Partiality

of the relationship is truly bothering Adriana, and she wants to know what is in it for her.[21] When Sanseverino tries to calm Adriana by saying that she is "with the good guys" Adriana hesitates – and the spectator, I contend, is not at all convinced.

There is one additional explanation for our antipathy toward the FBI agents that Howard overlooks. The FBI agents violate the trust, loyalty, understanding and empathy that come with friendship. Howard also points out that the FBI forces their informants to do a terrible thing when betraying their friends and family (Howard 2006: 175), and concludes that the series shows that "[a]bsolute justice is clearly a fiction, and personal justice is relative at best" (Ibid., 177).[22] However, the morality of partiality at work here should not be equated with relativism. It is sometimes claimed – even, as we shall see, voiced in meta-comments by characters in the series itself – that *The Sopranos*' morality is relativistic: there is no morally right or wrong, as it all changes depending on one's point of view. For example, in her paper about *The Sopranos*, Martha P. Nochimson writes that

> [w]e increasingly see Tony from a variety of perspectives, each of which has a truth equal to his, granting the viewer a prismatic, inconclusive view of all the characters. American mass culture has been profoundly hostile to ambiguity and nuanced ethical perspectives, but these are the essence of televisuality by virtue of what serial television does to narrative structure. Television, when permitted to operate along the grain of its narrative tendencies builds the nuances and ambiguity of relativity into the narrative.
>
> (Nochimson 2003)

I agree with Nochimson that the narrative complexity of *The Sopranos* has the potential for nuanced ethical perspectives. Nevertheless, I think it is a mistake to describe the overall morality of *The Sopranos* as relativistic. A more specific explanation, I think, is that *The Sopranos* explores the moral code of partiality, and how this morality challenges normative moral theory's demand for impartiality. Surely, in principle, most of us would agree that if it unveils a criminal network, pressuring Adriana to turn on her loved ones does serve the greater good. However, this series demonstrates how differently one ends up perceiving this matter if one knows these people personally, and knows what being deceived this way feels like. The FBI appears cynical and disrespectful. They use a mock friendship with Adriana to pressure her for information, while ignoring that in human psychology, friendship has no place for impartial concerns of the greater good. This, I suggest, is an additional explanation for the antagonistic appearance of the FBI in the series. *The Sopranos* not only builds on mechanisms of partiality to make sure the spectator sympathizes with its characters, but also explores these mechanisms thematically through stories such as Adriana's.

The Sopranos and Self-Awareness: Dr Melfi as Commentator on Engagement with Tony

Throughout *The Sopranos*, Dr Melfi is a character with a special function. Narratively, sessions with a psychiatrist are useful as they give the spectator transparent access to whatever is going on in Tony's life (or, more accurately, at least to what he decides to share with her). Dana Polan points out that Dr Melfi is one of several vehicles through which *The Sopranos* self-consciously plays with its target audience (Polan 2009: 84). Dr Melfi serves as a meta-perspective on the spectator's relation to Tony. As Bruce Plourde points out in a similar analysis of her role in the series, Dr Melfi is one of the characters most similar to us as spectators (Plourde 2006). In addition to the trivial fact that she is one of few characters in the series with no connection to the Mafia business – as we as spectators are not *Mafiosi* – with her highbrow cultural background and higher education, she is more similar to the intended spectator of *The Sopranos* than Tony is, with his one and a half semester of college. Furthermore, where we as spectators of a fiction are arguably willing to postpone a fully rational moral judgment of the main characters, as Tony's psychiatrist, Dr Melfi is not only warranted but also obliged to postpone moral judgment of her patient. Dr Melfi's professional role is to understand and help him. His sessions with her encourage the spectator, too, to understand and feel with Tony. As she as a psychiatrist sees things from his point of view, the spectator is meant to do the same; if Dr Melfi is willing to empathize with him, the spectator follows her example. It is as if Dr Melfi vouches for Tony.

Both Dr Melfi's ex-husband Richard and her own psychiatrist Dr Kupferberg are highly critical toward her treatment of the famous mobster, and try to talk her out of it. Richard mocks her, and states that "sooner or later you're going to get beyond psychotherapy, with its cheesy moral relativism. You're going to get to good and evil. And he's evil".[23] Here we see that the series self-consciously labels Dr Melfi's engagement with Tony as relativism (in line with Nochimson and Howard's suggestions addressed earlier).

Although Dr Melfi usually brushes this criticism off abruptly, time and again in the series she is reminded of the "animal nature" of her patient – as when he almost attacks her physically for suggesting that his mother is scheming to have him killed,[24] or when he hits on her and she is forced to spell out to him that it is out of the question for her to be with a murderer and a misogynist.[25] After she is raped by a stranger, she dreams of Tony attacking her rapist in the form of a vicious Rottweiler – and although the spectator is strongly encouraged to root for her unleashing Tony by letting him know about the rape, Dr Melfi ultimately and stubbornly answers no to his plea to tell him what is wrong.[26] Elsewhere, I argue that these scenes work as reality checks.[27] The spectator is reminded of what she would feel for a character like Tony in real life, or more specifically, what would be the consequences of befriending such a character in real life. In her engagement with the fiction, the spectator craves retribution; in principle, however, she does not condone the violence that by now she knows Tony will use.

54 *Partiality*

Figure 2.3 It is a reality check when Dr Melfi refuses to tell her patient Tony Soprano about her rapist, who got away with it (*The Sopranos*, HBO).

Finally, as the series is coming to an end, Dr Melfi is also confronted with psychiatric studies indicating that taking on sociopaths in talk therapy only makes them worse – more effective at what they do. Now Tony's insistence that he is basically a good guy because he loves his family, starts to sound hollow.[28] Reading these studies herself, she realizes with horror that Tony fits the descriptions perfectly – he is, as one study predicts, loving toward babies and animals; and he is more than willing to discuss and put the blame on his family background.[29] Finally convinced by this research, unsentimentally Dr Melfi ends the series-long treatment of Tony without any further ado in the series' penultimate episode. As the series is coming to its end, sympathy for Tony is thus questioned – perhaps he is nothing but a cynical sociopath after all, not someone we can or should try to understand. Notably, Tony's wife Carmela has also come to doubt the sad story about his childhood, accusing him of "playing the depression card until it is worn to shreds."[30] In the first episode, Carmela was thrilled to learn that Tony is seeing a psychiatrist, and enthusiastically comments that it is first and foremost his mother that they ought to talk about.[31] As the series is coming to its end, however, she is rolling her eyes, looking sceptical and distrustful when Tony repeats the same, old story about his tyrant mother is a session with their son Anthony Jr.'s (A.J.) psychologist – and Tony surely has this new psychologist's full attention, demonstrating for us yet again how effective this simple technique is in capturing the empathic listener.[32] Through Carmela and Dr Melfi's new insights into Tony, the narrative casts doubt on him. Perhaps he is merely cynically playing on his depression, anxiety, his loveless childhood and his horrible mother to gain sympathy, to deceive those around him to put up with his sociopathic nature – and even help him be a more effective

Partiality 55

sociopath. Other things contribute to complicating sympathy for Tony in this last season as well; for example, he kills his protégée Christopher, whom he refers to as his own nephew, when Christopher is wounded in a car accident. The important point here, however, is that Dr Melfi has been instrumental both in constructing sympathy for Tony, maintaining it, and finally questioning it. Up until this last season, she has postponed a fully fledged moral judgment of him – and so has the spectator. Dr Melfi, however, finally does pass moral judgment. Was her ex-husband right, then, in accusing her – and us as spectators – of "cheesy moral relativism"?

On the contrary, one could explain what is going on morally, both for Dr Melfi and for the spectator, not as moral relativism *per se*, but as bracketing or suspending moral judgment. Arguably, this kind of suspension of moral judgment is what friendship demands of us in real life. Turning a blind eye to your friend's moral flaws is to suspend moral judgment in a sense. Likewise, a psychiatrist is supposed to see things from the patient's point of view, and has taken on the professional role of trying to help this person. In a similar way the spectator allows herself to see things from Tony's point of view. The series explores the morality of partiality, with its emphasis on understanding, empathy and loyalty. When Dr Melfi promptly ends her therapy with him, Tony is infuriated, and yells at her that it is immoral of her to end it at a time when his son, A.J., has just tried to commit suicide. This seems to be yet another comment of self-awareness in the series. In a way, Tony is right. According to the morality of partiality, which is the very moral basis for the spectator's engagement with the series, ending therapy of or a friendship with Tony at that point in Tony's life, would almost be immoral. Dr Melfi, however, is now operating by another moral standard. Finally, she is refusing to be partial to Tony's perspective. She is judging Tony from an impartial point of view, and has come to the conclusion that if attempting to treat him only enables him to be a more effective sociopath her only morally viable option is to end her sessions with him.

Nevertheless, as if to demonstrate the very power of the psychological effects of partiality, the spectator's sympathy for Tony is not ended so easily. At least in my experience, I still felt suspense for Tony in the final showdown, and clearly wanted to see him survive, despite the severe reality check that Dr Melfi's ultimate rejection of her patient represents. Be that as it may, *The Sopranos* does in no way offer an uncomplicated case of sympathy for a mobster, as the spectator's sympathy is put to the test. Smith also points out that our sympathy for Tony is ambivalent – a case of partial allegiance (Smith 2011a). Another term he uses to describe our sympathy for Tony is 'fluctuating'. I think this is more precise, and my analysis demonstrates why: with Dr Melfi especially, but also through other narrative means, we as spectators are taken on a curve of changing sympathy for Tony. The spectator's sympathy for Tony oscillates. She is encouraged to reflect on the moral partiality that the series takes as its basis. I will pick up on this topic again in chapter 4 and argue that the authorial perspective in this series is that at

56   *Partiality*

the end of the day the experiment of sympathy for Tony should be rejected. In encounters with some people – such as sociopaths – partiality is probably not warranted. Nevertheless, partiality remains the very foundation of the spectator's engagement with the series.

Stubborn Sympathizers

After *The Sopranos* it has become standard for antihero series to copy this structure of sympathy; first enhancing sympathy with a morally bad antihero through various narrative means, and then deliberately putting the spectator's sympathy to the test, thus demonstrating time and again how much it takes for that bond to snap once it has been consolidated. The antihero's trajectory usually entails a flawed yet likeable protagonist slowly turning irredeemable: in the end Jackson Teller in *Sons of Anarchy* can no longer claim he does it all in order to protect his family as his criminal enterprise obviously brings them all in harm's way. *Breaking Bad* is another good example, and I will concentrate on this series here as, besides from *The Sopranos*, it is arguably the most well-known American antihero series. The initial episode makes a plea for excuses: the main character Walter White is a humiliated man. His wife seems to have little respect for him, demonstrated by her watching an E-bay auction on the Internet while unenthusiastically masturbating him (after all, it is his birthday). His chemistry class students at high school could not care less about what he wants to teach them. After school, he works in a car wash to make ends meet – and naturally, as he is ordered out to clean a car's wheels, some of his students see him, record the whole thing and put it on the Internet. As if this were not enough, he is also diagnosed with terminal cancer, and told he has little time left. How could one possibly not sympathize with this man? So, when he "breaks bad" and uses his abilities as a chemist to make the highest-quality methamphetamine that Albuquerque has ever seen in order to secure his family's finances before he dies, the spectator enjoys his assumption of control and wants him to succeed. The first episode is remarkably effective in constructing sympathy for Walter.

Other, conventional means of encouraging sympathy for Walter are also in use. In season 2, for example, the drug kingpin Tuco is portrayed as thoroughly cold-blooded and evil, and serves as a contrast character to make Walter appear morally preferable. Much suspense is created in the first two episodes of this season in relation to Tuco, and we as spectators root for Walter and his partner-in-crime, Jesse Pinkman. I explore the important function of suspense in making the spectator root for Walter in the next chapter.

Many spectators will experience doubt about their sympathy for Walter at various intervals while engaging in *Breaking Bad*, as Walter's criminal nature takes him one step further into the abyss. For example, one reality check is found in the finale of the fourth season, "Face Off".[33] Here, Walter and Jesse are up against drug kingpin Gus. Jesse's girlfriend has a son, little Brock, who suddenly falls ill and is hospitalized. In ferocious anger Jesse confronts Walter, and accuses him of poisoning Brock. But Brock recovers, and the doctors believe he had accidentally poisoned himself by eating Lily of the Valley berries. So, in the end, Jesse and Walter are reconciled. The final shot, however, cuts to Walter's back yard, where the camera zooms in on a plant – Lily of the Valley. Thus it is suggested that it was indeed Walter who poisoned Brock in an ingenious but deeply selfish and immoral plan to set things in motion and get to Gus. As a spectator, one is shocked – would Walter really do such a thing? Using an innocent boy in such a scheme is reprehensible, and again the spectator's sympathy for Walter is put to the test. As Walter is drawn into the shady world of drug dealing, from one season to the next, the spectator grows increasingly unsympathetic toward Walter. It creeps up on the spectator that Walter White is slowly losing his sense of compassion and loyalty. He seems to have no scruples.

In his analysis of *Breaking Bad*, Jason Mittell points out that it is hard to imagine one becoming involved in a series with a main character like Walter White as he stands at the end of the fourth season. He writes:

> Personally, I doubt I would get invested in the story of a pathetic and uncharismatic man who poisons a child to manipulate other criminals without any other clear protagonists with whom to align myself. Yet having watched from the beginning, I find myself connected to Walt (…).
>
> (Mittell 2015: 162–3)

In an interview, series creator Vince Gilligan points to a slow transformation of our feelings toward Walter, but also emphasizes how long it takes for us to stop liking him:

> Our hero has become, episode by episode, a villain. (…) *Breaking Bad* has been an experiment in television, as you said. Walter White has come very far down the road of badness, and he's pretty much an indefensible guy at this point. Viewers have noticed that, but it was interesting to me that they hung in there liking Walt as long as they did. It points out interesting things about the storytelling process. When we choose to invest in a story we're reading or watching, we invest a certain amount of psychic energy into the main character, and therefore it can be hard to come to the grips with the idea that this character may not be worth sympathizing with.
>
> (Gilligan quoted in Milligan 2012)

This testifies to how stubborn we are as sympathizers, if first encouraged to sympathize with someone. It is in itself a good illustration of the psychological force of partiality, that if we first like someone, we tend to want to go on liking her.

The spectator has a remarkable tendency to ease back into a sympathetic attitude toward Walter once the thought-provoking sequence is over. The same effect applies to Tony in *The Sopranos*. The sympathetic orientation we started out with plays a major role here: we like Walter and Tony, and

58   *Partiality*

we want to go on liking them. When the narrative explicitly reminds the spectator of the consequences of their actions through reality checks, she may momentarily drift out of sympathy, but, once the narrative moves on, she tends to bounce back into sympathetic allegiance.

Breaking Bad and *The Sopranos* are like long (suspenseful and amusing) tests of how stubborn the spectator's sympathy for a character can be. How long do the initial excuses hold? Perhaps it is Walter's betrayal of his partner Jesse that represents the greatest challenge to our sympathy with him: if Walter is treacherous toward his own allies, does he then deserve our loyalty? For some, his wife Skyler's suffering also represents a disturbing reality check (see chapter 6). And as we have seen, the last season of *The Sopranos* challenges the spectator's sympathy for Tony through several means. Furthermore, in addition to these narratively induced reality checks one can also argue that the mere temporal dimension of the medium of television enhances critical, rational reflection: the spectator is given ample opportunity to reflect on her own engagement and discuss it with others, in between episodes and seasons (and on most American TV channels except HBO and Showtime, during commercial breaks in episodes as well).[34] These temporal gaps may work as a kind of distancing technique and encourage a more critical take on one's own engagement.

Nonetheless, although the spectator's sympathy is repeatedly put to the test both through narrative means as well as extra-textual features, time and again, she seems to forgive and forget and return to the sympathetic orientation she started with regarding Walter and Tony. Tuning in to yet another episode of *Breaking Bad* or *The Sopranos*, she quickly once again allows herself to let a rational evaluation slip to the back of her mind and rely on the intuitive route – and intuitively, she still has a strong bond to those antiheroes. This is partiality at work, but also the fictional relief that I have argued for in the first chapter: when engaging with fiction we allow intuitive responses to lead the way. So even if the spectator has come to the conclusion that the antihero is irredeemably bad, in between episodes and in discussions with others, for example, one might still ease back into a sympathetic attitude toward the antihero when resuming watching. Activating deliberate moral evaluation of these characters makes the spectator distance herself from them; however, as the story continues, intuitively, what guides her engagement with these characters is the bond she have already formed with them. Getting to know these characters so well makes her overlook and explain away their many moral flaws. She cares for them; she likes them; she knows them very well. As with old friends, she cuts them some slack.

Familiarity with the Antihero Series

We have seen that who we get to know well in a narrative greatly influences our moral evaluation of the characters. I have argued that partiality with the antihero plays a central role. However, in two recent papers, Arthur Raney

Partiality 59

and colleagues have explored empirically the possibility that familiarity with the antihero genre is part of what makes a difference. For example, Daniel M. Shafer and Raney argue that "enjoyment of antihero narratives requires the development of story schemas over time" (Shafer and Raney 2012: 1028, see also Raney 2004). Generally, story schemas are "mental representations containing expectations about how a narrative is internally structured and how it will unfold" (Mandler paraphrased in Shafer and Raney 2012: 1030), and specifically, these story schemas are "cognitive pegs upon which to hang their initial interpretations and expectations of characters" (Raney 2004: 354). Story schemas are short cuts we as spectators use when engaging in a familiar genre, and Shafer and Raney argue that they may replace moral considerations. Instead of relying on moral monitoring of the characters, we rely on story schemas instead. If familiar with the genre, the spectator has a positive disposition toward the antihero as soon as she realizes that she watches an antihero narrative. Specifically, Shafer and Raney argue that the story schema that is activated by the antihero narrative is based on moral disengagement, as introduced in the first chapter. In line with the Affective Disposition Theory, Shafer and Raney postulate that a favourable disposition toward the protagonist in a story is of major importance in order for the spectator to enjoy engaging in that story. And they argue that such favourable dispositions "toward antihero characters – at least those held by viewers familiar with the genre – come not through the engagement of moral scrutiny but rather through moral disengagement-laden story schema" (Shafer and Raney 2012: 1043, see also Raney and Janicke 2013). Because the spectator is familiar with the genre, and knows that she will enjoy it if and only if she roots for the antihero, she morally disengages. Shafer and Raney write that

> the story schemas that viewers develop for antihero narratives necessarily contain moral disengagement information. That is, over time viewers learn that certain protagonists in certain narratives violate typical moral standards. To enjoy such stories, a viewer must take off the default lens of moral scrutiny and put on one of moral permissiveness and justification. Only with the alternate interpretive lens, which is forged by the process of moral disengagement, can the antihero protagonist be loved and the narrative enjoyed.
>
> (Shafer and Raney 2012: 1038)

They conducted several experiments in order to support these assumptions. In one study, they showed the participants either a traditional hero or an antihero feature-length film. They found that liking the character increased during viewing on both conditions. In the beginning, the hero was seen as clearly morally better than the antihero, and the participants liked the hero more; however, "the two characters were equally well-liked by the end of the film", despite the participants seeing the antihero as less morally good

60 Partiality

than the hero (Shafer and Raney 2012: 1034). Shafer and Raney conclude that this supports the assumption that viewers form story schemas for antihero narratives over time.

However, another explanation – which is arguably more plausible – is the one offered in this chapter: what is going on in this study is that the participants viewing the antihero narrative over time become partial to the protagonist's point of view, and start to like him due to the effects of familiarity. What might further support the idea that these participants become blind to the antihero's moral flaws over time, is that there is a dramatic increase of the morality scores for the antihero (from 21.5 at the beginning of the film to 41.9 at the end), much more so than for the traditional hero (from 40.8 at the beginning to 49.1 at the end). As should rightly be pointed out, there are differences between the ratings of the morality of the antihero and the hero at the end of the film – as the scores just quoted show, the hero is seen as morally better. So the participants never become fully oblivious to the antihero's moral flaws. However, the increase of the morality ratings of the antihero suggests that as the film proceeds, the participants do tend to begin to turn a blind eye to the antihero's flaws. One can speculate whether this effect would continue in a long-term narrative like a television series – that after a few more hours, and even seasons and years, the morality rating would even align with that of the hero. The main point here, however, is that there is nothing in this study specifically documenting the idea that this is due to the development of story schemas; on the contrary, the effects found are just as predicted by the effect of partiality alone.

The second study conducted by Shafer and Raney explores the influence of previous exposure to antihero games. Here the participants were shown an edited recording of live play of a video game, *Grand Theft Auto: San Andreas Stories*, where the antihero commits several criminal and violent acts (carjacking; beating; murder; and chainsaw murder). Participants with and without previous experience with this particular game series were compared. Those that had played the game before rated the antihero's morality as significantly higher (i.e., saw the antihero as morally better) than those without such experience. Those previously exposed to *Grand Theft Auto* saw the protagonist's actions as more justified. Shafer and Raney conclude that this suggests that "participants with previous exposure to the series (and possibly similar games in the genre) accessed existing schemas governing their expectations, leading to differential viewing experiences" (Ibid., 1036). However, again one can argue that nothing in this study specifically supports the idea that the respondents morally disengage because they access story schema; again it is just as likely that the effect that is observed is the result of partiality. Thus, these two studies may just as well be taken to support my arguments in this chapter that we become partial to the antihero when engaging in an antihero series. Notably, this is also an important part of the explanation that Raney offers in an earlier paper (Raney 2004). Development of story schemas may be an additional explanation pulling in

Partiality 61

the same direction, but because Shafer and Raney only investigated the effect of having engaged with this specific antihero narrative previously (i.e., this one video game), the effect of previous exposure to antihero narratives overall was not really tested.[35] Furthermore, they offer no explanation for how the antihero narrative may work even for spectators who have not engaged with such a narrative previously. How did the very first antihero narratives engage their spectators, when few if any story schemas were available to the spectator on which to rely? Partiality with the antihero is an effect that would be at work in spite of the lack of previous knowledge of or exposure to antihero narratives, and the partiality explanation is thus better suited in order to explain how this trend got started in the first place.

Nonetheless, despite these reservations, I agree that some of the conclusions they draw seem plausible. For example, they argue that "those who rely on existing schema to guide their perceptions of characters in antihero narratives are able to enjoy those narratives significantly more than those who lack such schema" (Shafer and Raney 2012: 1043). In fact, as the familiarity principle also predicts, familiarity not just with a person but with an object too increases liking. So familiarity with the American antihero series would quite plausibly increase a spectator's liking of any antihero story; or, if not directly and automatically increasing the spectator's liking, then at least facilitating engagement in a new antihero series because the spectator has gradually come to understand exactly what to expect, and how to engage with these series. Indeed, I think it has probably become easier and easier to sympathize with the antihero in American television series, simply because the spectator by now knows the trend or cycle very well. Perhaps fewer justifications and pleas for excuses are needed now than at the beginning of the trend – the spectator knows well that the antihero series offers certain pleasures (see chapter 4) and is enjoyable for those willing to bracket a rational evaluation of the antihero. Furthermore, she trusts that some limits will not be crossed (see chapter 5). Familiarity with the antihero series probably has an effect on our enjoyment both of the antihero, and the antihero series in its own right.

In this chapter we have seen that there is one kind of intuitive, moral response that undermines a fully rational evaluation of the antihero, namely partiality: we tend to become partial to those we know the best, and see them as morally preferable over complete strangers. In the next chapter I will turn to another way antihero series systematically undermine a fully rational evaluation of their flawed protagonists, namely how suspense can be used to make us root for immoral characters.

Notes

1. *The Sopranos*, "The Second Coming", season 6, episode 19.
2. *Breaking Bad*, "Pilot", season 1, episode 2, and "I.F.T", season 3, episode 3, respectively.

62 *Partiality*

3. *Sons of Anarchy*, "Burnt and Purged Away", season 4, episode 12.
4. Haidt and Kesebit (2010) describe these Western moral philosophies that all prescribe impartial moral evaluation as *the great narrowing* in Western morality – narrowing down what counts as moral questions to harm and fairness. I discussed this in chapter 1, and will return to it in chapter 5.
5. See, for example, Feltham and Cottingham (2010) and Helm (2013) for overviews of this line of debate.
6. For good overviews, see e.g., Eder (2006, 2010).
7. See e.g., Mittell's discussion of exposition in recent American TV series (Mittell 2010).
8. Which is not to say that they cannot change over time – but slowly.
9. Theory of fiction is only beginning to explore the mental mechanisms causing partiality and favouritism as an explanatory tool. In addition to Raney (e.g., 2004), see also Jones (2011) on humour. Although I argue in relation to television series here, I do think this point about the systematic way alignment influences allegiance holds for film as well, but it is beyond the scope of this chapter to investigate this effect more carefully (but see the research on how our rating of the morality of the antihero increases during one and the same film screening at the end of this chapter).
10. *The Sopranos*, "Second Opinion", season 3, episode 7.
11. *The Sopranos*, "46 Long", season 1, episode 2.
12. *The Sopranos*, "The Legend of Tennessee Moltisanti", season 1, episode 8.
13. After Vernezze's essay was published, the series suggested that Tony may be joining his mother and uncle in the Ninth Circle of Hell after all, as Tony kills his own distant cousin (and his wife Carmela's cousin) Christopher Moltisanti in the very last season. As I will come back to at the end of this chapter, this is arguably part of the last season's deliberate questioning of and attempts to decrease sympathy with Tony.
14. See also my discussion of the portrayal of female characters in the antihero series in chapter 6.
15. *The Sopranos*, "Down Neck", season 1, episode 7.
16. *The Sopranos*, "Army of One", season 3, episode 13.
17. *The Sopranos*, "Long Term Parking", season 5, episode 12.
18. *The Sopranos*, "No Show", season 4, episode 2.
19. *The Sopranos*, "Watching Too Much Television", season 4, episode 7.
20. *The Sopranos*, "Irregular Around the Margins", season 5, episode 5.
21. *The Sopranos*, "Rat Pack", season 5, episode 2.
22. One could argue that mobsters are also forced to kill their family and friends, as is Silvio Dante when ordered to kill Adriana. However, the mobster is asked to kill someone who is perceived as disloyal, whereas the FBI pressure their informants to turn on their own group. Arguably, this makes a difference for how the spectator perceives this morally.
23. *The Sopranos*, "The Legend of Tennessee Moltisanti", season 1, episode 8.
24. *The Sopranos*, "I Dream of Jeannie Cusamano", season 1, episode 13.
25. *The Sopranos*, "Two Tonys", season 5, episode 1.
26. *The Sopranos*, "Employee of the Month", season 3, episode 4.
27. I discuss this aspect of Dr Melfi further in Vaage (2013).
28. *The Sopranos*, "The Second Coming", season 6, episode 19.
29. *The Sopranos*, "The Blue Comet", season 6, episode 20.

30. *The Sopranos*, "The Second Coming", season 6, episode 19. See also Akass and McCabe (2002) for an analysis of the important function of Dr Melfi and Carmela in *The Sopranos*.
31. *The Sopranos*, "The Sopranos", season 1, episode 1.
32. *The Sopranos*, "The Blue Comet", season 6, episode 20.
33. *Breaking Bad*, "Face Off", season 4, episode 13.
34. Thanks to Ted Nannicelli for this suggestion.
35. They also conducted a third study intended to investigate the effect of watching an antihero narrative with and without clues for moral disengagement. I will not, however, discuss that study here as it seems less relevant for my discussion of partiality.

3 Suspense and Moral Evaluation

How Morality Is Shaped by Suspense and Style

Walter is set up with the big drug distributor Gus, but is in a hurry: he only has one hour to find the methamphetamine that he and his partner Jesse have produced, and hand it over to Gus.[1] From the moment Walter's car screeches into Jesse's driveway, I'm engaged in his search for the drugs. Accompanied by fast-paced music, Walter smashes in Jesse's door when he does not reply; he gets an answer out of a doped-out Jesse, and then struggles to find the drugs that are hidden beneath the kitchen sink. We see him emptying out the contents of the cupboard, getting halfway in there and desperately searching for those precious little bags of blue meth. Watching someone desperately trying to do something has an effect – it makes me engage in that action, the stress and adrenaline in the situation latching onto me. I want him to make the deadline.

This sequence is one example where the spectator is meant to feel suspense for a character in a situation where the character is doing something that is far from morally good and desirable: Walter should not be producing drugs in the first place, and there is no morally good, rational reason for me to want him to make it to the agreed meeting place with Gus in time. Indeed, this chapter will explore how we as spectators sometimes feel suspense with reference to the possibility of a character doing something morally wrong. The problem is that suspense is traditionally defined as grounded in moral evaluation, while this, and other examples that I will return to later, show that feelings of suspense are sometimes amoral.

A central claim in this chapter is that in order to establish what is the relation between a moral evaluation and feelings of suspense, one needs to keep various spectator responses apart. The film theoretical discussion about morality and suspense has often been restricted to the notion sympathy (or using the notion identification without clarifying exactly what this notion is taken to mean). However, in order to tease out the role played by a moral evaluation proper it is of the utmost importance that one carefully differentiates between *sympathizing, liking* and forming a fully blown *sympathetic allegiance* with a character, as explained by Carl Plantinga (Plantinga 2010). However, he suggests that it is counterproductive to clearly delineate the difference between sympathy and *empathy* (Plantinga 2009: 98–101), but I argue that for this theoretical exploration it is important to keep the two

Suspense and Moral Evaluation 65

apart. By way of introduction, empathy is to feel *with* a character.[2] Latching onto the stress Walter feels as he is searching for the drugs would be an empathic response to the sequence introduced above. One may also almost feel Walter's movements – or, if you do not experience this reflectively, perhaps you have observed others going through similar experiences as for example the micro-movements someone watching a football game may undergo without much conscious awareness – a small involuntarily jolt just as the player kicks the ball toward the goal, as if mirroring the player's movements. Or one can imagine what Walter should do next, going through his action alternatives and perhaps feeling like coaching him ("Look under the sink!")[3] Elsewhere I have developed an integrative account of empathy (Vaage 2010), arguing that there are two routes to empathy: one through low-level automatic reflexes, which I label *embodied empathy,* and another through more cognitively demanding efforts to put oneself in the other's shoes and imagine what it is like to be her. I label this *imaginative empathy.*[4] Note that the model of empathy that I use is a dual-process model, similar to and drawing from the same strain of research in current cognitive psychology as the dual-process model of morality. Understanding others around me through empathy is similarly either slow (through deliberate, imaginative efforts) or fast (through low-level automated mechanisms).

To reiterate, sympathizing with a character in Plantinga's sense would mean having some form of pro-feeling for the character, such as feeling sorry for her. One might also add rooting for a character as a form of sympathy; wanting the character to succeed with what she is doing at least locally in the narrative. Thus, if I root for Walter making it in time for Gus' deadline, I have started sympathizing with him as well. The spectator may also *like* a character because she represents some admirable or virtuous character traits, again following Plantinga, and Walter is showing determination and courage in this sequence, meeting up with the big player Gus. Finally, the spectator may form a long-term *sympathetic allegiance* with Walter, where she comes to see Walter as morally preferable (as in Smith's theory). Notably, as I have described these terms here we have moved from simpler, more automatized responses (such as low-level action simulation and the way I may latch onto Walter's emotions) that one might reasonably assume are quite local, to presumably more complex and lasting cognitive processes such as a more fully blown moral allegiance with someone. I will argue that it is a mistake to take the notion sympathetic allegiance as one's starting point in an analysis of the role played by moral evaluation in feelings of suspense. What is notable in examples such as the sequence with which I started this chapter is that this is not so much a case of the spectator's sympathetic allegiance with the antihero making suspense for him possible, as suspenseful situations being used in order to encourage, and maintain, sympathy for the antihero. "Just as I thought I was out, they pull me back in", Michael Corleone complains in *The Godfather Part III* (Francis Ford Coppola, 1990) (a line referenced numerous times in *The Sopranos*). Similarly, just as you might think that

66 *Suspense and Moral Evaluation*

you have definitely fallen out of sympathy with the antihero (e.g., after a particularly severe reality check), they (i.e., the creators) pull you back in. And suspense is one very effective way of pulling you back in.

Furthermore, empathizing with a character in suspenseful sequences can make the spectator root for a character or feel sorry for him, at least locally in the narrative, and can therefore make the spectator sympathize with and feel suspense for even immoral characters.[5] At the lowest, most automatic level, empathic engagement can be amoral, i.e., not determined by the spectator's moral evaluation of a situation. This breaks with the view of empathy in much of media psychology: as will be remembered from the first chapter, Zillmann claims that empathic responses are determined by the spectator's dispositions toward the characters. According to the Affective Disposition Theory, the spectator empathizes with a character if and only if she also sympathizes with him, i.e., sees him or her as morally preferable. This is also mirrored in the account Murray Smith gives of empathy, although again there are nuances in this theory some of which I will return to later in this chapter (Smith 1995: 95ff). Although the orthodox theory applies to much commercial film and television with Manichean moralities, I will argue that the spectator can sometimes feel with characters independently of her moral evaluation of them, or independently of whether she has also first sympathized with them. Sometimes merely watching someone do something, or suffer horribly, can make the spectator empathize even if she does not find the character morally preferable. At least locally in the narrative, experiencing empathy with a character can influence the spectator's moral evaluation and make her sympathize with that character: the spectator empathizes with the character and therefore she starts to feel sorry for him, or to root for him. This reflects the conclusion in chapter 2 as well: who the spectator is aligned with in a narrative greatly influences her liking and her moral evaluation. Whereas the previous chapter focused on the effects of partiality alone, this chapter will explore a related effect, namely how alignment with a character in a situation where he is desperately trying to do something has a remarkable tendency to make us engage empathically in that action – so much so that this may even undermine our moral evaluation of this character and/or the situation he is in. Contrary to the dominant models in cognitive film theory and media psychology, empathy is not determined by moral evaluation.[6]

First we shall see how morality has been discussed in relation to suspense. It is most notably Alfred Hitchcock's work that has triggered these debates in film theory, and therefore I will start by exploring how Hitchcock can be said to manipulate the spectator into empathizing with immoral characters. In the latter half of this chapter I will return to American television series. Equipped with a thorough understanding of the relation between morality and suspense I will investigate the use of suspense in *Breaking Bad*. Suspense is used to encourage empathy with the antihero in other American antihero series, too, but *Breaking Bad* is a prime example, so I will concentrate my analysis in this chapter on this series alone.

Classical and Hitchcockian Suspense

Noël Carroll argues that suspense is generated by a state of anxious uncertainty in a narrative: what will happen next? The spectator wishes for one outcome – the moral one where the hero conquers the villain – but fears an immoral outcome (Carroll 1996a: 94ff). In his book on Hitchcock, Richard Allen labels this *classical suspense* (Allen 2007: 39). In classical suspense feelings of suspense depend on two factors, moral desirability and uncertainty. Any event in a narrative functions as a question that begs for an answer, where the spectator feels suspense in anticipation of what will happen next. The feeling of suspense is tied to moral evaluation in that

> (...) in the main, suspense in film is (a) an affective concomitant of an answering scene or event which (b) has two logically opposed outcomes such that (c) one is morally correct but unlikely and the other is evil and likely.
>
> (Carroll 1996a: 101)

The spectator wants the hero to escape from the bad guy – but it seems unlikely that he will do so, because the bad guy is ingenious and pure evil and has the hero trapped in a situation that seems inevitably to lead to his death. Such a situation maximizes feelings of suspense, according to Carroll. Indeed, one can agree that in classical narrative film, this is the way that suspenseful situations are usually constructed. Notably, Zillmann also has a similar account of suspense. We evaluate what the character does as morally good and, therefore, we like her and feel suspense for her (Zillmann 1996: 204ff).

However, Carroll also discusses to what degree suspense may be generated without issues of morality arising. One important caveat he notes is that what is morally good in suspenseful films or sequences may be morally good only relative to the film's moral system: "initially more moral than the other morally relevant forces" (Carroll 1996a: 104, see also Carroll 1996b: 79). Also, he notes that what is constructed as morally good is often more Grecian than Christian in nature, in that a character may be constructed as morally good if he has virtues such as strength, fortitude, bravery, and so on, and if he is respectful and thoughtful in his treatment of other characters and especially protective of the weak (Carroll 1996a: 105). He then notes that "even an antagonist, if provided with some virtues, can at times serve as an object of suspense" (Ibid.). His claim about the morality of suspense is thus modified: suspense is tied to "what people are wont to call 'good' and 'bad' in a nonpractical, nonprudential sense in everyday language" (Ibid.). Notably, this is a weaker claim than what initially sounds like suspense being grounded in a fully blown moral evaluation. What Carroll points to here is that what we regard as right or wrong in the moral system of the film can in fact sometimes diverge from what we would, on reflection, regard as right or wrong proper. This is indeed in line with the main argument in this book.

68 *Suspense and Moral Evaluation*

Carroll discusses Hitchcockian suspense as a possible problematic case for his theory. He notes that some of Hitchcock's films represent counterexamples to his classical theory: "the audience worries because the success of some immoral action – 'immoral' even in terms of the film's point of view – is imperiled" (Carroll 1996a: 111). The Hitchcock cases are complicated, he argues, but he does concur that they raise the possibility that suspense is generated in relation to immoral acts. Notably, this is also the view that Hitchcock himself holds. He argues that we will "feel anxiety for" a snooper going through someone else's things if we are shown the things' owner approaching, "even if the snooper is not a likeable character" (Hitchcock quoted in Truffaut 1983: 73). The conclusion Carroll draws is that his theory of suspense is not universal, although it applies to most cases. His theory gives sufficient but not necessary conditions for suspense. In order for the theory to be universal and give necessary conditions too, one could "alter the morality component of the formula and replace it by the notion of desirability" (Carroll 1996a: 112). Suspense arises when a desired (not necessarily moral) outcome is improbable.

Carroll is right about the need for this modification in order to make his theory about suspense universal. Nonetheless, he downplays the importance of this finding when he concludes that "the general theory of film suspense is a more important discovery than the universal theory, for it pinpoints the centrality of morality in the vast majority of suspense films" (Ibid.). Hitchcock's inversion of the moral structure of suspense demonstrates an interesting fact about our moral psychology, namely that moral evaluation of a sequence can be undermined by certain narrative techniques. Suspense is used systematically in recent American television series to enhance engagement in morally dubious main characters, as my analysis of *Breaking Bad* will illustrate. Carroll's own observation that "subversion of the normal mode of film suspense gives such scenes an arresting, memorable, and even disturbing quality" (Ibid.) can at least partly explain why a series such as *Breaking Bad* is so intriguing. Before getting to *Breaking Bad*, however, let us explore Hitchcockian suspense in greater detail. How exactly do Hitchcock's films sometimes make the spectator root for immoral characters?

In his book on Hitchcock, Richard Allen argues that

> Hitchcock exploits suspense in order to foster in the spectator an allegiance to those forces that actually run counter to the resolution of the story that is ostensibly desired. In this way, Hitchcock turns the idiom of the thriller into a playfully perverse challenge to, and manipulation of, our customary moral responses.
>
> (Allen 2007: 39)

Allen sees Hitchcock films such as *Notorious* (1946), *Rope* (1948), *Strangers on a Train* (1951), *Psycho* (1960) and *Frenzy* (1972) as an ironic inversion of morality where we sympathize with villains, at least temporarily.

Suspense and Moral Evaluation   69

A much-discussed example of this is the sequence in *Psycho* where Norman Bates pushes the car, containing Marion Crane's dead body, into the swamp, and the car does not sink. Surely it is incorrect to say that the spectator is meant to root for the villain in this sequence, as Allen also carefully points out. At this point in the story it has not yet been revealed that Norman Bates is the killer. Nevertheless, the spectator has been aligned with Marion Crane, and so was shocked at her death, and there is no good reason for the spectator to want the car containing her dead body to sink – yet, as Allen and many others have pointed out, one tends to wish for the car to sink (e.g., Allen 2007: 53; Barratt 2006; Grodal 1997: 95; Truffaut 1983: 272). Hitchcock describes the audience's response as follows:

> When [Norman] is looking at the car sinking in the pond, even though he's burying a body, when the car stops sinking for a moment, the public is thinking, "I hope it goes all the way down!" It's a natural instinct.
> (Hitchcock quoted in Truffaut 1983: 272)

I will unwrap what Hitchcock could mean by 'natural instinct' and tie this to the notion empathy later, but let us first with Allen attend to the moral component in this suspense sequence. Allen argues that the spectator does not so much sympathize with Norman and therefore feel suspense for him, but rather, she is "made to feel anxiety on behalf of the character by being placed in his narrative situation and therefore sympathize with him" (Allen 2007: 53). Whenever Hitchcock makes the spectator sympathize with, and feel suspense for, immoral characters, Allen discusses this as moral inversion or subversion of suspense. Allen does not dig deeply into the spectator's response, but hints that

> our response to being in a character's situation is a more primitive or hardwired response, which our moral responses may support or counteract, but that is not reducible to them.
> (Allen 2007: 54)

Allen addresses this response variably as sympathy or identification, but I will argue that it is more precisely labelled as empathy, although it can lead to sympathetic responses such as rooting for the character and wanting him or her to succeed, more traditionally tied to the notion of sympathy. Sticking to a discussion of Hitchcock a little longer will help us disentangle this difficult question.

Hitchcock claims that suspense is maximized when the spectator knows more than the character (see e.g., Truffaut 1983: 73). However, as Susan Smith shows, in his films he just as often aligns the spectator with the character epistemologically in sequences of what she labels as *shared suspense* (S. Smith 2000: 16ff). Smith differentiates among three types of suspense in Hitchcock's films: *vicarious*, *shared* and *direct suspense*. Put briefly, the

70 *Suspense and Moral Evaluation*

difference between the two first has to do with the distribution of knowledge in the narrative. The spectator knowing more than the character gives us vicarious suspense, whereas being aligned with the character epistemologically gives shared suspense. The third type of suspense, direct suspense, is when the spectator feels anxiety and uncertainty on his own rather than on the characters' behalf – e.g., "we dread that this time it is *we* who are going to be assaulted with something quite horrific" (S. Smith 2000: 24, emphasis original). Direct suspense is experienced when the spectator fears not so much for the characters, but for the horrible turns that the story may take for her to watch and react to. This last type of suspense is interesting, but less relevant for my discussion here, so I will concentrate on the first two types.

The difference between vicarious and shared suspense, as Susan Smith delineates it, could be tied to a long-standing debate in cognitive film theory over whether films encourage sympathetic or empathetic spectator responses. Susan Smith does not use the terms empathy and sympathy systematically, but rather interchangeably, and does not engage this debate in her book. In cognitive film theory, however, it is sometimes argued that asymmetry between the knowledge that character and the spectator have, respectively, excludes the possibility of the spectator empathizing with the character (see e.g., Carroll 2008: 147ff). When one wants to warn the snooper (as is Hitchcock's own well-known example), this response is different from the character's state as the snooper is unaware of the approaching threat. Empathy is, as we have seen, defined as sharing some aspect of the character's state – through imaginative or automatically affective routes. But if the spectator knows more than the character knows one might want to argue that the spectator can only sympathize with her, as Carroll argues: the snooper is happily unaware of the approaching threat, and were the spectator to empathize with him she would merely be happily unaware, too – but the spectator feels distress and suspense, which is a radically different mental state from that in which the character is. Although I argue elsewhere that this line of reasoning is flawed (Vaage 2010), I need not engage this specific discussion here, as the sequences I want to look at do entail epistemological alignment with a character as in shared suspense.[7] It is not that epistemological alignment is by any means necessary for empathic responses to occur, but close alignment with a character does nevertheless tend to evoke empathic responses.

Smith's explanation for why shared suspense in particular has this effect is that shared suspense elicits "a fuller form of identification":

> By enabling the viewer to fear along with rather than simply for a character, shared suspense allows a much closer insight into a character's mental and emotional state, and by implication, offers the possibility of a fuller form of identification.
>
> (S. Smith 2000: 20)

Suspense and Moral Evaluation   71

However, the term identification is too obscure to pertinently describe what is at stake here – what is a fuller form of identification? Presumably because of this closer insight into the character's state, she later points out that shared suspense can "force the viewer into close involvement with a character whose earlier actions provoked revulsion and outrage (...)" (Ibid., 21). But narratives hardly force anyone to do anything. Smith's discussion here smacks of the fusion view found in psychoanalytical accounts of identification, which has been much criticized in cognitive film theory, as pointed out in chapter 1. The process that Smith points to should rightly be seen as the spectator's tendency to start empathizing with the ones with which she is narratively aligned, regardless of her moral evaluation of them: the spectator does indeed fear along with rather than simply for the character. Perhaps Smith uses the verb 'force' because this process of embodied empathy starts automatically and is perceived as something that is almost beyond the spectator's control. Smith concludes that shared suspense may in this way (i.e., in the terminology used here, when the morality of suspense is inverted) lead to an "uneasy sense of being entrapped in a character's pathological state of mind" (Ibid., 22). In order to try to explain how this can be so, let us return to the sinking car sequence in *Psycho,* and Daniel Barratt's discussion of it.

Barratt concurs that we empathize with Norman, and his paper discusses what mental mechanism underpins empathy (Barratt 2006). As the cognitive underpinning of empathy is not my focus here, I will ignore this debate, and merely focus on his discussion of the *Psycho* example.[8] Barratt is right to point out that it is indeed empathy with Norman the spectator feels in this sequence, and the use of sympathy by other writers, such as Allen and Smith, possibly obscures the question at hand (namely, the role played by moral evaluation). So, although Barratt does not discuss the role moral evaluation plays, his discussion of *Psycho* brings us one step closer to a clarification of the spectator's response.

Barratt explores the sinking sequence in its narrative context and points out that before this sequence we have seen Norman carefully clean Marion Crane's motel room in order to hide all traces of her being murdered. Barratt asks why the cleaning sequence is so long – it lasts for over eight minutes, and is thus remarkably long, especially considering that nothing much happens. The spectator merely attends to the minute cleaning process.[9] Barratt suggests that in addition to Hitchcock giving the 1960 audience a chance to recover from the shock of having the film's major star killed early in the film, another explanation for the length of the sequence is that Hitchcock

> wanted to give the viewer, from both then and now, a sufficient opportunity to 'switch' their 'loyalties' from Marion [with whom we have been aligned until her death] to Norman.
>
> (Barratt 2006: 47)

72 *Suspense and Moral Evaluation*

The notion 'loyalty' might denote sympathy, or even stronger, a sympathetic allegiance here. However, in line with Barratt's overall analysis, I think empathy is a better term than loyalty: the cleaning sequence gives the audience time to start empathizing with Norman. This is a point Torben Grodal makes in relation to this sequence as well. He suggests that we start identifying with Norman as there is no one else in the sequence that we might identify with (Grodal 1997: 95). A more accurate explanation is that the mere length of the cleaning sequence encourages empathic engagement because we have little else to do as spectators. Surely, the spectator can admire the film aesthetically, but yet, one would try to find some narrative meaning for the characters in most sequences in narrative film, and this sequence offers seemingly little by way of narrative relevance. Norman's cleaning is all that is going on, and empathizing with him is arguably what appears to be the most relevant response. Furthermore, I do not think the spectator experiences this as a choice at all: slowly, most spectators will tend to start empathizing with the character. These responses are automatic and pre-reflective, but they do make the spectator focus on Norman. Empathic engagement even at this low level will be experienced as one's attention being directed at the character. One will perhaps start to engage in imaginative empathy as well, trying to imagine what is going through Norman's mind as he is cleaning.

Barratt's own further suggestion is interesting. He proposes that

> [a]lthough the cleaning sequence may be mundane in terms of content, the fact that we are exposed to that content is anything but: the close shots of Norman washing his hands and mopping the bath provide us with an optical approximation of the views we would have if we were washing our own hands or mopping the bath ourselves. First, it is plausible that certain levels of the mind/brain do not make a distinction between the proposition, '*Norman* is wiping away the traces of the killing,' and the proposition '*I* am wiping away the traces of the killing.' Second, in the way that some psychologists propose that emotional contagion occurs when we are allowed to witness another person's facial expressions, perhaps something like 'goal contagion' occurs when we are allowed to witness another person's actions: this process of contagion results in the activation of the goal structures which correspond to Norman's situation (as a person attempting to cover up a crime) (...).
>
> (Barratt 2006: 48, emphasis original)

Most relevant for my discussion here, this solution suggests that what is at work here has less to do with evaluating Norman morally or switching loyalties. Rather, the natural instinct that Hitchcock himself points to in relation to the sinking car sequence, is triggered already by the cleaning sequence: watching someone do something has a remarkable tendency to make us engage empathically in that action. This is embodied empathy – a low-level automatic response mirroring someone else's emotions and bodily experiences.

As Zillmann points out, in the psychological literature on empathy it is often seen as the archaic action coordinator – I empathize with others' bodily movements instinctively because their movements (e.g., fight or flight) might be important for my survival (Zillmann 2013: 134).[10] As mankind evolved it would have been useful if one were instantly primed to start running when seeing someone flee from something – before the need to reflect deliberately on the need to flee. Recent research on our natural mirroring mechanisms, as explored by Vittorio Gallese and colleagues in the Embodied Simulation approach, for example, provides empirical support for this claim. Our brain re-uses parts of its sensory-motor neural resources to map other's behaviour. "When witnessing actions performed by others, we simulate them by activating our own motor system" (Gallese and Guerra 2012: 185). Not only do we simulate another person doing an action – merely seeing an *object* "recruits the same motor resources typically employed during the planning and execution of actions targeting the same object" (Ibid.). Later in the same paper Gallese and Michele Guerra analyse a sequence from Hitchcock's *Notorious* to demonstrate how the viewer "is almost ready to grasp the keys" in the sequence where Alicia is planning to steal her husband's keys to the cellar (Ibid., 201). This, I propose, comes quite close to what Barratt might mean by goal contagion.

In line with the heuristics and biases approach, one can argue that the intuitive, automatic, low-level nature of our tendency to simulate actions easily supresses the cognitively demanding – and much slower – process of evaluating the sequence's moral dimension rationally (cf. Kahneman 2011). The tendency we have to empathize with a character can circumvent a moral evaluation of this character. Empathizing with a character can thus be amoral. This, I propose, can explain why there is not necessarily an intrinsic moral structure to suspense. The spectator can be encouraged to feel suspense on behalf of characters doing immoral actions through manipulation of alignment. This is due to local, low-level empathic responses that should be analysed separately from the spectator's fully blown moral evaluation of the character's actions, as captured by the notion sympathetic allegiance.

Murray Smith also ties the *sympathy for the devil* effect in relation to Hitchcock films to the powerful effects of affective mimicry (e.g., in relation to *Saboteur*, see Smith 1995: 103ff).[11] Notably, in Smith's theory, too, empathy is given a central role when explaining the puzzling sympathy for the devil effect. Smith emphasizes the effect of close-ups of the character's distressed state – an important point that corroborates the tight spot the character finds himself in, and fits with another criteria he gives for sympathy for the devil, namely "a local situation in which an otherwise undesirable character is herself victimized, or is placed in a dreadful situation" (Ibid., 217–8). I suggest that being in a tight spot narratively is the most important point here – the close-ups of the character's face underline the desperation of the situation. The close-ups make the spectator latch onto the character's feelings, as Smith argues – but even more importantly, feeling this desperation makes the spectator simulate the character's action alternatives. The automaticity with which

74 *Suspense and Moral Evaluation*

this occurs might explain Susan Smith's use of the verb 'force' to explain such responses.[12] The sequences discussed as 'sympathy for the devil' or moral inversion of suspense typically involve some kind of action that the immoral character is desperately trying to perform. The more clearly and convincingly this desperation is communicated to the spectator, the easier she probably engages. The so-called sympathy for the devil effect thus often arguably starts with low-level empathy – it is the spectator's action and affective simulation of these villainous characters that thwart her moral evaluation. The amoral nature of empathic responses can make me feel with – and because of this also root for – immoral characters.[13]

When moral inversion of suspense is enhanced in Hitchcock films, the sequences intended to thwart the spectator's moral orientation in the narrative are usually fairly short and limited, and they are embedded in a narrative where the spectator is clearly aligned both spatiotemporally and morally with some other, morally preferable character. Arguably, feeling with the villain is thus designed only to have local effects. In *Breaking Bad* moral inversion of suspense plays a prominent role in enhancing sympathy for Walter and Jesse. Along with the effects of partiality, moral inversion of suspense is intended to continually ease the spectator back into feelings of sympathy after each and every time Walter simply goes too far. When used repeatedly and systematically, moral inversion of suspense can have more long-lasting effects on the spectator's engagement, and in *Breaking Bad* moral inversion of suspense contributes to the formation of, and maintenance of, a sympathetic allegiance with Walter and Jesse.

To conclude, the reason empathy may effectuate a moral inversion of suspense is that both empathy and morality make use of automatic, low-level responses. Whereas we can deliberately empathize with someone by making a cognitive effort to understand her (a process I label imaginative empathy), often, however, empathy is an automatic, low-level response where we simply mirror the actions and feelings of a person we see. The related dual-process model of morality postulates that we rely heavily on automatic, low-level intuitive and emotional responses when evaluating something morally. It is thus likely that empathizing with someone can – and will – influence our moral evaluation of the situation that person finds herself in. If there is a prolonged focus in the narrative on her distress and pain, for example, or the emphasis is on her desperately trying to perform an action, the spectator will be prone to start feeling with her and see things from her perspective. The point of view of the character with which one is narratively aligned might then influence one's moral evaluation of the character.

Immorality and Narrative Desires

The low-level, amoral nature of empathic engagement, however, is not the whole solution to the problem of moral inversion of suspense. The empathic response in relation to Norman's situation should also be seen as tied up with *narrative desires* (cf. Currie 1999). Norman cleaning the room satisfactorily, and his succeeding in sinking the car, seem like the most relevant actions in these local situations that can bring the narrative forward. A narrative desire has to do with desires regarding the story, and may, as Gregory Currie notes, depart from character desires in the story. One example could be somebody who likes romantic comedies, and wants the boy and girl to get together (at the level of character desires) but she also wants to enjoy some interesting and unusual complications before that happens (narrative desires).

Moral inversion of suspense cannot be explained only by exploring processes internal to the fictional world. The spectator has desires both in relation to characters (internal to it) and in relation to the narrative (external to the fictional world).[14] Two mechanisms are at work in moral inversion of suspense: first, our 'natural instinct' to begin empathizing with characters we see trying to do something, and second, our narrative desires regarding the development of the story. The spectator wants the story to be engaging. She desires actions that bring the narrative forward. When the spectator empathizes with Norman and simulates his action alternatives that will lead to him hiding Marion's body, this should be seen as linked to narrative desires. It is an expression of the spectator desiring an action that will bring the narrative forward locally.

This might seem to contradict my earlier suggestion that the spectator allows herself to rely on low-level, automatic responses instead of a full-blown rational evaluation of the events and characters because the latter is cognitively taxing. Indeed, I have argued that the spectator of fiction allows her intuitive and emotional moral responses to suppress the slower and more demanding cognitive moral evaluations (indeed, that what characterizes engagement with fiction is that one relies more heavily on intuitions). The suggestion that our responses and desires when engaging in a story are also influenced by narrative desires – external desires directed toward the story as an object made by someone – seems to fly in the face of this logic. Keeping various story levels in mind, and having narrative desires externally in addition to character desires internally to the story may indeed sound like an onerous cognitive operation. Furthermore, this may also sound counterintuitive: most spectators will probably not typically experience having explicit thoughts about which direction they would like the narrative to go in order for the story to be engaging, for example. This, however, can perhaps also be a clue to how we experience narrative desires. Take the example of tragedies. We would want the story to go badly (narrative desire for a sad story), but also that the characters make it (character desires). One would typically not think reflectively that one wants the story to go badly. This is not a desire that I am consciously focused on. Perhaps this narrative desire would become evident for the spectator only if her expectations are breached. If the tragedy has an artificially induced happy ending, I might dislike the film because it did not give me what I desired. Only then might I notice that I did in fact have narrative desires relating to the story.

76   Suspense and Moral Evaluation

Narrative desires may thus take centre stage when I appreciate (or do not appreciate) a story aesthetically. I would also be able to access and articulate my narrative desires were someone (e.g., a researcher) to stop the film at regular intervals and ask me about them. So it is not that narrative desires are inaccessible to the spectator's reflective consciousness, only that we are often not reflectively focused on them throughout our viewing experience. I will return to appreciation in chapter 4.

Similarly, in relation to suspense I do not suggest that the spectator typically experiences reflectively explicit desires regarding outcomes of suspenseful sequences, or that she usually thinks things like "At a narrative level, I want this story to...". Basically, narrative desires in relation to suspense sequences become evident in that she wants the story to be engaging. The spectator wants to maximize suspense because it makes the story engaging. There may be various reasons for suspense just being naturally engaging. Perhaps this is so because suspense sequences have a tendency to make the spectator focus on the character's actions, and that this makes her maximally interested, and interest is a basic function of story engagement (cf. Tan 1996, 2008). Or because the tendency to draw me into engagement with the character's actions and/or feelings makes me maximally transported or immersed in the story. It is beyond the scope of this chapter to explore why suspense is so engaging. But suspenseful sequences do seem to be instantly gratifying: we find them enjoyable. It is hard to find a commercial film and television series that is not suspenseful.

To sum up, the narrative desires in relation to suspense sequences should not be seen as high-level, cognitively reflective thoughts about one's story engagement, but are rather very simple expressions of what we want stories to do. The narrative desires we have regarding suspense are perhaps best described as an attitude we take toward the story: we want stories to engage us.

It is also important to point out that narrative desires can quite ordinarily be seen as inverting morality, and less puzzlingly so than the impression given by the 'sympathy for the devil' discussions of Hitchcock. It is often the case that the spectator wishes for unfortunate events to befall even liked characters in fiction because it makes a good story. Characters behaving well and leading good, uninterrupted everyday lives without any obstacles whatsoever might not make the best entertainment – we want challenges, transgressions and violations. Even if we want the hero or heroine to put a stop to these transgressions in the end, and the story thus to end happily (unless it is a tragedy), at the level of narrative desires we nonetheless want immoral elements to be introduced in the story. So, narrative desires are commonly immoral, in the sense that we desire immoral events in stories (and not in the sense that it is immoral of us to have such desires). In sequences where suspense is inverted from its usual moral coordinates, I propose that we empathize with the immoral character because his or her success in that sequence is what would drive the story forward. Seen as a narrative desire, this is in many ways indeed unsurprising. I will return to this discussion of desiring immoral events in fiction in the next chapter.

Suspense and Moral Evaluation 77

I can now sum up my theory as follows: *moral inversion of suspense* is when the spectator empathizes with characters who are immoral, who are not necessarily presented as morally preferable in the narrative and may thus otherwise have been perceived as unsympathetic, and feels suspense in relation to a situation where it seems unlikely that this character will succeed. Empathizing with the character makes the spectator root for this character, wanting him or her to succeed – more traditionally seen as sympathetic engagement. Moral inversion of suspense occurs most easily if the spectator is narratively aligned with a character, and the narrative dwells on a situation where the character has a clear goal or is trying to perform an action, but is in a tight spot where it seems unlikely that he or she will succeed, but the character's succeeding will bring the narrative forward in a narratively desirable way locally. Hitchcock can be said to have explored and exploited this effect systematically. And one of the strategies recent American television series use to ensure engagement with their morally bad main characters is moral inversion of suspense. Thus, the phenomenon that Hitchcockian suspense is perhaps best known for is being exploited and explored further in contemporary American television. I will concentrate on *Breaking Bad*, as suspense is one of the main ways this series enhances a sympathetic engagement with its antihero Walter White.

Moral Inversion of Suspense in *Breaking Bad*

As will be remembered from the previous chapter, initially the spectator meets Walter White as the all-too-common husband and high-school teacher, and follows him through his rise and fall as a drug kingpin in the Albuquerque criminal underworld. Walter transforms from a passive and humiliated man to an active, assertive, secure and even aggressive man, becoming known as Heisenberg. I explored how mere familiarity with him influences the spectator's sympathy – the spectator becomes partial to those she knows best, and *Breaking Bad* first and foremost aligns the spectator with Walter. A number of techniques are used to ease the spectator into such a personal relation initially – such as the many pleas for excuses in the very first episode, emphasizing how disempowered and humiliated he is as a father, husband and teacher. Although we would not normally condone cooking methamphetamine as a way to secure one's family's finances, in this case the spectator is invited to turn a blind eye to this.

However, there is more to the spectator's engagement with Walter in *Breaking Bad* than this. Suspense is also used to enhance engagement with Walter. The suspense structure of *Breaking Bad* contributes to pulling the spectator back into engagement with Walter after the many reality checks with which this series challenges her. Moral inversion of suspense plays an important role in the way these suspense sequences work, and the series' style bolsters this effect, too.

Let us first see how moral inversion of suspense is at work in the suspense sequences in this series, making us root for Walter although his actions are morally wrong. Walter and Jesse typically find themselves in a tight spot from

78 *Suspense and Moral Evaluation*

which it seems they cannot possibly escape. As amateurs in the drug business, time and again they get into situations that it seems they cannot possibly wriggle their way out of – being up against the truly bad guys, unscrupulous and psychopathic drug lords. Walter and Jesse have a way of getting themselves into trouble, often opting for desperate solutions to save themselves.

The pilot episode starts with such a sequence, representative of suspense sequences throughout the series. More specifically, this suspense sequence is a prologue to the pilot episode, and a flash-forward to the situation Jesse and Walter will find themselves in as the pilot episode comes to its end. In the prologue the narration starts *in medias res* with Walter's trousers flying through the air in the desert – then there is a cut to Walter, driving an old and worn RV stark naked except for his white underwear, an apron and a gas mask; Jesse is fully clothed and also wearing a gas mask, and is half-sitting, half-lying knocked out beside him. Walter is panting and driving wildly on a dirt road – it seems something or somebody is chasing them. Eventually he crashes into some bushes, and as he runs out of the camper we hear distant sirens, coming closer. Walter is crying and as he hurries into the RV again to collect a camera he also picks up a gun from a dead body lying on the floor. He records a farewell message to his wife and son, leaves the camera along with his wallet on the ground and walks toward the approaching vehicles with his gun aimed at them. Then there is a cut to the short title sequence, and the pilot episode proper starts with Walter living his everyday life before being diagnosed with cancer. We return to this suspense sequence only at the end of this first episode, where we learn how Walter and Jesse ended up in this situation – and it is, of course, only now that we know them as Walter and Jesse.

However, this very first prologue is typical of the suspense sequences in the series in that they often contain chases or escapes, where Jesse and Walter find themselves in such hopeless and often near outlandish situations that the story becomes absurdly comical. Both the chase elements and the comical valence in these sequences may facilitate moral inversion of suspense, as Carroll also points to in his discussion of suspense. He points out that one may wonder if "races, chases, rescues and escapes (…) generate suspense without any special issue of morality arising" (Carroll 1996a: 102), and also discusses how "morality ratings are not applicable to gags" in comedies as the spectator takes "pleasure in all sorts of sadistic spectacles" (Ibid., 109–10). Both chases and escapes, especially if a comical slant is added, can thus be expected to aid moral inversion of suspense – i.e., the spectators will root for immoral characters in a suspense sequence more easily if it contains a chase, race, rescue or escape, and also if it is constructed as being comical.

Furthermore, let us linger on the prologue of the pilot episode in order to see exactly how the spectator is invited to feel suspense on behalf of Walter in the very first two minutes of the series. It is important to note that as the prologue starts, the spectator knows nothing about the two characters

Suspense and Moral Evaluation 79

she sees. She has no reason to sympathize with them; she has not formed a sympathetic moral allegiance with them, neither has she developed antipathetic feelings for them. She has not yet any background for doing so. The series starts with a suspense sequence where the spectator is invited to feel with Walter – quite simply to empathize with him. Several narrative techniques are used to ensure empathic engagement. Once the spectator is aligned with him in the RV, subjective narration is used to communicate the feeling of being in Walter's shoes (cf. Branigan 1984; 1992). There is a blend of external focalization, seeing him desperately trying to steer the RV, intercut with long shots of the RV careering down the dirt road, and with internally focalized POV shots showing us the road ahead as Walter sees it and reaction shots focusing on his hyperventilating, panicky state. Adding to the internal focalization is the use of a shaky, handheld camera when filming Walter's face in reaction shots, and later in the sequence also a foggy POV shot to illustrate for us that Walter's view is being distorted by damp building up inside his gas mask. A reaction shot shows that he is agitatedly trying to wipe away the condensation – but it is, of course, inside his mask and not on the outside of it. The RV ends up in the ditch, shown to us externally from outside the RV.

As Walter jumps out of the crashed RV, gasping for air, the spectator is again invited to feel with him. The spectator sees the desperation written on his face, and communicated clearly through his body language also. Intermittently he sobs and swears, looks hysterically around and holds his head in his hands as if instructing himself to "Think! Think!"

Figure 3.1 Walter is in a tight spot in a suspense sequence typical of *Breaking Bad*. Through moral inversion of suspense the spectator can be made to root for immoral characters (*Breaking Bad*, AMC).

80 *Suspense and Moral Evaluation*

We hear sirens in the distance – are they coming for Walter? The spectator might start to search for action alternatives – can he run? Can he hide under the RV? What can he do? He spots his shirt hanging out of the window of the RV and fumblingly he puts it on; at a low-level of awareness the spectator might feel with him performing this action.

In these first two minutes there is an elaborate mix of narrative strategies intended to work together to give the spectator the feeling of what it is like to be in Walter's situation – and thus pulling her into engagement with this character before knowing him, and before knowing whether this is someone she should sympathize with in the first place.[15] The sequence is already suspenseful – before she has evaluated it morally. Through the effect of low-level empathy, the spectator feels suspense on behalf of Walter, engaging in his perspective. However, had she known that this is a criminal mind she is watching, someone indeed trying to cover up a crime, arguably she would have felt suspense on watching this sequence nonetheless – indeed, similar sequences are used throughout *Breaking Bad* in order to secure engagement with Walter. This very first suspense sequence cannot be said to be a moral inversion of suspense proper, as the spectator does not yet know that this character is in fact morally bad. Even so, the sequence works in the same way in that it is designed to induce the spectator to engage empathically independently of a moral evaluation due to the amorality of the low-level responses evoked by such sequences. Later in the series the amoral nature of empathic engagement in such sequences is used for moral inversion of suspense proper – making the spectator feel suspense for and root for Walter despite knowing that what he is trying to achieve is not morally good. The suspenseful sequences are so enjoyable that they make the spectator circumvent moral evaluation of what Walter and Jesse are doing. They offer the spectator instant gratification. As we have seen, suspense can make the spectator engage in a character's perspective on its own, and humour and chases further facilitate the pleasurable and thrilling feeling of suspense. Suspense is used to enhance feeling with Walter (and Jesse) throughout *Breaking Bad*.

A Suspense Structure in Fits and Starts

Although *Breaking Bad* is perhaps best known for and most greatly appreciated by its many fans for its highly enjoyable suspense sequences, the series does not merely consist of such material. In fact, throughout *Breaking Bad*, Walter and Jesse's journey into the drug making and dealing underworld of Albuquerque serves as an enjoyable contrast to Walter's home life. Long sequences take place in the family context, where Walter seems trapped and is rendered passive. These sequences are filmed with a steady camera, there is no non-diegetic music – often, long stretches of conversation with Skyler has a clock ticking as the only sound breaking the awkward silences. These sequences are often remarkably uneventful and long. They are slow, and typically they emphasize the disillusionment and entrapment that Walter

Suspense and Moral Evaluation 81

feels. He is diffident and disempowered; their lives are boring and conformist. Their house is not particularly stylish, looking like any middle-class house; neither is Skyler or Walter particularly appealing. Even though other recent American television drama series, such as *The Sopranos*, also dwell on Tony Soprano's family context, family life is never presented as slow and as uneventful as it is in *Breaking Bad*. The family sequences in *Breaking Bad* often seem to have the primary function of emphasizing the dullness of Walter's family life – and to serve as contrasts to the sequences where Walter descends into criminality and deception.

These latter sequences typically differ from the family sequences dramatically. When Walter and Jesse are making meth, there is often use of cool, speedy non-diegetic music (e.g., rap, reggae, ska, punk), the filming is often more experimental – using different camera angles,[16] fast editing, more subjective narration – making these sequences stand out as visually enjoyable. This stylistic change piggybacks on the far more enjoyable narrative content in these sequences: when Walter and Jesse are engaged in the drug trade there is more action, more adventure, more humour and not least of all, more suspense. The visual rhetoric underlining the contrast between these two types of sequences found in *Breaking Bad* clearly seems to suggest that it is much more fun when Walter is bad than when he is not. *Breaking Bad* contains two types of narration, one of them close to social realism, where Walter is humiliated, passive but morally good, and the other an action-adventure suspense thriller, where Walter and Jesse are active and bad. The suspense sequences serve as an attractive relief from the dullness of the family sequences. In this sense the suspense structure in *Breaking Bad* is one of fits and starts: fast paced, stylistically enjoyable suspense sequences are interspersed sparingly into a narrative dominantly consisting of much slower – titillating, or sometimes bordering on tedious – sequences, typically in the family context.

One example of this contrast is found in an episode where Skyler is angry with Walter for not wanting to go through treatment for his cancer and decides with her sister Marie and brother-in-law Hank to confront Walter (in what Marie ultimately labels "an intervention").[17] So there they are in Skyler and Walter's living room, Skyler starting as she is holding the 'talking pillow', allowing her to air her concerns uninterruptedly. I suspect many spectators with me find the scene both cringe-worthy and comical, at least in the beginning (when their son, Walter Jr., gets the talking pillow, both we as spectators and Walter listen more carefully, emphasized by zooming in on Walter as he listens, tears filling his eyes). But at least initially, the spectator is invited to see Skyler's intervention as humiliating, as does Walter. The context is claustrophobic, with the ticking of the clock and the nervous gazes of the characters involved. Walter clearly does not want to be there. Skyler is portrayed as unsympathetic in the sense that she even breaks her own rules about the 'talking pillow' when her sister Marie changes her mind mid-way and supports Walter's decision not to get treatment, as she points out that

82 *Suspense and Moral Evaluation*

it is his own right to decide what to do with the last months of his life. Skyler yells at her for not supporting her view. Thus this family meeting is portrayed as staged by Skyler first and foremost to communicate her views to Walter, and to make him listen to her. The talking pillow will probably provoke some male spectators in particular – embroidered with 'Find joy in the little things', the talking pillow becomes the symbol of a domestic life where a boring and conventionally minded wife is the boss. Skyler's unwillingness to listen to other opinions will probably confirm their suspicion that the talking pillow is a scam: only some are allowed to talk freely – namely the wife introducing the pillow. When Walter is finally allowed to talk at the family meeting, he tries to explain how he never feels he has had a real say in his life, how he wants to make his own choices – and this one choice, about *living* the last time of his life properly, instead of desperately trying to *survive* for a little longer, is something he wants to decide for himself.

Intercut with these sequences from the family meeting, is a sequence with Jesse. Jesse has decided to cook meth with another partner, Badger (after a break-up with Walter earlier in the season). They are heading out into the desert in the old RV, and this sequence is filmed in the stylistically experimental and pleasing way described above. The contrast to the silence and stuffy atmosphere of the family meeting is striking – so striking that it is comical. The family meeting is intercut with sequences from Jesse and Badger's cooking escapade – unsurprisingly, it does not go well, they start fighting, and the sequence is funny, action-filled and suspenseful – in stark contrast to the slowness of the family meeting. In this example, Walter does not take part in the drug adventure, but in many earlier and later examples, similarly dull and unpleasant family sequences, or sequences where Walter is getting treatment for his cancer for example, are intercut with pleasurable drug sequences where Walter too is present, always accompanied by the marked change in style, always portrayed as much more upbeat, funny and suspenseful.

The attractive relief that the suspense sequences offer, both narratively and stylistically, is important in order to explain the spectator's rooting for Walter aka Heisenberg in addition to the isolated effect of moral inversion of suspense. Feelings of suspense in *Breaking Bad* do not merely rely on narrative development *per se* (that is, narrating about suspenseful events) – but on stylistic features as well. Greg M. Smith (2003) explores how stylistic features influence and shape our engagement in film, and he argues that this is just as important in order to explain the spectator's emotional responses as is character engagement. However, I do not argue that these stylistic features are more important for feelings of suspense than our engagement with Walter; rather, I argue that the stylistic features are used to corroborate our character engagement. They work in concert, one not replacing the other, but mutually reinforcing one another.

Furthermore, the suspense structure of *Breaking Bad* is not merely one of fits and starts, but fits and starts of suspense aligned with fictional reliefs and

Suspense and Moral Evaluation 83

reality checks. As the series develops, increasingly the enjoyable, fast-paced suspense sequences are intercut with sequences where Walter and Jesse face the consequences of their actions – reminding the spectator of the atrocity of making and selling a harmful and addictive drug. The suspense sequences make us enjoy Walter's transgressions, circumventing moral evaluation and cheering for him even when it is a matter of killing competing drug dealers, while slower sequences continue to remind Walter and the spectator of the consequences this way of life has not just for Walter and Jesse, but especially for Walter's family. The spectator's narrative desires here are arguably immoral – she wants Walter to be bad because *Breaking Bad* is more entertaining when he is. The reality checks work all the more effectively because the series corroborates the pleasurable side of transgression stylistically: engaging in the series entails not just enjoyment of Walter's transgressions, but longing for more of them, as they are intercut, delayed and postponed by these long, slow sequences of humiliation and disempowerment. The transgressive suspense sequences are enjoyable in contrast to this. Thus, when the narrative reminds the spectator of the consequences of this way of life – the immorality of Walter's transgressions – and the thought-provoking nature of our cheering for them, this is striking.

Carefully Orchestrated Suspense in Fits and Starts: Season 2 as a Case Study

Although the general sympathy structure of *Breaking Bad* can be described as one, long downward spiralling loss of sympathy with Walter – after the initial construction of sympathy for him in the very first episode – each season is carefully constructed as a series of interchanging fictional reliefs and reality checks. Let us look at season 2, and my own response to it, as a case study. This season starts with clear-cut sympathy for Walter (and Jesse – more about him later) in that the psychopathic maniac Tuco serves as a contrast character. Tuco is a drug lord portrayed as a sick and very violent man, beating even his own men to death in horrible tantrums. When Walter and Jesse are up against Tuco, we naturally root for them. The first three episodes are enjoyably suspenseful because of this conflict, and feelings of suspense for Walter and Jesse can be said to be more or less classical in that Tuco is so clearly portrayed as morally worse (so there need not be any moral inversion of suspense at work here, strictly speaking). When Tuco kidnaps both Walter and Jesse and wants to take them to Mexico to cook, we as spectators clearly want Walter and Jesse to kill him and escape. These episodes can all be said primarily to evoke fictional relief.

A fourth episode brings more of the family life, strengthening the spectator's desire for Walter to continue his other, secret life in the drug world. When they are back on track in the fifth episode, the spectator craves for more. Now, however, the narrative takes a challenging turn. Two drug addicts hold one of Jesse's dealers up, and Walter instructs Jesse to deal

84 *Suspense and Moral Evaluation*

with it: it is essential that they are respected in the drug world. Walter gives Jesse a gun. In the next episode Jesse locates the two drug addicts who held up his dealer, and ventures into a nightmarish household slum to confront them and make them give the money back. What makes this a particularly effective reality check is the presence of a little boy, the drug addicts' son – a four- to five-year-old little dirty, snotty, hungry and totally neglected child left to his own devices among the garbage and broken furniture in the house. When Jesse arrives the boy is all alone, and Jesse feeds him and watches TV-shop with him (the only channel available) until the two junkies return home.

Figure 3.2 Jesse is, as always, the one truly facing the consequences, and the neglected child of two drug addicts represents an unpleasant reality check (*Breaking Bad*, AMC).

To make a long story short, it ends up with Jesse being beaten half unconscious only to witness the woman junkie kill her partner by tipping an ATM machine they have stolen over him so that it crushes his head. Jesse calls 911 and carries the boy outside, instructing him to wait until the police arrive. These miserable people are the ones Walter and Jesse are making a fortune from. The little boy's depraved childhood is the consequence. This sequence reminds Jesse, and us as spectators, exactly what it is they are responsible for, and it is for this reason disturbing and thought-provoking.

How can one as storyteller bring the spectator back into a pleasurable enjoyment of Walter's drug escapades again after such a reality check? First, this is merely one of a series of reality checks intended to make the spectator question her sympathy for Walter specifically: typically, Jesse pays a much higher price than Walter, and it is first and foremost Walter the spectator is

Suspense and Moral Evaluation 85

beginning to dislike. Jesse comes off as someone one feels sorry for – he suffers more and is manipulated to do things by the far more eloquent Walter. When a devastated Jesse tells Walter about the horror of that house, Walter does not seem very interested in hearing about the little boy at all, but is merely coaching Jesse to "get back on that horse". And when it becomes evident that everyone in the drug underworld thinks that it was Jesse who crushed the junkie's head with the ATM machine, Walter enjoys their new status and does nothing to correct this misunderstanding. Walter wants to increase their number of dealers and gain new ground. Our sympathy for Walter decreases, being replaced by sympathy for Jesse.

In addition to this adjustment, where Jesse becomes the (temporary) focal point of our sympathy instead of Walter, the series brings in a lot of comedy to ease the spectator back into engagement. In episode 8 the creators bring on the lawyer Saul Goodman, who is to become an important partner in Walter and Jesse's criminal enterprise. Saul lives up to the expression 'devil's advocate' as it is Saul who hooks them up with some of the big players who will be important for several seasons (such as the major player Gus, and his hit-man Mike). Saul is best known from the cheesy commercial he airs on television. He is unscrupulous, but adds much comedy to the series because he is amoral in such an entertainingly straightforward and almost naïve way. When he comes up with the incredible idea of paying the ex-con 'Jimmy-in-and-out' to take the fall for one of Jesse's dealers, Badger, because Jimmy simply loves to be in prison, we as spectators are drawn into one of *Breaking Bad*'s irresistible mixes of farfetched suspense and comedy. It is absurd, very funny and suspenseful – and surely again we root for Walter and Jesse, without even remembering our second thoughts about what exactly it is they do.

This enjoyable use of suspense and humour is continued and deepened in episode 9 that focuses dominantly on only one storyline about Walter and Jesse heading far out into the desert with their camper to cook for four days – and of course, when they are nearly out of water and food, and ready to go home, the RV's battery is flat. They are in a tight spot, and, true to form, the solution will, of course, be the most outlandish one. We are eased back into engagement, even with Walter. After having built one cell of a battery with sponges in plastic cups filled with mutters and screws and whatever else they can find made out of galvanized metal, and hooked this onto the RV's battery, they find their seats in the vehicle, Walter with key in hand, ready for this one final attempt at getting the thing started. As he turns the key, we are fully focused on this movement. As it starts, I cheer with them, and silently coach them from my sofa: "Drive! Before the damn thing stops again! Drive!" A fully fledged moral evaluation is out of the question. Quite simply, the sequence makes me engage in what he is doing and hope that he will get the vehicle started.

When Walter thus announces that he will probably withdraw from cooking in episode 10, at the level of narrative desires I do not really want him

86 *Suspense and Moral Evaluation*

to. Again, the family context humiliates Walter, and slows the narrative down – when he encounters an amateurish meth cook in a store, obviously buying what he needs to set up his own little meth lab, I feel a flash of intense enjoyment when Walter hisses that he should "stay out of his territory". Heisenberg is back. It is a fictional relief; I crave the suspense it brings along, and welcome Walter's having once again changed his mind. So, in the sequence with which I started this very chapter, when Walter is desperately searching for the drugs they have hidden in Jesse's house, I want, as already pointed out, Walter to make Gus' deadline. This also becomes evident to me when his pregnant wife Skyler's birth commences just as Walter is frantically searching through Jesse's kitchen for the drugs. She alerts him to this by sending him a text message ("BABY IS COMING!!") when he does not reply on his cell phone. Walter slows down when reading this, giving himself a moment to reflect what to do – and me with him. And I find myself quietly urging him to ignore it! I want him to keep on hurrying to make Gus's deadline, as this is the storyline bringing the most pleasurable suspense with it. Notably, the participatory response that Walter should ignore the text message and hurry up is all I reflectively experience of what should rightfully be seen as a narrative desire to maximize suspense. Again, long gone is the resistance toward Walter's (and Jesse's) way of making a living – the suspenseful situation easily supresses moral evaluation. I do not care whether it is wrong or right. Such reflections do not even strike me as relevant at this point in the narrative. My engagement with Walter, at the edge of my seat (or rather, my sofa) hoping he will make it in the nick of time, relies on low-level, automatic responses triggered by seeing someone desperately trying to find something and make it somewhere. Low-level empathy contributes to low-level moral inversion of suspense. I root for Walter not because I have rationally evaluated the situation and feel that his making it in time to meet Gus's deadline would be morally preferable. On the contrary, this will pull Walter further into the criminal abyss. And rationally speaking, Skyler is morally preferable, she is giving birth and naturally wants her husband to be there – yet it is not her I root for in this sequence. Watching Walter desperately trying to make it makes me engage in his perspective, and the pleasures offered by this and other suspense sequences makes me desire downright immoral turns in the narrative – because they are more entertaining. The suspense sequences make me engage through moral inversion of suspense, and they are also immediately rewarding in that they are enjoyable.

This pleasurable feeling of suspense is disturbed again by one massive and horrible reality check in the penultimate episode. Jesse has hooked up with his next-door neighbour, Jane. They are very much in love, and although she is eighteen months clean from drugs, actively going to NA meetings, she is tempted by Jesse's drug use, and soon they are shooting heroin together. Walter clearly does not approve of Jesse turning into a proper drug addict. One evening he comes to Jesse's house to find him and Jane knocked out

Suspense and Moral Evaluation 87

by a heroin high in bed. As he tries to wake up Jesse to talk sense into him, Jane rolls over on her back. She is always careful to instruct Jesse never to fall to sleep on his back when he is high, as he might choke on his own vomit were he to throw up in his sleep. This is exactly what happens to Jane. Walter's first impulse is to help her, but we see him decide not to – and he stands by their bed and watches as she chokes and dies. Is this really the man we have been rooting for? Walter reveals himself to be monstrous there and then, and this evokes antipathy toward him. Arguably this very antipathy for Walter lasts until the end of this season – being corroborated with other, small reality checks, such as intercutting Jane's father picking out a dress from her locker for her funeral with Walter cuddling happily with his own new-born daughter; the speech his own son Walter Jr. gives to some journalists interviewing him, where he explains that "my dad is my hero" all the while the camera zooms in on Walter's troubled face; and finally, his wife Skyler throwing him out of the house when she finds out that he has been lying to her incessantly. I do not feel sorry for Walter when this happens – he had it coming. When a plane crashes close to Walter's house because of Jane's father's grief after her death (he is a flight controller, and distractions can be fatal), the narrative spells out how Walter's actions have consequences. *Breaking Bad* thus keeps reminding the spectator of the consequences of what Walter and Jesse are doing. Toward the end of this season, again it is only Jesse I feel sorry for, having drifted out of sympathy with Walter. In a similar manner, the continuing seasons orchestrate the spectator's sympathetic feelings by use of suspense sequences intermittently contrasted with slower sequences, where suspense plays an important role in inducing pleasurable fictional reliefs.

To sum up, suspense plays an important role in *Breaking Bad*, time and again easing us as spectators into empathic engagement with Walter through moral inversion of suspense, typically often also leading to sympathetic engagement with him due to fictional reliefs and the mere pleasure that such suspense sequences offer, in stark contrast to the dull and slow family context.

One interesting implication of my theory of moral inversion of suspense – as is evident, I give embodied empathy a central role in it – is that it predicts that we will more easily engage in the perspective of those characters who are actively trying to do something. It is primarily simulating actions that trigger moral inversion of suspense according to this view. As I will explain further in chapter 6, this may start to explain why the antihero's wife gets a raw deal in these antihero narratives. She is typically a passive and resistant observer to her husband's wild moral transgressions. I argue that because we find her husband's transgressions so enjoyable, and she continually wants those very same transgressions to stop, many spectators dislike the antihero's wife. I will return to this in chapter 6, but before then, let us in the next chapter continue exploring what attraction there is for us as spectators in engaging with the antihero. Why an *anti*hero instead of a regular hero?

88 *Suspense and Moral Evaluation*

Notes

1. *Breaking Bad*, "Mandala", season 2, episode 11.
2. In film theory, empathy has traditionally been discussed as imagining the characters' states, labelled *central imagining* (e.g., Choi 2005), *imagining from the inside* (e.g., Smith 1997), or *empathetic re-enactment* (e.g., Currie 1995). It has also been seen as important for spectator engagement as understanding the meaning of narrative events for the characters (e.g., Tan 1996, 2013). Furthermore, empathy has in addition been used as a matching feeling with the character (e.g., Grodal 1997; Plantinga 1999; Smith 1995). For careful discussions of empathy and neighbouring phenomena, see (Coplan 2004, 2006, 2009, 2011a, 2011b) and Tan (2013). For critical discussions of the notion and its usefulness in film theory, see e.g., Plantinga (2009: 98–101) and Carroll (2008: 165–6). In Vaage (2010) I discuss some of the counterarguments against empathy, such as Carroll's. For a good overview of empathy in philosophical and psychological literature, see also Maibom (2014).
3. In line with Polichak and Gerrig (2002) I will label this sort of response *participatory responses* (e.g., experiencing wanting to warn the spectator or in other ways responding verbally to their experiences on-screen). Participatory responses are perhaps observed most explicitly in children, who will often actually shout warnings and recommendations to the characters as they watch: adults will have learned not to do, but may still experience the desire to thus communicate with the characters – notably, in my theory, this is because one has put oneself in the character's situation.
4. An early exploration of this model is found in Vaage (2006).
5. This model also has the advantage of being able to explain feelings of suspense in relation to situations where nothing moral is at stage, such as sport events, although this is beyond the scope of my analysis here.
6. This complicates the view that moral judgments are based on empathy (basically a heritage from Hume). As Heidi L. Maibom points out, "[o]ne concern with a view of moral judgments based ultimately on empathy is that empathy is fragile and biased" (Maibom 2014a: 28). See the essays in (Maibom 2014b) for further discussion. Space does not allow me to explore these implications of my claims here.
7. Although Hitchcock's own example of the snooper is in fact an example of moral inversion of suspense in a case of vicarious and not shared suspense. Also, note that epistemological differences is not the only problem Carroll sees in theories making use of the notion empathy to explain the spectator's response to film – he consistently argues against the value of this notion, and might thus disagree with my use of it nonetheless. I hope to defend the notion by demonstrating its explanatory value.
8. However, I will briefly note that he argues that while most empathy theorists use simulation theory to explain what empathy is, he sees appraisal theory as a more plausible alternative. Barratt's discussion boils down to the spectator primarily engaging with Norman himself (simulation theory) or the situation he is in (appraisal theory). The spectator switches to Norman's situation in both cases, and simulates, imagines or appraises what he can do in order for the car to sink. For my purposes in this chapter it makes no difference which of these descriptions of empathy is correct, but see chapter 4 for a more careful discussion of empathy.

Suspense and Moral Evaluation 89

9. As Greg M. Smith points out, the only significant narrative event is Norman finding the newspaper where Marion has hidden the money she had stolen (G. Smith 2003: 80). Arguably, this narrative event nonetheless hardly warrants eight minutes screen time.
10. See also Tan (2014) for an empirical investigation of viewers' action readiness.
11. See also Smith (2011b: 102), though he does not discuss the 'sympathy for the devil' effect of Hitchcock's films here – but does connect his discussion of sequences in Hitchcock's films where one is made to empathize with characters on-screen to the literature on mirror systems, in line with my argument here.
12. The expressivity of the actor surely adds to this effect. For example, one could argue that one of the reasons that Norman "short-circuits" moral rationalism is also due to the charisma, ambiguity, and emotionalism that Perkins brings to the role. Thanks to Aaron Taylor for pointing this out. I discuss his theory further in chapter 4.
13. Thanks to Robert Stecker for pointing out that I need to clarify what I argue about amoral vs. immoral responses – I think saying that empathic responses can be amoral and may thus lead to empathizing even with immoral characters gets it right.
14. On the difference between internal and external perspectives on fiction, see Lamarque and Olsen (1994: 143). A related vein of research in film theory is found in Ed Tan's differentiation between fictional (F) and artefact (A) emotions; see Tan (1996: 81ff). See also Currie (1999, 2010). I will elaborate on this in chapter 4.
15. The sequence surely has other notable effects as well, such as posing a whole lot of questions that will make the spectator wanting to see the rest of the episode in hope of getting some answers, in line with Carroll's point about the film experience typically being shaped by a structure of question-response (see Carroll 1988: 170–81). I am thus not suggesting that the sequence's only intended effect is to make the spectator empathize.
16. *Breaking Bad* often explores highly weird and innovative camera angles, such as attaching the camera to the end of a brush filming Jesse cleaning a tank in their lab, and the like. Fans typically celebrate *Breaking Bad* for this use of strange camera angles, and notably, they are used in sequences related to Walter as Heisenberg. Skyler and their family life are never afforded such camerawork. I remember only one sequence where Skyler is filmed and there is non-diegetic music. Typically, all the stylistic bravura that *Breaking Bad* is celebrated for is absent in the family context. In the final chapter I will return to how this adds to an unsympathetic portrayal of Skyler.
17. *Breaking Bad*, "Grey Matter", season 1, episode 5.

4 Why so Many Television Series with Antiheroes?

The Attraction of the Antihero's Very Immorality

Why are there currently so many antiheroes on American television? In this chapter I will try to find an answer to this question by discussing two related ones: why does the spectator empathize and sympathize with the antihero, and even enjoy doing so – as I will claim – when they are severely morally flawed? And what role does immorality play in our appreciation of stories? Notably, in order to make the spectator sympathize with the antihero, narrative stage setting is required. I have mentioned several such strategies already – most prominently explored by Noël Carroll and Murray Smith – such as making other characters in the narrative appear morally worse (e.g., Carroll 1996a, 2004, 2013; Smith 1995, 1999, 2011a). However, I have also shown that the spectator typically merely perceives the antihero as morally preferable due to several low-level effects: the long duration of television series capitalizes on the effects of partiality, and antihero series in particular often use this long-term alignment with the antihero to plead for excuses on his behalf. The spectator is blinded by familiarity with him, and perceives others as morally worse. Suspenseful sequences are also used to undermine a rational evaluation of the antihero. Now, when various narrative strategies are required to facilitate sympathy with the antihero, there must be some pay-off to be found in his very immorality. If there is no attraction to be found in the antihero being immoral, why not just tell stories about conventional heroes? Why an *anti*hero in the first place?

We need to tackle the very immorality of the antihero head-on; the spectator does not merely sympathize with the antihero in spite of his bad sides. The antihero's bad sides offer enjoyable attractions.[1] One such attraction is the enjoyable experience of empathizing with someone in power. Power is nature's own drug, and there is good reason to think that even aligning ourselves with and feeling with powerful people on-screen gives rise to pleasurable bodily effects. In addition, watching those whom we perceive as even morally worse than the antihero get what we feel they deserve, is inherently gratifying for us as pro-social punishers, a notion to which I shall return in due time.

However, ultimately the question of why the spectator enjoys antiheroes cannot be answered without investigating what she wants not just from characters in stories, but also from a fictional story in its own right. Surely, the

Why so Many Television Series with Antiheroes? 91

spectator wants a plurality of pleasures from fiction, and I will not discuss all of these here. I will focus on merely a few related aspects, which are particularly relevant in order to explain the appeal of antihero series – namely the role played by narrative desires and by aesthetic appreciation of the morally transgressive. The spectator appreciates stories that are engaging, and adding immoral elements to a story makes it even more so. Furthermore, villainy can be aesthetically pleasing, and the antihero borrows some character traits from proper villains in this regards. At the end of the day, the antihero story is also emotionally and morally disturbing, and I argue that the intended spectator in the trend of American antihero series is the spectator who is both willing to allow herself to enjoy the antihero's moral transgressions, but who also firmly adheres to the common norms in our society, by which the antihero is clearly morally bad.[2] The intended effect of engaging with an antihero story is to both like and dislike the antihero. The dual-process model of morality can explain both of these responses, and why we find ourselves feeling conflicted about the antihero. This thought-provoking feature of antihero stories is pivotal to explain its appeal.

However, this also entails that there are several groups of spectators who fall outside of the scope of this study, or what I will discuss as the antihero series' intended spectator. One of these is the spectator who sees the antihero as heroic, perhaps because he truly believes the values the antihero stands for are morally good, or because he completely fails to reflect on the implications of the antihero's actions – I will discuss such spectators as bad fans. The bad fan only likes the antihero. Another group is made up of those who are too rigidly moral and/or political to be seduced by the antihero's transgressions in the first place, thus coming only to dislike him. One example could be those who were unable to enjoy *The Sopranos* because of what they saw as a misogynistic portrayal of women (a perfectly understandable resistance, at least based on a first impression of the series). Another example could be the viewer who is simply too morally minded to enjoy the antihero's criminal trajectory, never letting go of the (again, from a rational point of view, perfectly legitimate) critical meta-perspective that this is just *wrong*. Antihero stories probably offer little attraction for this group – with the caveat that if the series is a proper ensemble cast series, where the spectator is both aligned with and given access to a number of characters in addition to the antihero, one can perfectly well engage in the series, finding other kinds of pleasures than the ones offered by the antihero. In my case, for example, *Mad Men* (AMC, 2007–2015) is such a series: I have never really liked Don Draper (but know that many spectators do, and for them, he does offer some of the attractions of the antihero). The reasons I do not like Don Draper may not be moral or political strictly speaking, but that is not the important point here: rather, note that as a dedicated *Mad Men* fan, he has never been of central importance to my engagement with this series. I strongly feel for some of the female characters, such as Peggy, Betty and Joan. The myriad plotlines explored by this series, where

92   *Why so Many Television Series with Antiheroes?*

some of these other characters take centre stage, offer me plenty of opportunities to engage with the series. I do not explore such negotiated readings of antihero series in this book, but focus on the main, intended response – which I will argue is both liking and disliking the antihero – and I do offer an explanation for the appeal of this particular viewer position.

Does the Spectator Like the Antihero Because of or in Spite of his Immorality?

Do we not sympathize with the antihero *in spite of* his morally bad sides, because we like his morally good sides – such as his caring for his family, for example? Do we really enjoy his moral transgressions? This is a question to which Smith has returned several times.[3] A main question in his work is why we as spectators can sometimes sympathize with characters with whom "we would have either no interest in or an active aversion toward in reality" (Smith 1995: 194). As will be remembered from the first and second chapter, Smith gives moral evaluation an important role in spectator engagement. In his careful discussion of this he also explores cases where the moral status of the character with which the spectator sympathizes is trickier. He points out that whereas what he labels the classical moral system requires a moral resolution (the moral status of its characters is clear) and a moral centre (there is a locus of positive moral value in the narrative), films in other traditions may either refuse a moral resolution or flatten all moral dynamism, i.e., no character is perceived as morally better or worse than any other character (Ibid., 214ff).

Interestingly, it appears incorrect to say that antihero series have neither a moral resolution nor a moral centre. Rather, when engaging with an antihero series, the spectator is arguably intended to perceive the antihero as morally preferable – although as I have shown, the spectator is also regularly encouraged to take a step back and reflect critically on her own engagement. A fourth type of moral structure Smith discusses seems a more accurate description of the antihero series, namely that its moral structure is dynamic or unstable (Ibid., 216). The antihero series does have a moral centre in the sense that the antihero is perceived as morally preferable to other characters in the story – but the intuitive morality on which the spectator allows herself to rely in order to see the antihero as the moral centre breaks radically with what she would hold as morally right in real life. Because of this, the series can make her question her own engagement through reality checks. During reality checks, the antihero series momentarily changes from a sympathetic narrative to a distanced and ambiguous one, in Carl Plantinga's terminology, meaning that the antihero series temporarily becomes a narrative in which one does not sympathize strongly with anyone (Plantinga 2009:170ff). In his discussion of antiheroes, Alberto N. García makes a related point when he argues for what he labels cyclical re-allegiance in the antihero series: sympathy for the antihero is put to the test, and then re-established, again and again (García, unpublished manuscript).

Why so Many Television Series with Antiheroes? 93

Dan Flory discusses morally ambiguous characters in what he identifies as a *film noir*-influence in Spike Lee's films, and argues that similarly morally complex characters, who are both good and bad, in that setting makes a *flawed moral centre* (Flory 2008: 97). For example, he argues in relation to *Do the Right Thing* (Spike Lee, 1989) that there is "a centre of positive moral value [in the character Da Mayor], even if that moral orientation is substantially complicated by moral flaws" (Ibid.) This could be said to be true about the antihero series as well – the antihero makes a moral centre, but this centre is complicated because the antihero is morally flawed. However, in order to account for the dynamic nature of the spectator's engagement in the antihero series it may be more accurate to say that during reality checks in the antihero series the moral resolution of its main character changes drastically – from being portrayed as morally preferable, understandable and all human, to being portrayed as alien, monstrous, reprehensible. As Dr Melfi puts it, we sometimes see Tony's animal nature. The spectator does not continually see the antihero as morally flawed; conveniently, the spectator allows this to slip to the back of her mind. She engages in, and enjoys engaging in, his perspective. It seems wrong to describe this moral centre as being continually perceived as morally flawed. Sometimes, however, the spectator is reminded of the antihero's moral flaws. The moral structure of the antihero series is unstable. If we think of the antihero as somewhere between a regular hero and a villain, borrowing something from both, during reality checks he should stand out as more villainous than heroic. The spectator wavers in her dedication to the antihero. But what role does the antihero's *villainous* qualities play in the spectator's engagement with him?

Smith doubts that the spectator sympathizes with characters because they are bad. He argues that the spectator's sympathy for morally bad characters, such as Hannibal Lecter in *The Silence of the Lambs* (Jonathan Demme, 1991), are in spite of him being a murderer and a cannibal, and not because of this (Smith 1999). The spectator's engagement with Hannibal is only a partial allegiance, where she sympathizes with his attractive sides but not with his morally bad sides. He argues that truly perverse allegiances, as he labels them, in which the spectator sympathizes with deliberate violation of moral precepts, are rare – the narrative will usually ultimately elicit morally approbatory responses. The reader will recognize this argument, as I emphasised this aspect of Smith's account in chapter 1: the spectator's engagement with fiction is ultimately seen as morally grounded. Nevertheless, Smith does modify this view slightly in later papers by suggesting that it is not only the case that we sympathize with the antihero's (morally) attractive sides, but that his immoral sides also have some degree of appeal to us. Let us look at Smith's discussion of responses that seem less than morally good step by step.

One explanation for Tony's appeal that Smith discusses is amoral fascination, where the spectator watches someone truly evil with the same kind of

94 Why so Many Television Series with Antiheroes?

fascination as she would watch an alien creature like a shark hunting its prey. Smith dismisses this as an explanation for the attraction of *The Sopranos* – the spectator is not merely fascinated by Tony in such a detached, amoral fashion (Smith 2011a). The crux of the question is indeed how it is we as spectators come to feel with, sympathize with and like the antihero, and merely being fascinated by him does not explain these responses. However, in some cases there may be an element of fascination, too – *Dexter*, for example, plays upon the alien nature of its serial killer protagonist. He may seem common and humdrum, just the regular guy next door – but he is nothing like us, as emphasised by the everyday breakfast ritual rendered grotesque in the series' opening sequence.[4]

The TV series *Hannibal* can also be said to emphasize and explore the alien nature of Hannibal the cannibalistic serial killer, and again an amoral fascination can be said to be an intended response. In one episode, for example, in a flashback (marked as such in black and white) we see Hannibal strangle the FBI trainee Miriam Lass, who is on to him.[5]

Figure 4.1 Hannibal is strangling a victim into unconsciousness. This is a moment he cherishes for its beauty, making the spectator watch him as if he were a strange animal indeed (*Hannibal*, NBC).

She is standing in his office as he sneaks up from behind her; he has taken off his shoes in order not to be heard, and approaches silently, like a giant feline predator. He grabs her from behind with his hands around her throat. The spectator is bound to be taken aback as Hannibal is strangling her into unconsciousness, shown in a lingering close-up. The victim's facial expression, as she is fighting for her life and is slowly asphyxiated, is surely hard to watch – but Hannibal is perhaps even more disturbing. He is not expressing

Why so Many Television Series with Antiheroes?   95

hatred, anger, aggression, or any of the sinister emotions one would expect from a proper villain. His face is calm, solemn. He has an air of dignity. As he is strangling her, he softly tilts his head so that he leans his head onto hers. It looks as if he is almost trying to comfort her, or to communicate to her: do not worry, I will do this well. I will strangle you well. This kind of sequence can elicit a kind of amoral fascination. Watching Hannibal kill is like looking at a strange animal indeed; he is nothing like normal people. His killing is portrayed as a moment of beauty for him; an intimate moment; a moment he cherishes. The angrily hissing, aggressive traditional villain is perhaps even slightly more comprehensible than Hannibal is in this sequence – killing because one seeks revenge for something, or because one is carried away by one's passions somehow – but Hannibal's killings are nothing like that.

Adding to amoral fascination for antiheroes such as Dexter and Hannibal is also the fact that they are portrayed as hugely talented, and at least in Hannibal's case, as an awesome genius. Furthermore, perhaps Dexter and Hannibal, both serial killers who enjoy the very kill immensely, and kill first and foremost because they enjoy it (although Dexter's killings serve a greater function as well), stand at the border of what the spectator is willing to allow herself to engage with imaginatively, and more so than the gangster Tony or the meth-cook Walter, who both importantly do what they do for their families, at least initially. As an antihero, Hannibal is nudged much closer to a regular villain than is Tony and Walter, or most of the other antiheroes I discuss in this book. So to some degree the question of fascination with the *villain* also becomes a pertinent question in this debate.

A third solution Smith discusses, as part of his discussion of good-bad characters ('an alloy') is that the spectator can use fictional stories to enjoy immoral wish-fulfilment in a sort of imaginative slumming (Smith 1999). However, this is not a truly perverse allegiance either, he argues, insofar as the good-bad characters are often "only apparently or temporarily characterized as morally undesirable" (Ibid., 225). Smith will thus typically emphasise how seemingly perverse allegiances are only partial – rather than truly forming an allegiance on the basis of the character's immorality, the spectator's allegiance will typically be enhanced by other, morally approbatory responses. Later he discusses Tony Soprano as offering the spectator such an opportunity for imaginative slumming, or more specifically, that "the transgressive aspects of [Tony's] character (...) may make him appealing, and an object of care [because of] his ability to flout moral and other constraints with impunity" (Smith 2011a: 80). In this later paper Smith suggests that it is not only the case that the spectator likes Tony's morally good sides, but that his moral transgressions are also alluring, most notably through the enormous power Tony has. The very immorality of the antihero thus comes to play a more important role in this explanation of the appeal of Tony than Smith's theory has previously allowed for. He argues that Tony has a paradoxical appeal: the spectator is attracted to his regularity, and sees him

96   *Why so Many Television Series with Antiheroes?*

as morally grounded to some degree. She forms a partial moral allegiance with Tony – to his heroic side, one might add. However, at the same time the allure of the transgressive is also important for the spectator's engagement with Tony. Tony's ability to flout moral and other constraints with impunity is enjoyable, too. Smith's observation is supported by an empirical study of British men's engagement with *The Sopranos*, where especially the middle-aged interviewees say that they both identify with Tony as a husband and father, earning and living under stress – but also enjoying the escapist, fantastic potential offered by the gangster (Lacey 2002). As one respondent puts it: "You feel for the guy, you can identify with him, at the same time there's the fantasy, looking at him and thinking wouldn't it be good to be able to dot, dot, dot" (Lacey 2002: 102). Lacey concludes that what appeals most to this particular respondent is "the gangster as a fantasy figure (...) his ability to live a life beyond accepted social structures and expectations" (Ibid., 106).

Returning to Smith's theory, he touches upon the way the spectator can take pleasure in immorality here. The spectator's enjoyment of and sympathy with Tony thus becomes paradoxical in Smith's account: he is both moral and immoral. There is indeed something paradoxical about the spectator's ability to enjoy in fiction what she would condemn in real life. As Smith acknowledges, he has not solved this paradox, but concludes that the paradox is "not a product of faulty thinking about an aspect of behavior, but, rather, a description of our behavior. (...) The real 'solution' (...) may be to stare hard in the face of the complexity, and even inconsistency, of certain aspects of human behavior" (Smith 2011a: 80). However, there is more to be said about this complexity. In order to do so yet again we need to focus on lower-level responses, and on how they often differ radically from the slow thinking of our rational mind.

The Attraction of Empathy with the Antihero

Both imaginative slumming as vicarious wish-fulfilment and the allure of the transgressive are easier to explain and appear less paradoxical and puzzling if seen as low-level intuitive responses. The spectator enjoys the antihero's transgressions through low-level bodily mechanisms and moral intuitions. Without such low-level responses there is a missing link in the explanation of imaginative slumming. For example, there are several instances in the series where I would argue, in line with Smith's latter paper, that the spectator is intended to enjoy Tony's murderous violence (a sort of imaginative slumming). Take the relationship between Tony and Ralph Cifaretto in season 3, for example. In one of the most brutal and disturbing episodes of the series earlier in the same season, Ralph's relationship to his stripper girlfriend Tracee is one of the main storylines.[6] Ralph and another man have sex with Tracee at the Bada Bing – she is weeping, but Ralph seems sadistically to enjoy it. Later in the episode, Ralph beats Tracee to death during a quarrel.

Why so Many Television Series with Antiheroes? 97

Ralph is portrayed as a fully blown psychopath, and is arguably one of the characters that make Tony appear morally preferable in the series. In the fourth season, Ralph finally gets what he deserves: Tony kills him in exactly the same way as Tracee was killed in the previous season.[7] I predict that most spectators see Ralph's violent death as deserved in this fictional context, and that one enjoys this justice sequence (a sequence where justice is restored through punishment of a criminal who has caused an injustice, cf. Raney 2002). As Ralph is portrayed as morally worse than Tony, one can surely say that Tony's vengeance is intrinsically moral. Nevertheless, few of us would at the end of the day applaud beating trespassers to death as retribution, and the sequence where Tony kills Ralph is exceptionally violent. Arguably, the spectator's enjoyment of this sequence is not grounded in a fully rational evaluation of what Ralph deserves. A more accurate description of the spectator's response again turns to our moral – or sometimes immoral – intuitions.

Spectators of crime drama seem to "expect (and perhaps even demand) a retribution that is greater than what is morally acceptable in reality" (Raney 2002: 320).[8] Rationally speaking, one would probably not applaud taking the law into one's own hands as Tony does in this sequence. Perhaps the spectator prefers greater retribution and harder punishment in relation to fiction than what she would find acceptable in real life because, intuitively, we find watching a deserved punishment emotionally rewarding, probably more than most of us would be willing to admit in real life. Joshua Greene discusses what he labels *pro-social punishment* (also often referred to as altruistic punishment) as one of the core features of human morality (Greene 2013: 57).[9] As humans we have an in-built willingness to punish wrongdoers, even if nothing wrong has been done to us personally. Remember that we have evolved to co-operate in groups, and it is in everyone's interest that the group collaborates as smoothly as possible. In this picture, our intuitive moral emotions have evolved mainly to secure such co-operation. Cheating, freeloading and other kinds of wrongdoing pose a threat to group harmony; indeed, were too many to get away with it, the collaborative group would fall apart altogether. Humans in a group need to trust each other. Our willingness to punish others regardless of self-interest is one mechanism to secure co-operation. As will be expected from our morality at such a basic, intuitive level, it is driven by an emotion – righteous indignation. When seeing someone we are sided with punish a wrongdoer in a fiction, feelings of righteous indignation are triggered, and we take pleasure in seeing the perpetrator punished. Indeed, Greene also points out that

> Nowhere is our concern for how others treat others more apparent than in our intense engagement with fiction. Were we purely selfish, we wouldn't pay good money to hear a made-up story about a ragtag group of orphans who use their street smarts and quirky talents to outfox a criminal gang. We find stories about imaginary heroes and

98 *Why so Many Television Series with Antiheroes?*

> villains engrossing because they engage our social emotions, the ones that guide our reactions to real-life cooperators and rogues. We are not disinterested parties.
>
> (Greene 2013: 59)

In relation to real-life moral trespassers, we might want to, or try to, overrule such pleasures – perceived as primitive perhaps – by rational evaluation, and think of the rule of being innocent until proven guilty, for example, or be concerned about a humane penal system. Again, restricting my argument to us as people in contemporary Western societies, our taking pleasure in retribution does not seem to be a feature of our moral make-up to which we are willing to admit. In relation to fiction, however, and in the privacy of our very own imaginative engagement with a story, undisturbed by observing strangers, we may not feel the need to evaluate something rationally in such a way, and then we enjoy Tony's revenge. On a basic level of bodily feelings, it is to some degree pleasurable to watch Ralph be treated the same way he treated Tracee (an eye for an eye!)

As will be remembered from chapter 1, Raney argues that we morally disengage when we engage with fiction. In Raney and Janicke's discussion of what they label morally complex characters – who display qualities of both heroes and villains – they argue that moral judgment plays an even less significant role in our liking of such characters than in our engagement with regular heroes (Raney and Janicke 2013). The reason they give is that enjoying the fiction is perceived as of the utmost importance, and in order to avoid cognitive dissonance when engaging with fictions with morally complex characters, the spectator morally disengages. Because she wants to enjoy the narrative the spectator finds ways of liking the protagonist even though this figure is morally bad. Raney and Jackie point to several explanations for the appeal of such morally complex characters. First, they argue that we enjoy the antihero's restoration of justice; it is pleasurable because we want to believe in a just world.[10] This is in line with my suggestion about taking pleasure in pro-social punishment. Furthermore, they also point to the pleasure of seeing the antihero flout social conventions, and argue that "morally complex media characters are appealing because they help us to vicariously exercise our constantly suppressed selfishness" (Ibid., 163). The pleasure we take in seeing the antihero being selfish is tied to the suggestion Smith makes as well about the allure of the transgressive in his account: Tony is enjoyable because he is powerful (Smith 2011a: 78, see also 1995: 94). In the sequence where Tony kills Ralph there are thus other sources of pleasure to be found, beyond enjoyment of punishment. Ralph has been challenging Tony for a long time. He has grown more and more disrespectful. A very important reason for the antihero being enjoyable, I propose, is that he is powerful.

In the sequence where Ralph is killed, Tony puts his foot down and restores himself as the leader. Who would not want to be in a position of

Why so Many Television Series with Antiheroes? 99

power? I am obviously not suggesting we all secretly wish we could beat our colleagues to a pulp. But who would not want to be the one who makes the decisions, at least; the one to whom others must listen? The one pulling the strings? A central theme in the gangster genre is the pursuit of power.[11] The ageing Don Corleone laments the power struggle in which he leaves his son Michael in *The Godfather* (Francis Ford Coppola, 1972): he always thought he would leave his son as the one holding the strings (rather than having to move about to someone else's will like a puppet). The antihero series has inherited from the gangster genre this exploration of power. Walter White transcends his disempowered state to become the supreme drug kingpin, and enraged by his wife Skyler's concern about someone, sometime, coming to knock on their door to harm their family, he informs her that *he* is the one who knocks. He is the danger.[12] The antihero rises to power (e.g., Tony Soprano, Walter White, Jackson Teller, Enoch "Nucky" Thompson in *Boardwalk Empire*, Vick Mackey in *The Shield*). He struggles to maintain power. What attraction does this depiction of powerful men (and some women, see chapter 6) offer the spectator?

In a recent meta-study power is defined as "having the discretion and the means to asymmetrically enforce one's will over others" (Sturm and Antonakis 2015: 139). Having power has distinct cognitive, affective and behavioural effects. Power increases confidence (Fast et al. 2012). Power holders demonstrate less loss aversion and take greater risks (Inesi 2010); they are more inclined to experience positive affect such as desire, enthusiasm and optimism (Keltner et al. 2003, Anderson and Galinsky 2006); they are more likely to take action (e.g., Galinksy et al 2003); and more sensitive to potential gains (Keltner et al. 2003). All of these effects of power can be seen as evolutionary based: it makes sense that a leader is confident, optimistic, able to take action and able to identify potential gains. Ian Robertson summarizes this in his popularized account of the effect of power as the powerful's "can-do orientation" (Robertson 2012: 117). He also points to the strong effects of power on what he labels the brain's reward network (2012: 24ff). The system is fuelled by the hormone dopamine, which is released when we do something that is good for evolutionary survival, such as eating something sweet or having sex. Experiencing power also results in a flush of dopamine in the brain, and is perceived as pleasurable. Other hormonal effects are at work, too: the levels of cortisol, the stress hormone, decrease when experiencing power and increases when one feels powerless (Pruessner et al 2005).[13] Furthermore, winning makes testosterone levels rise. Testosterone is associated with more aggressive behaviour and increased appetite for risk (Cashdan 2003; Mazur et al. 1992). These effects are all part of that feeling, one hopes familiar to most of us, of rush of power that one may experience when having won something, or successfully taken the lead on something.

Power need not be sinister; e.g., caring for one's family can also give a sense of power. The important thing would be having more influence over others than they have over you (i.e., as parents have over children; as a boss has over her employees, etc.). Furthermore, the antihero's display of power need not be violent. The antihero Jackie Peyton in *Nurse Jackie* (Showtime, 2009–2015) is cheating on her husband and she is a drug addict, but within her ER environment in the hospital, Jackie is the vigilante nurse who will circumvent inhuman bureaucracy created by administrators looking for economical profit and tending to their own careers. Jackie is the one who stands up them, insisting on putting the patients' interests first. In season 4, for example, there are economical cutbacks and the ER is severely understaffed. No one dares speak up to the administrator who is responsible for making these changes. Jackie, too, tries to adhere to the new rules. But finally she puts her foot down. She cries out: "I'm in charge!", and calls in more temporary nurses.[14] Jackie is a small-scale vigilante – not saving the world by throwing train cars at metaphysically evil bad guys, but ensuring that her ER room is devoted to giving care to its patients. In this series, too, ultimately sympathy with the antihero is put to the test by emphasizing the consequences Jackie's lying and cheating has for her, for her colleagues, her family and, in the latter seasons, ultimately also her patients. However, for a long time her willingness to violate rules and cross boundaries makes her enjoyably powerful.

Figure 4.2 "I'm in charge!" When nurse Jackie puts her foot down in an act of defiance, this is an enjoyable display of power (*Nurse Jackie*, Showtime).

When watching powerful characters on-screen, engaging with them over a long period of time and empathizing with them, some of these effects might also latch onto the spectator. Temporarily, when watching, perhaps we feel some of those pleasurable feelings that come with a "can-do orientation". Aligning ourselves with powerful antiheroes might give us a momentary relief from our more-or-less stressful everyday lives. Just as one might feel the power of the action hero remain in one's body for a few minutes after coming out of the screening of any action film, perhaps after having watched Tony Soprano win the respect of unruly subordinates for a couple of hours, one finds oneself breathing a little like him; his heavy breathing signalling that he might have a fit of rage at any moment. Indeed, exposure to violent media may make the spectator more aggressive as a short-term effect, e.g., through mechanisms of priming or excitation transfer (see e.g., Bryant and Miron 2003; Zillmann 1983).[15] This should not be taken to mean that spectators necessarily will display more aggressive *behaviour* – nor do I deny that such effects may be found.[16] However, rather than reviewing the literature on potential long-term effects of watching media violence, or on the effects of violent media on real-life violent behaviour, it is merely my aim here to argue that in the short-term, i.e., immediately after having watched aggression and violence on-screen, it seems plausible that the spectator is left in a physically excited state which, from what we know about the physicality of emotions, simply takes time to abate. The debate about the effects of violent media naturally focuses on the potential negative effects (and understandably so, in the sense that we need to know who are mostly prone to be influenced negatively, and what kind of violence might be more harmful than other kinds, etc.). However, the state in which the spectator may find herself after media exposure can also be seen as a pleasurable and positive experience – the experience of being powerful and in control. As emphasised by some media psychologists, the research on media exposure should also ask why spectators are attracted to media products in the first place (see e.g., Tamborini 2013). I will merely concentrate on the attractions such media products can offer. Tony is willing to escalate any conflict in order to win, and just as he feels powerful perhaps the spectator, too, feels a slight testosterone rush. The mere pleasure of being in this powerful affective state may be one of the reasons why the spectator seeks out narratives about powerful antiheroes.

It is not that the antihero must be immoral in order to be powerful – regular heroes surely also have power. However, perhaps it is part of the wish-fulfilment offered by the antihero series that one allows oneself to take pleasure even in the immoral side of power, or the negative effects of power. There is a danger for people in power over time to become less empathic and more selfish, and near megalomaniac, suffering from the potential negative effects of boosted self-confidence and hardnosed faith in one's own decisions.[17] The antihero, too, can often be said to suffer from some of these effects – Walter White, for example, continues to produce drugs long after he has secured his family's finances, as was his initial excuse. He simply does it because he enjoys it, ignoring the suffering he brings upon his wife and children. Nevertheless, as he enjoys his power trip, so does the spectator (at least up until a certain tipping point). The antihero is ultimately self-serving, allowing for plenty of displays of power. Perhaps this, too, is pleasurable – as Raney and Janicke also suggest.

Furthermore, Jean-Baptiste Du Bos made a relevant observation hundred of years ago in his discussion of the pleasures of engaging with representational art that stir up negative feelings such as suffering when engaging with tragedies (the paradox of negative emotion).[18] Du Bos argues that we use representational art primarily to alleviate boredom, and that

> [l]ooking at pictures depicting positive events can be pleasant, but the feelings to be had in this way may lack the intensity and so fail to forestall boredom. Pictures of violent, disturbing, and risky events, on the other hand, can stir up stronger feelings and are thus more likely to alleviate boredom.
>
> (Du Bos paraphrased in Livingston 2013: 401)

It is difficult to be indifferent to violent and disturbing images on-screen, and because they capture our interest so effectively, this can partly explain the prominent role they take in entertainment. This alternative explanation for violent and disturbing content in entertainment deserves more space than I can give it here, but we can include this suggestion on our list of reasons for why creators aiming at making a story that is maximally engaging would want to include immoral, disturbing and violent images – simply due to the fact that such images stir up strong emotions and capture our interest very effectively.

In conclusion, there are bodily pleasures offered by the antihero's very immorality. Slight feelings of power might be pleasurable because they put the spectator vicariously in the position of a winner. The feelings triggered by seeing justice be done are rewarding, regardless of the punishment being much more severe than what one would condone in real life. Notably, these payoffs are only evident in a model of spectatorship where low-level responses are given an important role, such as moral intuitions and embodied empathy. The apparent sympathy for the devil effect has in large parts perhaps less to do with the spectator finding reasons for defending the antihero's misdeeds rationally as she watches, and thus truly deliberating about him as morally preferable, and more to do with some relatively simple and basic feelings of pleasure by feeling with the top dog. Perhaps she finds good reason to like him only after the fact, once she starts discussing the series with others and reflecting on her own engagement – and feels the need to defend it. It is exactly by pushing the pleasure we take in Tony's immorality to the far end of low-level bodily feelings of empathy and moral intuitions that the paradox of our sympathy with immoral main characters in fiction can be properly explained: we come to sympathize with them because we have empathized with them first. And we find it hard to explain rationally why we find them morally preferable. The paradoxical air of our engagement with and enjoyment of the antihero can thus be solved in a dual process model of morality.

Why so Many Television Series with Antiheroes? 103

Yet one can still argue that this does not fully explain why the antihero strategy has become so common in American television. If we enjoy displays of power and seeing justice be served, would it not be easier to simply make epic series where the heroes use their powers to impose Good over Evil? In order to come to the bottom of this question, we need to turn to the function of villainy in a story.

On the Narrative Importance and Function of Immorality

The important function played by villains in fictional stories has surprisingly been explored only to a limited degree. Carroll points out that in addition to sympathy for the protagonist, antipathy for the antagonist is an equally important driving force in the spectator's emotional response to a story (Carroll 2008: 182–4). Thus, feeling antipathy for a villain, wanting to see him get what he deserves, are central parts of the spectator's emotional response to a story. In chapter 5 and 6 I discuss antipathetic responses to proper villains in the antihero series that serve to make the antihero appear morally preferable. Now, however, let us focus on another question: do we *only* feel antipathy toward the villain? Or can we sometimes, at some level, also like the villain in some special sense? Immorality is important to stories in the sense that villains and their immoral acts fuel the spectator's emotional engagement and truly get the drama in a story going. As pointed out in the previous chapter, the spectator quite commonly desires immoral events to befall characters in fiction simply because it makes a good story (cf. Currie 1999). Surely mere unfortunate events or difficulties of other sorts could make a dramatic story, too, but without having some person on which to put the blame, one would miss out on a cluster of intense emotions triggered by antipathy – dislike, hatred, disgust, righteous indignation – and also, when the villain is getting his just deserts, the rewards of witnessing his punishment. One can see why a personified evil force – as in a villainous character – makes stories more engaging by giving us somebody to hate. In fact, villains play such an important role in stories that we would sometimes say that we 'love to hate' them. What this means is arguably that we appreciate the strong emotions they give rise to, and the way they make the story engaging in turn. A villain is thus narratively desirable. Let us then explore how giving the antihero some villainous character traits is rewarding at a narrative level, i.e., how adding immorality makes the story more engaging.

One way to start exploring these narrative desires in relation to immorality is a point Flory makes in relation to the attractive-bad characters in the *noir* films that he analyses. He suggests that one way

> these characters' moral complexity, ambiguity, and at times their immorality help to foster greater suspense and interest in many *noir* narratives [is] because such traits help to create still greater uncertainty in the viewer.

(Flory 2008: 77–78)

104 *Why so Many Television Series with Antiheroes?*

Because the morally complex character is an alloy of good and bad characteristics, he is more difficult for the spectator to predict. One never knows whether the alloy will be good or bad, as he is an amalgam of both. Flory argues that this adds to the spectator's "interest in these protagonists because they are to some extent unpredictable" (Ibid., 78). This explanation is related to my suggestion about the role played by narrative desires in the sense that what I take Flory to be suggesting here is that the spectator comes to be interested in the alloy – and perhaps also appreciate the alloy narratively – because he adds to the suspense. The spectator never knows what he will do. The alloy is thus narratively desirable.

Among the antihero series, *Sons of Anarchy* offers good examples. The main characters are, in their own words, 'mechanics and motorcycle enthusiasts' – but they are in fact operating on the wrong side of the law, mostly making a living through trading with illegal weapons. Through rivalry with other motorcycle gangs, murder is also common. Among the main characters are the leader of Sons of Anarchy Jackson Teller, and his mother, Gemma Teller. Both Jackson and Gemma are alloy characters who are unpredictable, and therefore interesting and entertaining, because they are such a complex mix of good and bad. Jackson wants to make his motorcycle gang legit, but ends up killing an awful lot of people in the effort to get there. Although Gemma argues that she is no psychopath because she sees that what she does is bad, she also keeps on doing bad things. And of course, in line with my argument in chapter 2, it is all for the family – both Jackson and Gemma are simply doing what needs to be done in order to protect the family. A whole family of unpredictable antiheroes! In the two last seasons of this series, for example, Gemma hooks up with Neron "Nero" Padilla, a pimp who appears sensitive and kind – morally preferable – in this brutal biker setting. Will her love for Nero make Gemma kinder? Will the boundaries that he is still able to track help her delineate between right and wrong? Flory's argument about the felicitous effect of uncertainty makes sense in relation to *Sons of Anarchy*. It adds to the suspense in this series that one never knows whether the antihero – both the younger, male one (Jackson) and the older, female one (Gemma) – will choose right or wrong.

Another good example is *Bloodline* (Netflix, 2015-present), where the oldest brother Danny Rayburn is the one bad apple in a seemingly shiny, happy family running a hotel in the sunbathed Florida Keys. One of his three siblings, John, is the local sheriff, and the family are ambivalent when Danny returns after a long absence, as he usually simply mocks up. However, things are not always as they seem, and at the end of the first episode, as we see John drag an unconscious Danny through the swamp in a flash-forward, we hear in voice-over the sanctimonious John reassure us that "We are not bad people. But we did a bad thing." Thus the set-up in this first season is to find out how bad Danny really is, and whether he deserves the resentment his family feels toward him. This makes for engaging viewing, as Danny is notoriously hard to predict, and as the season evolves the spectator is

Why so Many Television Series with Antiheroes? 105

continually asked to re-evaluate him and the others. Morally complex characters who are an amalgam between the morally good and the villainous are less predictable, making it intriguingly difficult for the spectator to foresee what they will do.

In order to narrow in further on the narrative function of villainy, Aaron Taylor's exploration of the spectator's enjoyment and appreciation of the villain is helpful. Discussing the villain in *Sunset Boulevard* (Billy Wilder, 1950) Taylor argues for the important function of aesthetic appreciation of what he labels melodramatic villainy (i.e., a villain in the melodramatic tradition) (Taylor 2007).[19] The excessive theatricality of the melodramatic villain affords the spectator a pleasure that overrides her moral reservations against him: because the villain's performance is so entertaining, spectacular and charismatic, it encourages the spectator to appreciate the character's immoral art. "Taking pleasure from a melodramatic representation of evil is often a complex form of aesthetically oriented appreciation" (Ibid., 14). Taylor thus argues that our appreciation of villains is "aesthetic approval rather than moral disapproval" (Ibid., 24). Because the spectator wants a fictional story to be entertaining and enjoyable, her narrative desires for the entertaining and spectacular override a moral evaluation per se – similar to the effect of suspense, as we saw in the previous chapter.

Gyp Rosetti in the third season of *Boardwalk Empire* represents an excellent example of these effects of aesthetic appreciation. At the beginning of the season, Rosetti is but a slightly annoying minor character in this tale about the antihero Nucky Thompson as the kingpin in Atlantic City's prohibition period gangster underworld. Rosetti is disrespectful and full of himself, and I found myself being annoyed with Nucky for not putting him in his place (wishing for greater display of power!). Increasingly, however, this loudmouth brute – almost a cartoonish parody of the gangster – becomes such a pleasurable spectacle in and of himself that I start to enjoy Rosetti's appearances. Rosetti takes the narcissistic anger and aggression that drive the gangster one notch forward. In once sequence, for example, what starts out as a humble prayer in church, where he interrogates the Lord's plans for him, soon turns into rage against his God, accusing Him of being a "sick fuck" for treating him this way.[20] The actor's performance of Rosetti's anger is impressive and the sequence is hilarious; Rosetti surely makes a magnificent display.

Other sequences, too, revolve around Rosetti as a spectacular character. One episode opens with a disconcerting series of grunting noises off-screen.[21] As the camera slowly closes in on the source of these noises one is given ample time to imagine what it is we are about to see – someone being tortured, tormented, killed slowly perhaps. It turns out to be Rosetti having sex; he climaxes only if being stimulated at the same time as he nears asphyxiation. Roberta, his lover, has obviously been instructed to suffocate him with his own belt while he masturbates. Later in the same episode as a similar sex sequence with Gyp takes place, a group of men are approaching

106 *Why so Many Television Series with Antiheroes?*

to take Rosetti out. The fight that continues ends with Rosetti, stark naked, covered in blood and with his own belt still hanging from his neck, walking through the hallway, stepping over dead bodies as the camera hovers over him in a very unusual, unnatural angle seldom used in this series. The sequence is both outlandish and massively spectacular, inviting appreciation both of Rosetti's performance; the spectacular and perverse display offered by his sexual habits and his naked body covered in blood; as well as its cinematography.

Figure 4.3 A spectacular sequence with Giuseppe "Gyp" Rosetti which may be appreciated aesthetically even to a point where moral responses are rendered less relevant (*Boardwalk Empire*, HBO).

Rosetti also offers aesthetic appreciation as a dandy villain – as does the entire cast of *Boardwalk Empire*: these gangsters are all men of exquisite taste, always well groomed and elegantly dressed in the most refined suits. Appreciating their appearance is arguably an important part of watching this series. The important point here, however, is that slowly my engagement with Rosetti changes – he is introduced as a villain in this antihero series, and serves as a contrast to the seemingly more civilized and dignified Nucky. Nevertheless, as the season progresses I stop wanting Nucky to take Rosetti out, and start simply appreciating Rosetti aesthetically. Aesthetic appreciation seems to undermine moral responses – rendering them less relevant somehow. Rosetti's performance gives me what I desire from a good story.

The antihero can borrow something from the melodramatic villain's performance in this sense. The spectator is invited to take pleasure in and appreciate the very performance in itself, which is often excessive and theatrical. In between a villain and a hero, the spectator's response to the antihero borrows from the aesthetic appeal of the villain while downplaying the antipathy that traditional villains also trigger. Through various techniques, empathy with the antihero is triggered – by making him recognizably human, similar to me and part of my in-group. Equally important is the fact that the antihero is pleasantly powerful and vengeful, and often also aesthetically pleasing by offering spectacular sequences. Finally, the moral disgust often used to mark proper villains as repulsive is downplayed.[22]

Why There Are so Many Series with Antiheroes

In his discussion of Hannibal in *The Silence of the Lambs* as a Nietzschean exploration of the will to power (Taylor 2014) and of the melodramatic villain in *The Night of the Hunter* as our moral shadow in a Jungian framework (Taylor, unpublished manuscript), Taylor argues that villains serve an important function in that they help the spectator revalue the dominant ethics in our society, namely Judeo-Christian ethics. The villain serves as a trigger for moral reflection. Raney and Janicke make a similar point: we seek out morally complex characters because of the "post-hoc moral scrutiny" that they encourage (Raney and Janicke 2013: 164). One can thus say that at a narrative level, the spectator desires immoral characters in fiction because they give her the opportunity to reflect on, and perhaps even revise, her ethical stance. This argument emphasises the way engagement with fiction can sometimes trigger very deliberate, rational moral evaluation indeed. As such, it can be seen as a counterargument to my theory in this book. However, although I do not think that the spectator typically engages in such deliberate moral evaluation and reflection throughout her engagement with most fiction, surely there is something to the idea that at least post hoc, and perhaps most prominently in conversation with other spectators, the spectator can use the fictional story as a starting point for her own exploration of and critical interrogation of her own morality. Large parts of the press that the various antihero series have received – *The Sopranos* and *Breaking Bad* especially – have been concerned with the ethical questions these series raise. The debaters scrutinize their own sympathy for the immoral antihero after each episode and season – potentially adding up to a prolonged ethical reflection. Thus, there have been plenty of post-hoc discussions about morality in relation to these series, and if the antihero had not been immoral, there would not have been as much to discuss.

Narrative desires in relation to fictional stories, appreciation of an actor's display and of the story's triggering of deliberate reflection on moral issues all point to spectator responses beyond mere immersion in the story world. These desires and appreciation are external to the fictional world, not internal to it (as are sympathy and empathy for the antihero, for example) (Cf. Lamarque and Olsen 1994). In addition to the enjoyment of engaging in a narrative, arguably an important attraction of the antihero series is a response I will label *appreciation*.[23] We can differentiate between enjoyment and appreciation by saying that enjoyment is tied to involvement

108 *Why so Many Television Series with Antiheroes?*

or engagement in the unfolding narrative as entertainment. This may give rise to various emotions, such as empathy and sympathy – both of which Ed S. Tan would label F (fiction) emotions (Tan 1996: 32ff). Appreciation, on the other hand, is tied to awareness of the narrative as an artefact—to its plot and style elements. In Tan's account, appreciation gives rise to A (artefact) emotions, such as admiration of the series' beautiful style, or feeling annoyed with the writers' bad choices in relation to a particular, liked character. These emotions take as their object the film or series as an aesthetic object made by someone. Relatedly, appreciation can also be tied to a narrative's more thought-provoking features (Oliver and Bartsch 2010).

There are many ways in which Quality TV series enhance appreciation, including highly rated actors; high budgets affording film-like quality and style; intertextuality or other forms of playful narration; and so on. In the literature on Quality TV, appreciation plays an important part. For example, Jason Mittell argues that what he labels complex TV is characterized by *operational aesthetics* (Mittell 2015). Operational aesthetics is when a TV series is highly reflexively aware about a mode of plotting where the spectator is intended to find pleasure not merely in the story development ("what will happen next?") but in the very mode of storytelling ("how did they do that?"). In online discussions one can find fans dissecting the narrative in great detail (what Mittell labels *forensic fandom*), testifying to the pleasures operational aesthetics in complex TV offer its spectators. Mittell sums this up as follows:

> We watch these series not just to get swept away in a realistic narrative world (although that certainly happens) but also to watch the gears at work, marveling at the craft required to pull off such narrative pyrotechnics.
>
> (Mittell 2015: 43)

Marvelling at the skills it takes to construct a narrative is certainly a kind of A-emotion in Tan's account, a form of appreciation that is distinctly different from engaging in the on-going story world *per se*. Furthermore, interestingly, when Mittell discusses *Breaking Bad* as complex TV, he suggests that Walter White's moral complexity invites a sort of character engagement specific to operational aesthetics, namely *operational allegiance*. In his analysis of our attraction to Walter White he argues that endeavouring to understand this complex character and engaging in the construction of his character are of central importance. Indeed,

> one of the pleasures of watching complex television is engaging with a sense of ludic play and puzzle-solving analysis, and attempting to read the minds of nuanced, multifaceted characters is fertile ground for such playful viewing practices.
>
> (Mittell 2015: 132)

In this account, the spectator enjoys trying to figure out what makes Walter tick.[24] Furthermore, in line with Mittell's account of operational aesthetics overall, the play and puzzle-solving activities that take centre stage when engaging with this complex character are responses not merely internal to the fiction, but a type of engagement that also entails an ongoing evaluation of the construction of this character – aesthetic appreciation, external to the fiction. This is in line with what I have discussed previously as the added value of a morally complex hero (in comparison to a traditional hero): complex characters do not merely add to the suspense, making it more rewarding to engage in the fiction through boosting various F-emotions, but also potentially makes us marvel at the way they are constructed – a kind of A-emotion.

Furthermore, the appreciation that the antihero series evokes specifically is the puzzled questioning of why it is I, as the spectator, like this character so much, despite his many serious moral flaws. As explored in this book, through various low-level, intuitive responses the spectator comes to perceive the antihero as morally in the right. On reflection, however, she does not actually think he is morally right. Thus, if the narrative reminds the spectator of this conflict, she marvels at the fact that she likes this character so much.[25] The spectator finds his or her liking of, and sympathizing with, these characters puzzling and fascinating. These television series thrive on their antiheroes because they add a thought-provoking, puzzling effect in addition to their engaging narratives. That is the proper effect of operational aesthetics and operational allegiance in antihero series: making me question not just what makes the antihero tick, and how the antihero is constructed, but also to reflect on the effects this story has on *me*. It is one of the ways in which these series enhance appreciation of their construction. In a related response to the one Mittell discusses as the response invited by operational aesthetics ("how did they do that?"), the antihero series makes the spectator reflect not merely on how the creators pulled off various story elements and plotlines, but how they made me engage this way ("how did they cause me to like the antihero?"). Making us empathize with, like and sympathize with these immoral antiheroes is something we are intended to admire.

In order to cash in on the spectator's tendency toward empathy and sympathy with the immoral antihero, these television series regularly put the spectator's pro-attitude for the antihero to the test through reality checks, as we have seen in the case of *The Sopranos* and *Breaking Bad*. It is particularly at these moments in the story that the spectator is supposed to reflect on, and appreciate, what these series make her go along with. The success of *The Sopranos* truly sparked the trend. One can speculate that the critical acclaim and audience success of *The Sopranos* triggered the creators and producers of other recent American Quality TV series to copy this aspect. Indeed, through interviews with various TV executives and producers, television critic Alan Sepinwall shows how others deliberately tried to copy *The Sopranos*, for example AMC executives saying, "We need a *Sopranos*"

110   *Why so Many Television Series with Antiheroes?*

(Sepinwall 2012: 302). The spectator comes to admire the construction of a series that makes her engage, almost despite herself, and that regularly encourages her to contemplate this very fact. The oscillating sympathy structure in *The Sopranos* is thus copied in the later antihero series. First, the spectator is made to like and sympathize with the antihero and then this sympathy is repeatedly put to the test. As it turns out, adding to other features meant to enhance aesthetic appreciation (acting, cinematography, complex storytelling, etc.), this is a winning formula.

Anne W. Eaton comes to a similar conclusion in her discussion of *The Sopranos* as a compelling case of *immoralism* in art (Eaton 2012). Immoralism in art is

> a peculiar sort of aesthetic achievement that has its basis in the immorality of the work in question. (...) [T]he capacity to make an audience feel and desire things inimical to their considered views and deeply held principles is for this very reason and to this extent an aesthetic achievement. In this way, moral flaws of a particular kind can make a significant contribution to a work's aesthetic value.
>
> (Eaton 2012: 281)

According to Eaton, Tony Soprano is a rough hero – a label she takes from David Hume. A rough hero is a character whom the spectator is meant both to like and sympathize with, but at the same time she is also meant to be "acutely aware of [his] profound and irredeemable moral flaws" (Ibid., 284).[26] This gives rise to deep-seated conflicted attitudes in its target audience. Whereas the artwork's perspective encourages the spectator to overcome imaginative resistance so as to like a rough hero such as Tony Soprano, she remains ambivalent about him because the artwork also makes it clear that the rough hero is morally flawed. We are in a conflicted state of "dividing ourselves-against-ourselves", and it is bringing about this state that is aesthetically valuable (Ibid., 287):

> we are moved to simultaneously approve and disapprove of the same character yet are offered nothing to resolve the conflict. This (...) is precisely what makes [works with rough heroes] so disturbing and compelling. (...) [A] moral defect can be an aesthetic merit.
>
> (Eaton 2013: 379)

Whereas Eaton does not have the conceptual terminology available to describe exactly of what this conflicted state consists, I do: the dual-process model of morality neatly explains the spectator's simultaneous approval and disapproval of Tony Soprano. Furthermore, Eaton's argument about the appeal of immoral artworks is closely linked to my argument here about the trend of antihero series – they are appealing exactly because the spectator finds the conflicted state in which they leave her thought-provoking and puzzling.

Why so Many Television Series with Antiheroes?   111

Eaton's paper on immoralism defends a specific position in a long-standing debate – indeed, harking back to Plato – on whether moral flaws in artworks are aesthetic flaws or not.[27] Carroll defends another position, *moderate moralism*, holding that "sometimes a moral defect in an artwork counts as an aesthetic defect" (Carroll 2013: 371). I will not discuss the relation between moral flaws and aesthetical defects here, as my goal is to say something about audience appeal, and not strictly speaking whether or not moral flaws make artwork better as *art*.[28] Nevertheless, Carroll's reply to Eaton's paper on immoralism is relevant to my discussion here (Carroll 2013). Carroll argues against her that Tony "clearly occurs in a narrative context where he is unblinkingly framed as a character whom the audience should regard as evil" (Ibid., 372). To corroborate this claim, Carroll points to Tony's wife Carmela and her encounter with the psychiatrist Dr Krakower.[29] Dr Krakower clearly condemns Tony, and Carroll takes this to be a warning to the spectator not to turn a blind eye to Tony's crimes. The authorial disapproval of Tony is thus made clear, according to Carroll. Where there is ambivalence and conflict in Eaton's account of *The Sopranos*, in Carroll's there is moral clarity. Against Eaton, Carroll argues that this series is not immoral. Rather, seeing Tony as someone the spectator is supposed to like is committing the narrative fallacy, namely failing to see the character's place in the overall narrative. The spectator is only invited to see Tony as attractive (due to his loyalty to his family, for example) in order to serve an ethical function: *The Sopranos* serves as a cautionary warning against "the seductiveness of bad guys with (nonmorally) attractive traits" (Carroll 2013: 373).

There are several problems with Carroll's reply to Eaton. First, Eaton never claims the spectator is only meant to like Tony – central to her argument is indeed the claim that the spectator is both meant to like and dislike him. Moral disapproval of Tony plays an important role in Eaton's argument. Furthermore, as Carroll points out at the end of his piece, the spectator is encouraged to like Tony through a series of, by now, familiar narrative techniques, in line with my discussion in this chapter.[30] This, however, gives Carroll's reply a contradictory air: when the spectator is given so many reasons to like Tony, how come it is clear that she is supposed to not like him? In the ensemble cast of *The Sopranos*, why should Dr Krakower, a minor character in the grand scheme of things, be seen as the creator David Chase's mouthpiece? As Eaton also points out, it is Carroll who seems to commit the narrative fallacy here (Eaton 2013: 378). Perhaps he sees Dr Krakower as voicing the creator's perspective simply because Dr Krakower is, in fact, right: Tony is morally reprehensible. This, however, is not sufficient to prove that he articulates the authorial slant or perspective in *The Sopranos*. Arguably, settling the question of authorial perspective in a long and complex series such as *The Sopranos* is no easy task, and much more careful analysis and argument would be needed than to point to the brief episode where Dr Krakower condemns Tony.

112 *Why so Many Television Series with Antiheroes?*

Be that as it may, my analysis of the interspersed reality checks in this and other antihero series arguably provides a starting point for such an analysis, and I do agree that *The Sopranos* ultimately encourages a moral condemnation of Tony Soprano; indeed, that it is typical of the antihero series to remind the spectator of the morally flawed nature of its protagonist through regular reality checks, especially toward the end of the entire series. Notably, however, these reality checks serve as a contrast to the spectator's liking the antihero, encouraged through fictional relief. This supports the view that the spectator is left in a conflicted state, such as the one Eaton describes, more than the moral clarity that Carroll finds in *The Sopranos*. The thought-provoking nature of this conflicted state is indeed what characterizes antihero series.

However, in favour of Carroll's view, one could for example point out that the antihero is usually punished at the very end of the series (though Tony is not – or who knows, as the series finale notoriously leaves Tony's fate open for interpretation). The end does seem especially important when looking for the 'moral in the story' – or the authorial perspective on the story's characters. Without revealing too much, think for example on the difference between the endings of the lives of antiheroes Albert "Chalky" White and Nucky Thompson, respectively, in *Boardwalk Empire*'s last season. One of them is arguably portrayed as a decent man after all, who might have made some wrong choices in life but who finally reveals that he has a moral, deeply empathic and noble character inside him.[31] The other is rather revealed, in an almost twist ending, to be by far less dignified and civilised than the spectator has been lead to believe. Thus the spectator is given a sense of closure for each of these characters, and in this closure it is suggested that their true moral character is revealed. The endings of their stories carry special weight when the spectator tries to tease out the moral of the story, as Martin Zeller-Jacques also points out in his exploration of the moral function of television series' endings, as one of several expectations we have toward what makes a good ending (Zeller-Jacques 2014: 125). Unfortunately an exploration of endings is beyond the scope of this present chapter.

The Antihero Series and the Problem of the Bad Fan

Let us say that there is an authorial perspective in *The Sopranos* that, at the end of the day, presents Tony as morally bad. What follows is a problem facing both Eaton and Carroll, and my own theory, too: what if the spectator does not get it? What if there is no uptake of the intended reality checks – a complete failure to recognize the authorial perspective asking the spectator ultimately also to dislike the antihero, even if she has been asked to like him initially? What if the spectator simply likes Tony Soprano? Carroll argues that *The Sopranos* is a cautionary tale, but one may fear that the spectator does not "come to *appreciate how our moral compass can be* demagnetized" (Carroll 2004: 136, my emphasis),

Why so Many Television Series with Antiheroes? 113

but rather, plain and simple, has his moral compass demagnetized. Both Eaton's immoralism and Carroll's moderate moralism assume that the target audience is sufficiently moral to feel either ambivalence/conflict (Eaton), or more strongly, moral clarity (Carroll). What if some take a liking to the series for all the wrong reasons? Television critic Emily Nussbaum has discussed this in relation to *Breaking Bad* by use of the term *bad fans*. She ties the phenomenon of bad fans to

> the much lauded stream of cable "dark dramas," whose protagonists shimmer between the repulsive and the magnetic. As anyone who has ever read the comments on a recap can tell you, there has always been a less ambivalent way of regarding an antihero: as a hero. Some of the most passionate fans of "The Sopranos" fast-forwarded through Carmela and Dr. Melfi to freeze-frame Tony strangling a snitch with electrical wire. (David Chase satirized their bloodlust with a plot about "Cleaver," a mob horror movie with all of the whackings, none of the Freud.) More recently, a subset of viewers cheered for Walter White on "Breaking Bad," growling threats at anyone who nagged him to stop selling meth. In a blog post about that brilliant series, I labelled these viewers "bad fans," and the responses I got made me feel as if I'd poured a bucket of oil onto a flame war from the parapets of my snobby critical castle. Truthfully, my haters had a point: who wants to hear that they're watching something *wrong*?
>
> (Nussbaum 2014a, emphasis original)

The bad fans are those who simply root for Walter, and hate Skyler vehemently (see chapter 6), and refuse to take notice of the authorial perspective portraying Walter as slowly becoming irredeemably bad. In both Eaton's and Carroll's theories, there must be an uptake of the authorial intention also to dislike Tony in order to cash in on its moral and aesthetical merits. Nussbaum's bad fans do not. Some spectators might simply see the immoral antihero as good entertainment, and may not take up a more distanced, reflective spectator position.

Flory discusses a related case of missing uptake of what he sees as the intended complex argument in relation to racism in Spike Lee's films as *cognitive insensitivity*. A white viewer's (pre-conscious) racial bias may prevent her from

> judging [the sympathetic racist character Sal in Spike Lee's *Do the Right Thing*] negatively as a racist because they know him well and have become firmly attached to his character. [They] might be inclined to overlook or excuse the depth of Sal's wrongdoing because their attachment to the character – based on both racial and nonracial elements of the narrative – is too powerful.
>
> (Flory 2008: 55)

114 *Why so Many Television Series with Antiheroes?*

This is not just the result of partiality, as I have discussed in chapter 2, but of what Flory discusses as *empathetic impairment*: even whites who do not desire to be racist will be "unable to detect the cognitive importance of race in situations where antiblack racism impinges on African Americans in day-to-day interactions with whites" (Janine Jones paraphrased in Flory 2008: 56). However, as the viewer is arguably intended to recognize Sal as both sympathetic *and* a racist – and Flory carefully explores how the narrative portrays him as such – it seems accurate to say that these viewers do not get what they are supposed to get. Spectators cheering uncritically and unreservedly for Tony, Walter and other antiheroes do seem to suffer from cognitive insensitivity – they do not pick up on textual cues that clearly also encourage them to recognize these characters as bad.[32] They reduce a morally complex series to a simple tale of heroism, which it is arguably not intended to be. The bad fans seem to be impervious to the idea that their own beliefs and values could be mocked or critiqued, and they fail to pick up on the authorial perspective on the antihero as a morally flawed human being.[33]

A critic could say that these viewers, or bad fans in Nussbaum's terminology, simply allow themselves the fictional relief that I have argued that we typically do afford ourselves when engaging with fiction. Indeed, if the spectator seeks out antihero series for entertainment, why is the reality check important? Again, this problem takes on the full force of the question of harmful effects of bad entertainment, as for example whether engaging with violent films, television and videogames make us more prone to violence, and I will not engage this debate here. However, independently of the question of harmful effects on real life behaviour one can question whether it is morally right to sympathize with these immoral characters imaginatively. Is the bracketing of moral principles in fictional reliefs, and thus enjoying the antihero's rise to power, his vigilante killings and criminal actions, intrinsically morally wrong? Some argue that it is wrong to enjoy merely imagined evil (e.g., Smuts 2013). This position is labelled *response moralism*: spectator reactions to works of art can be morally bad (Hazlett 2009).[34] In response to antihero series, the spectator surely does imagine things that are morally bad. Is it wrong of us to do so? Not according to Brandon Cooke, who argues convincingly that "[p]romting one's audience to fictively imagine some immoral *x* or to take pleasure in so doing is not in itself wrong. What is wrong is recommending for export [from the fiction to the actual world] some blameworthy belief or attitude" (Cooke 2014: 325). It is not the fictively imagining *per se* that is intrinsically wrong, but exporting to real life beliefs and attitudes that should not be encouraged.

So, with regards to the antihero series, one could say that it is not intrinsically wrong to engage imaginatively in the antihero's transgressions, so long as one does not export the beliefs that we hold as (fictionally) true when engaging (e.g., "Walt is in the right to cook methamphetamine because he may be dying of cancer and wants to secure his family's finances"). Because

Why so Many Television Series with Antiheroes? 115

this is only a fiction, we allow ourselves to believe things and take on attitudes that we do not truly have. This is the fictional relief. In real life, I do not think that people who are dying of cancer have the right to kill other people and engage in criminal activities. But part of the fictional relief is to avoid thinking of morality in terms of universal, moral principles that I may or may not defend rationally. The question of whether it is morally wrong of me to allow myself this fictional relief would, according to Cooke's line of reasoning, be whether the fiction – *Breaking Bad* in this case – encourages export of these attitudes to real life. Am I meant to truly think that Walt is morally right? No, the reality checks remind me that he is not. Arguably, the authorial perspective in *Breaking Bad* is thus clear. These beliefs and attitudes are not to be exported, and it is not morally wrong of me to engage in this fiction.

At first sight it might seem that bad fans clearly export morally blameworthy attitudes and beliefs, such as praise for Walter's misdeeds and misogynistic attitudes toward Skyler, for example (see the final chapter). Then again, perhaps this is not so much a case of exporting blameworthy attitudes as *importing* such attitudes to one's engagement with a fiction in the first place: would the proper Skyler haters – the online bloggers who called her a bitch and who even posted death threats toward the actress playing her in *Breaking Bad* – feel this way if they did not already have misogynistic attitudes? This is a complex empirical question, and not something I can settle here. I will leave this debate with the following tentative conclusion: if any spectators were to truly come to believe that what Walter is doing is right when he is cooking meth, and that Skyler is morally worse than him because she is cold and nags, and export these beliefs to real life, this would be a case of exporting a blameworthy belief – and a blameworthy belief mistakenly attributed to the creators due to the inability or unwillingness to recognize the complex intention behind this fiction. In line with Cooke's theory, I conclude that only then is it morally wrong to engage in *Breaking Bad*.

So, when Nussbaum writes that the bad fan "watches something wrong", she is basically arguing – correctly, in my view – that these series' target audience is able and willing to "get it": the antihero is likeable and morally in the right (fictional relief), but surely not really (reality check). As mentioned in the preface, what got the trend of antihero series going was the segmentation of the audience, and the quest for a segment not traditionally attracted to regular TV – the affluent, urban, highly educated audience who would only allow themselves to become hooked to a television series if convinced that "it is not TV". Thinking about the antihero series in an intention-response communicative model, one could say that the intended audience of the antihero series is a spectator who might appreciate something for being challenging and thought-provoking. In line with the Bourdieuian perspective taken up by Michael Z. Newman and Elana Levine in their critical, polemical dissection of the Quality TV trend (Newman and Levine 2012), one could argue that the alienating effects of the reality check is part of a strategy the

116 *Why so Many Television Series with Antiheroes?*

creator uses to render the series inaccessible – a strategy precisely intended to exclude those who are not properly trained for, or motivated for, recognizing and appreciating the distancing and alienating effects of 'high art'. Quoting Lawrence W. Levine, Newman and Levine write that

> [p]opular art is transformed into esoteric or high art at precisely that time when it in fact *becomes* esoteric, that is when it becomes or is rendered inaccessible to the types of people who appreciated it earlier.
> (Levine quoted in Newman and Levine 2012:
> 9, emphasis original)

It is not that the bad fan does not appreciate the antihero series – but he appreciates it for the wrong reasons. What the bad fan appreciates is not what has elevated this series to status as art.

However, one need not agree with Newman and Levine's Bourdieuian perspective and tie this to notions such as class, nor to see it as a strategy intended to distinguish between those trained to recognize such complex creator intentions, and those who are not. Perhaps one can simply argue that those who do not interpret these series as is intended, whoever they are, could be labelled as unintended fans – with an unintended response. Elaborating on an observation Dana Polan makes in relation to *The Sopranos*, namely that the viewer of *The Sopranos* is supposed to enjoy the ironic or tongue-in-cheek playfulness with lowbrow conventions (Polan 2009), the intended effect of liking the antihero can be seen as ironic. The spectator is merely supposed to "like" the antihero. These series invite the spectator to do some imaginative slumming, but the creator knows, and the viewer knows that the creator knows, that surely the viewer will get the idea that the antihero is actually morally bad. Indeed, the authorial perspective in the antihero series can often be said to be mocking the spectator for coming to like the antihero so much. Dana Polan comes to a similar conclusion in his analysis of *The Sopranos* as a work of postmodern irony:

> *The Sopranos* satirizes some of the very values the targeted viewer would bring to the show and even assails the very assumptions held dearly in the life world of that viewer. The self-mockery that upscale viewers engage in by watching *The Sopranos* [connect up with the appeal of the show's as] a chance to slum.
> (Polan 2009: 84–5)

Without exploring the notions irony and postmodernism here, one can certainly tie this observation to the playful oscillation between fictional reliefs and reality checks. I do not claim that all antihero series are ironic, but they do generally tend to enhance a conflicted response of both liking and disliking the antihero – which can typically be seen as near mocking the spectator through reality checks for the sympathetic allegiance she has formed with the antihero.

Why so Many Television Series with Antiheroes?   117

The spectator of the antihero series should thus allow herself to be entertained by the series through fictional reliefs, but is also intended to *appreciate* the mockingly alienating effects of the reality checks. The antihero series is part of a trend that has been elevated to the status as television art – as Quality TV – and often heralded as something completely different from regular TV. One can wonder if it would have been so, had these series not deliberately left the spectator puzzled and confused – that is, if the intended response was only to like and enjoy the antihero. Through rendering the antihero series difficult their status as art or Quality is secured. When discussing the latest episode of *Breaking Bad* in a water cooler moment at work, one is not intended to merely cheer for Walter as a hero, but to discuss some of the moral complexities of the series. This is what grants this series its status as art.

This could be seen as corroborating Eaton's point: immoralism can sometimes make something more valuable as art, at least in the eyes of critics and commentators, in which case it is the conflicted state in which it leaves the spectator that is seen as particularly valuable. And the bad fan does not seem the least bit conflicted. Not getting the reality checks appears as missing out on the full force of what the antihero series can do: it can offer both entertainment and appreciation; suspenseful engagement and lingering reflection. I hope that pointing out that although the root of our liking of the antihero lies in intuitive moral responses, the reality checks reminding the spectator of the immorality of the antihero are also an intended, central part of the experience of engaging with these series. The thought-provoking effect of having enjoyed something immoral is core to the very attraction of the antihero series.

Notes

1. I do not argue that this applies only to recent Quality television series. Soap opera audiences might have enjoyed and appreciated these effects long before the recent boom of antiheroes. For example, in his study of Norwegian spectators watching *Dynasty* (ABC, 1981–89), Jostein Gripsrud notes that although his respondents claimed only to identify with the (good) female protagonist Crystle, he observed "laughter of ambivalent relief at Alexis's [the main "bad" female character] actions when watching *Dynasty* with very mature housewives (in their sixties)" (Gripsrud 1995: 158). There are also other antecedents in TV as well, such as morally complex characters in *Hill Street Blues* (NBC, 1981–87) and *NYPD Blue* (ABC 1993–2005) as well as antiheroes in both film and literature – but exploring these lies beyond the scope of this study.
2. I will not offer a theory here about the role played by the author's intentions in appreciation and interpretation of fiction, but rely broadly on the idea that they play an important role. See e.g., Livingston (2005, 2009).
3. As I discussed Carroll's theory at some length in the previous chapter, I will concentrate on Smith's here. See also Currie (1997) on what he discusses as the problem of personality.

118 *Why so Many Television Series with Antiheroes?*

4. See also the next chapter for a discussion of *Dexter*.
5. *Hannibal*, "Entree", season 1, episode 6.
6. *The Sopranos*, "University", season 3, episode 6. See also Merri Lisa Johnson's perceptive and insightful analysis of this episode (Johnson 2007), where she argues that this is one example of *The Sopranos* actually qualifying as primetime feminism: "although the narrative of 'University' may seem to move toward the restoration of the patriarchal order, the monstrous oppressiveness of the order has been exposed, and the episode's attitude toward this restoration is, if not ironic, at the very least tragic"(Ibid., 291).
7. *The Sopranos*, "Whoever Did This", season 4, episode 9.
8. On enjoyment of retribution, see also Zillmann and Bryant (1975).
9. See also Fehr and Gächter (2002) and Marlowe et al. (2008).
10. See the next chapter for a discussion of so-called Just-World Theory.
11. As Robert Warshow argues in a classical essay entitled "The Gangster as Tragic Hero", the gangster is under an obligation to succeed: he is "what we want to be and what we are afraid we might become" (Warshow 2001 [1948]: 101). See also Taylor (2014), to which I return shortly.
12. *Breaking Bad*, "Cornered", season 4, episode 6.
13. There are individual variations here – some personality types become more anxious with power. Those who have a high need for power, e.g., who want to be in control, however, will experience lower cortisol levels with power. See Robertson (2012: 122ff).
14. *Nurse Jackie*, "Are Those Feathers?", season 4, episode 9.
15. See e.g., Cicchirillo and Eastin (2013) for a short overview on the research on media and violence.
16. Although some point to methodological weaknesses in the literature on harmful effects of media violence, see e.g., Ferguson and Savage (2012), others conclude that despite some such weaknesses the overall empirical support for harmful effects is robust and strong (Zacks 2014: 113ff). See also Bryant, Thompson and Finklea (2013: 155ff) for a discussion. There is reason to believe that watching on-screen violence does have a (relatively small, but statistically significant) negative effect on real life behaviour. Although I will not discuss such behavioural effects here, I will return to the potential negative effects on the spectator in the form of flawed attitudes toward the end of this chapter.
17. See Robertson (2012) for a popular account.
18. See Paisley Livingston's discussion of Du Bos (Livingston 2013).
19. See also Allen (2007: 83ff) and Flory (2008: 71) on the dandy villain.
20. *Boardwalk Empire*, "Sunday best", season 3, episode 7.
21. *Boardwalk Empire*, "You'd be surprised", season 3, episode 5.
22. In the next chapter we will see that there are some limits that the antihero does not cross, in particular tied to feelings of moral disgust.
23. There is much literature in philosophical aesthetics on aesthetic appreciation that I cannot go into detail on here, but a good starting point is Iseminger (1981, 2004).
24. This would be a kind of imaginative empathy in my account – but as Mittell describes it, when taking the form of a puzzling solving activity, it is surely a reflective activity to a much greater extent than what is usually the case when we are trying to understand characters in fiction.
25. Raney (2011) explores a similar point about thought-provoking turns in a narrative activating moral reasoning, but does not tie this to television series specifically.

Why so Many Television Series with Antiheroes? 119

26. Eaton dismisses the notion antihero as a pertinent label for Tony Soprano. The antihero, she argues, is but plagued by human frailties (Eaton 2012: 283); in comparison to the antihero's mild moral flaws the rough hero's moral flaws are grievous. I use the notion antihero as synonymous with her notion of rough hero here. For Hume's discussion of rough heroes – whom he claims will disfigure a poem if their vicious manners are not marked with proper blame – see Hume (1987: 246).
27. For an overview, see e.g., the introduction given by Gaut (2007).
28. Although I will not discuss as what we appreciate the antihero series, a tempting answer is that we appreciate such series as works in the popular art of television. However, I will not explore this notion here. For relevant discussions of television art in general, see e.g., Cardwell (2006, 2007, 2013, 2014) and Nannicelli (2012; forthcoming).
29. *The Sopranos*, "Second Opinion", season 3, episode 7. See also Smith's discussion of this sequence in Smith (2011a).
30. See also Carroll (2004).
31. See also Flory (2008: 54) for a related point about how characters can sometimes be perceived as basically having a good moral character, despite having made some bad choices.
32. And, in relation to the often hateful response toward the antihero's wife, from empathic impairment: perhaps a misogynist male spectator is unable to see that the antihero's wife is worthy of sympathy. However, I also argue that these female characters are often given a raw deal in the antihero series, and that antipathy for them is to some extent encouraged: see chapter 6.
33. Thanks to Ted Nannicelli for this observation, and for pointing me to Nussbaum's discussion of bad fans.
34. Thanks to Paisley Livingston for pointing me to this debate.

5 Crossing the Line
On Moral Disgust and Proper Villains in the Antihero Series

I have investigated how the spectator is invited to empathize and sympathize with the antihero, and argued that a series of narrative techniques are used, capitalizing on our moral psychological make-up – or more specifically, our moral intuitions and emotions. While it may indeed be puzzling that the spectator likes, sympathizes and empathizes with the antihero from a rational point of view, knowing how our moral intuitions and emotions work explains this more easily. However, as mentioned in the previous chapter, in order to fully explain our engagement with fiction, one cannot merely focus on positive feelings towards the protagonist. One must also attend to feelings of antipathy towards the villain. I have investigated how villains are important to stories and how the antihero borrows some traits from villains – but more needs to be said about who the proper villains in the antihero series are. Not all villains are aesthetically pleasing, as suggested previously. Some villains simply serve the function of stirring up strong feelings of antipathy. Carroll writes that

> the complex emotive relation of sympathy-for-the-protagonists *plus* antipathy-for-the-antagonists (...) [i]s a psychological condition that most moving pictures strive to raise in audiences. They aspire to dispose the viewer to feel emotionally allied to the protagonist and against the antagonist. The antagonist is designed to instill anger, indignation, hatred, and sometimes moral disgust in us.
>
> (Carroll 2008: 184, emphasis original)

This observation applies to antihero series as well. In order to make the antihero morally preferable, there are always proper villains who are perceived as morally worse. In this chapter I explore one strategy used to clearly mark the antagonist as such, namely rape. I explore why the antihero in these series is typically a murderer, but rarely a rapist. *The Wire* is a good case study for a start; I then move on to I show that this observation is valid across the antihero series trend.

Rape in *The Wire*

The Wire is a celebrated television series, part police procedural and part contemporary gangster drama. Although it is not an antihero series strictly speaking, there can surely be said to be antiheroes portrayed in the series'

Crossing the Line   121

huge ensemble cast – characters who are portrayed as morally flawed, but that the spectator is nonetheless encouraged to like. In numerous interviews, creator David Simon emphasizes that *The Wire*'s portrayal of Baltimore city life is *true*. Part of the background for the show is found in Simon and co-writer Ed Burns's nonfiction writing after spending a year with African-American drug dealers and addicts in Baltimore, which was published as a book entitled *The Corner: A Year in the Life of an Inner-City Neighborhood* in 1997 (Simon and Burns 2010). The book was later made into a drama mini-series *The Corner* (HBO, 2000), one of *The Wire*'s closest predecessors.[1] Another writer on *The Wire*'s team, Raphael Alvarez, explains the many steps taken to ensure a *realistic* portrayal in the series (Alvarez 2009). The most charming of these is perhaps the story about the orange sofa in "the Pit" in the first season, where D'Angelo Barksdale and his crew of young drug dealers often sit and contemplate. The worn down sofa is actually an expensive prop; the crew meticulously copied an old sofa they spotted in a container as some had collected it before they had the chance to pick it up for the set. From background sound to accent, from props to police work, emphasis is on the realism in the portrayal. The creators' emphasis on realism and truth is echoed in the nothing short of celebratory academic reception of the series. According to one writer, *The Wire* offers a "troubling realistic representation" (McMillan 2009: 53), and is "a comprehensive, faithful portrait of contemporary urban life" (McMillan 2008). Two others write that *The Wire*'s stories "scream of verisimilitude" (Marshall & Potter 2009: 9), and have "an authenticity that bleeds through the screen" (Ibid., 10).

However, in an interview, Jason Mittell warns that one ought to be aware that *The Wire* is a fictional narrative, and that choices have been taken concerning what to portray – and what not to portray. He points out that one telling example of an issue that *The Wire* only rarely and to a very limited degree touches upon is rape. When portraying crime-ridden environments – and when the goal is that the reader or spectator should understand and sympathize with the criminals – depiction of rape is especially problematic.

> Faced with a choice between verisimilitude and drama's demand that the audience identify with the characters, the show's creators, Mittell believes, went with the latter. "It could be that with the specific types of dealers and users that Simon and Burns spent time with, rape was not really part of their culture. The other explanation, which I think is more probable, is that if you portrayed these people as rapists you would lose the ability to make them at all sympathetic and human," says Mittell.
>
> Viewers are willing to sympathize with murderers, whether it's Stringer Bell, Avon Barksdale, or Omar, because there's a sense that they still have a certain code. Portraying them as rapists would make that much harder, Mittell argues. "Rape is a more taboo and emotionally volatile crime to portray on-screen than murder," he says.

122   *Crossing the Line*

"Imagine the show *Dexter*, except instead of being a serial killer, he was a serial rapist".

(Mittell quoted in Bennett 2010)

Mittell argues that taking scholarly research on similar communities into consideration, it is perhaps unlikely that rape is uncommon in this environment. For example, in an anthropological study of a crack dealing community in New York's 'El Barrio', Philippe Bourgois unwillingly and disappointedly testifies to the commonality of rape (Bourgois 2003). It is worth quoting the anthropologist at length:

> Despite the almost three years that I had already spent on the street at the time of this particular conversation, I was unprepared to face this dimension of gendered brutality. I kept asking myself how it was possible that I had invested so much energy into taking these "psychopaths" seriously. On a more personal level, I was confused because the rapists had already become my friends. (...) They had engulfed me in the common sense of street culture until their rape accounts forced me to draw the line.
>
> From an analytical and a humanistic perspective, it was too late for me to avoid the issue or to dismiss their sociopathology as aberrant. I had to face the prevalence and normalcy of rape in street culture and adolescent socialization. In any case [the two main informants] would not let me escape it, and over the next year, as if peeling off layers from an onion's core, they gave dozens of accounts and versions of their direct participation in sexual violence during their earliest adolescent years. Few people talk about rape – neither the perpetrators nor the victims. In fact, rape is so taboo that I was tempted to omit this discussion, fearing that readers would become too disgusted and angry with the crack dealers and deny them a human face (Ibid., 207).

Again, Bourgois was reluctant to report about rape because he wants the reader to understand the challenges these crack dealers face. He wants us to see things from the perpetrators' point of view. But we do not willingly sympathize with all kinds of perpetrators.

On the other hand, perhaps Simon's informants did in fact not rape. In *The Corner*, the book-length journalistic reportage, rape is only on the agenda once. The daughter of one of the main informants, Miss Ella, was brutally raped and murdered by a man not from the neighbourhood, a man just released from a sentence for sexual assault. Simon and Burns write:

> These were by no means crimes of the corner. You look at [the rapist] and you saw nothing but an ugly hunger behind hollow, empty eyes – that otherworldly stare to which [the corner regulars] could never pretend. At their worst, the corner regulars were petty and larcenous and tragic; [the rapist] was evil.

(Simon and Burns 2010: 565)

Crossing the Line   123

It is thus made clear that rape is an evil crime, a world apart from the crimes committed by the corner regulars.

Nonetheless, rape is not fully omitted in *The Wire*. Let us look more closely at the few episodes in *The Wire* where rape can be said to occur. Arguably (but potentially controversially) we see three examples of rape. In the first season, drug dealer hit man Wee-Bey takes advantage of a woman who has snorted too much cocaine at a party. While she has passed out, he rapes her, and it is D'Angelo Barksdale who later discovers that she lies dead in his bed, probably of an overdose. I will explore this sequence further shortly. Second, Dennis 'Cutty' Shark, a former hit-man just released from prison whom we follow in his struggle to embark on a new, law-abiding life, sees some of drug dealer Marlo's men receive a blow job in a dark back alley. This might be rape, or she could be a prostitute – it is left indeterminate. Third, in the fourth season one of the young boys we are narratively aligned with, Randy, is asked by some older boys to stand guard outside a restroom at school while they have sex with a girl. Later, the girl reports to the school authorities that she was raped in the restrooms.

In a five-season narrative about crime-ridden inner-city life, showing just three cases of rape confirms Mittell's observation that rape is not really on the agenda in *The Wire*. Furthermore, none of these sequences are portrayed as clear-cut cases of rape; rather, it is left indeterminate what is going on. The rape itself is not shown explicitly, and the narrative context also fails to make clear the nature of these events. In none of the cases is the spectator aligned with the female characters involved. The spectator does not get to know any of the three women in the three respective sequences, neither before nor after the event. In fact, throughout *The Wire*, little access is given to women in this community, and one is left wondering what it is like specifically for girls to grow up in these neighbourhoods. In feminist film theoretical literature on rape, a common critique is the lack of attention given to the victim in general – and most prominently to African-American rape victims. Depictions of rape are often highly racialized, where white women are typically the victims (e.g., Projanski 2001: 154ff).[2] Although the rape victims in these sequences in *The Wire* are African-American, the narrative gives little access to their point of view, so overall one can say that this series does little to change this tendency.

However, rather than a feministic critique of the (lack of) depictions of rape, and the lack of focus on the women's perspectives in *The Wire*, my concern here is the narrative function of rape in this narrative *per se*. I suggest that rape has a clear effect on, or function for, the sympathy structure of this series. Let us take a brief detour into the history of depictions of rape in American prime-time series in order to explore this function.

As Lisa M. Cuklanz argues in her study of the portrayal of rape in American television series from 1976 to 1990, rape is typically used to focus on what is considered acceptable (or, in her terminology, hegemonic) masculine behaviour. Rape is most often portrayed in detective or cop drama in what she labels the *basic plot*. Here, a very violent rape committed by a stranger is typically used to contrast this thoroughly evil and sick rapist with the compassionate,

124 *Crossing the Line*

understanding police detective, who is righteously angered and disgusted by the rape, and who often seeks revenge for the victim. She sums up the basic plot as follows:

> the victim is attacked by an unseen rapist who clamps a hand over her mouth, grabs her forcefully or throws her to the ground, and speaks lines filled with threats, sexist stereotypes, and outmoded ideas about women and sexuality. (...) The beginning of the attack often emphasizes the rapist's intense depravity, which is condemned by the (male) protagonist and contrasted with his own actions, belief and character. (...) Rapists are depicted as identifiably outside the mainstream through their language, clothing, habits, or attitudes. (...) The detective's sense of morality, and often his need for revenge on the criminal, thus culminate in a successful triumph of the "good guy," which is often accomplished through violence against the rapist.
>
> (Cuklanz 2000: 6)

As part of her critical feminist approach, Cuklanz points out that the individualistic explanations these series give for rape – the rapist as pathological and crazy – downplay how masculine gender role socialization in general may cause rape. In a study of rape in teen heroine series (to which I will return), Susan Berridge elaborates on the problems with the portrayal of individual 'baddie' rapist by arguing that they are portrayed as "isolated aberrations of an otherwise functioning patriarchy" (Berridge 2013: 495). Again leaving aside this critical aspect, my interest here is in Cuklanz' analysis of rape narratives in their own right. The narrative function of rape is traditionally to create strong feelings of antipathy for a criminal, and equally strong sympathy for a detective (both male). These portrayals of rape fit well with a Manichean moral – a polarization between an evil criminal and a good policeman. It is this polarizing function of rape that is my focus here.

Traditionally, the spectator is either meant to side with the policemen or the gangsters (in the police procedural and gangster genres, respectively). But in *The Wire*, the spectator is encouraged to sympathize with some drug dealers and murderers, but not all, and, likewise, to loathe some of the police officials (the corrupt ones, for example), but root for others (the 'good police'). However, probably for dramaturgical reasons, a clear 'goodie-baddie' axis is still useful, in line with Carroll's point introduced above. There is a moral ambivalence and complexity in *The Wire* that is rarely seen in American television series, but even in these morally murky waters some intuitive and easily accessed means of separating the good from the bad are needed – lest the narrative be thoroughly taxing and morally confusing for us to engage with. Rape is one narrative technique used to effect such a separation. Let us look more closely at the first instance of rape in *The Wire* to illustrate.

D'Angelo Barksdale is born into a drug dealing family, and his uncle Avon Barksdale is in control of the drug trade in the Western district. D'Angelo runs his own crew of dealers in what is known as 'the Pit'. Nonetheless, D'Angelo is increasingly troubled by his way of life and tells his girlfriend that it sometimes feels as if he cannot breathe. When a witness to a murder he committed (but was acquitted for) is killed, he asks his uncle whether violence is really necessary. When detectives Moreland and McNulty have him believe that the witness has left behind two children – now orphaned – D'Angelo weeps and shows signs of truly feeling guilty. D'Angelo is one of the criminals we are narratively aligned with, and we are given access to his doubt and guilty conscience. In this way, sympathy for D'Angelo is encouraged.

D'Angelo is invited to a party with Barksdale crew men Little Man and Wee-Bey, a party especially advertised as offering strippers from uncle Avon Barksdale's strip club.[3] It turns out that the party is also well supplied with cocaine, which the women present are offered in generous quantities. Wee-Bey carries a woman, Keisha, half unconscious, over to one of the bedrooms and throws her on the bed, despite her muffled complaint that she is not feeling well. There is a cut to another scene. When D'Angelo returns to the party after picking up more alcohol, the party is already over and all the girls are gone. Wee-Bey and Little Man are sitting on the sofa and watching TV when D'Angelo spots Keisha still lying naked in the bedroom. He asks Wee-Bey about her, who replies nonchalantly that he had indeed "Fucked her silly. What can I say?" D'Angelo walks over to her, and discovers that she is dead. He is shocked and shouts over to Wee-Bey again. In a close-up shot of Wee-Bey, we see him turn his head half indifferently, half annoyed for being disturbed, to brush D'Angelo off. In the background of the shot, we see a horrified D'Angelo.

Figure 5.1 The antihero D'Angelo Barksdale is horrified at discovering Keisha raped and dead (*The Wire*, HBO).

126   *Crossing the Line*

A critic might object that it is not clear that Keisha was raped. We never see this, and it is not referred to in the narrative as rape. Indeed, many summaries of the episode do not label this incident as rape. However, in order to clearly spell out why I discuss it as rape, I assume Keisha did not consent because the last thing we see before there is a cut to another plotline is that she says she is not feeling well. She can hardly walk, and looks clearly unwell. Also, in the next episode, Detectives Greggs and Freamon try to convince one of Keisha's colleagues from Orlando's strip club, Shardene, to spy on kingpin Avon Barksdale for them.[4] They show her Keisha's dead body and inform her that there was semen from three different men found in her mouth, her vagina and in her anal cavity. Based on this information, too, it sounds highly unlikely that Keisha, in the state she was in, would have consented to this. The most reasonable conclusion is that this was a gang rape.

In contrast to D'Angelo's reaction of horror and repulsion, Wee-Bey is portrayed as cold blooded and remorseless. Although it could very well be said that D'Angelo did little to help Keisha when he saw Wee-Bey carry her into the bedroom, D'Angelo's reaction gives him more human dignity than Wee-Bey has. It corroborates the sympathetic impression we have of D'Angelo. In parallel, the scene adds to an already antipathetic portrayal of Wee-Bey. It was Wee-Bey who killed the witness, an ordinary citizen, to D'Angelo's murder. Wee-Bey also tortured and killed the stick-up man Omar Little's lover Brandon in revenge for robbing one of Avon's stack houses. Omar is another character among the criminals whom we as spectators are strongly encouraged to like (Vaage 2013), and the murder of Brandon is thus portrayed as a monstrous act. After the rape sequence, Wee-Bey also shoots detective Greggs working undercover – one of the most likeable police officers. At the end of the first season, Wee-Bey is sent off to prison, taking the fall for many murder charges that he confesses to nonchalantly while eating sandwiches. Wee-Bey is one of the criminals who is portrayed as all bad – a man without conscience or compassion. The only mitigating human trait Wee-Bey is portrayed as having in this first season is perhaps that he cares about the fish he keeps in tanks. And as mitigating factors go, this is not much.

The main point here is that it is Wee-Bey who rapes. D'Angelo is shocked. Even when a main protagonist character is a criminal, such as D'Angelo is, he is not a rapist. Cuklanz's study shows that traditionally, rapists are villains – and this basic fact is preserved even in the complex moral structure in *The Wire*.[5]

The portrayal of Wee-Bey the rapist deviates from the basic plot depiction of rape, as Cuklanz' describes it, in that we do not see use of violent force, and in that it is a date or acquaintance rape, and not a stranger rape.[6] This rape sequence in *The Wire* could thus be seen as more progressive than basic plot depictions of rape in that its depiction of an acquaintance rape is more realistic in the sense of being closer to how most rapes, statistically speaking, are committed in real life. On the other hand, *The Wire* blurs the lines about this and other rape sequences by leaving it indeterminate whether or not it is in fact a rape: the events are typically not referred to as rape by other characters in the narrative, and by not aligning us as spectators with the victim in order to give access to her thoughts and feelings, the narrative also misses out on the opportunity to hear her side of the story. Thus one can say that there is nothing progressive about the portrayal of rape in this series. This is also corroborated by the portrayal of what may – or may not – be a rape in season 4. Randy is one of four eighth graders at Edward Tilghman Middle School who are the main characters in this season. One day at school two other boys recruit him to stand guard outside the restrooms.[7] A girl accompanies them into the restrooms. From the context we understand that they have sex with her. Later, however, we see the same boys mock her,[8] and as this plotline plays out across several episodes, she reports what happened in the restrooms as rape to one of the school officials. However, the most likely interpretation of this plotline as it is portrayed in the series is arguably that she did have sex voluntarily, but then regrets doing so because the very same boys reject her. Only then does she claim it was rape. She also later withdraws the accusation. Thus it is suggested that this girl takes revenge by accusing the boys of rape although it was not. Again, as spectators we are not aligned with her and get no access to what happened in the restroom or to her thoughts and feelings afterwards. The problem of adolescent date rape – as this may or may not have been – is thus downplayed, and instead presented as an insulted young girl's vengeance over two innocent boys. Be that as it may, in this case also Randy, who is one of the sympathetic main characters, does not participate in the restroom incident directly – two other boys whom we never get to know do. Problematic as it may be, the restroom incident is again used to mark our man Randy as morally preferable – he did not know what they intended to do in the restrooms. Although rape is not really on the agenda in *The Wire*, it seems safe to conclude that when rape occurs, the main sympathetic characters are not the perpetrators.

The Narrative Function of Rape

Furthermore, this observation seems to be applicable to other antihero series as well, such as *The Sopranos, Sons of Anarchy, The Shield* and *Dexter*.[9] As a rule, the antiheroes in these series murder (to focus on the gravest moral transgression they have in common), but they do not rape. I suggest that rape has predominantly two narrative functions in these recent television series. First, rape marks some characters as antagonists. The raping characters are used as contrast characters – unsympathetic characters with the main function of making the antiheroes morally preferable. As will be remembered, this is one method standardly used to make the spectator sympathize with an antihero. Someone is portrayed as morally worse, which – to a remarkable degree – secures the spectator's rooting for the morally preferable. Second, rape is used as justification for vigilante revenge, and to make

128   *Crossing the Line*

the spectator applaud this. The analysis above of the portrayal of D'Angelo and Wee-Bey exemplifies the first function of rape, and before moving on to other American television series I will now concentrate on another example from *The Wire* in order to demonstrate the second function.

There is a fourth instance of sexual assault in *The Wire* that I have not yet mentioned, but that is especially relevant for the revenge function of rape. It is an even more indirect portrayal of rape. As already mentioned, in the fourth season the narrative aligns us with four adolescent West Baltimore boys, Michael, Duquan, Randy and Namond. Michael lives with his drug addict mother, and works hard to take care of his little brother Bug. When his stepfather suddenly turns up after being released from prison, however, Michael is obviously disturbed. Angrily, he refuses any kind of physical contact with his stepfather, and tries to keep him away from Bug. In other sequences we see that attention from other (well-meaning) adult men, such as coach Dennis Shark, freaks him out. When Michael confers with his friends about what to do about his home conditions and his worry about Bug (discreetly and without revealing why he loathes his stepfather), their advice is clear: Michael cannot contact social services, as they will only separate him and Bug, and put both of them in dreaded group homes. In desperation, Michael turns to drug dealer Marlo, and asks him to deal with his stepfather. When pointing out his stepfather to two of Marlo's henchmen, Chris and Snoop, they inquire why he wants his stepfather killed. When Michael does not answer, Chris grows troubled and we get the impression that he understands why. When Chris and Snoop take Michael's stepfather away to kill him, Chris goes berserk and kicks the man to death – instead of shooting him in a vacant house, as planned.

The narrative thus hints about Michael being sexually abused by his stepfather – and about Chris knowing all too well about the anger this incites. Michael feels he cannot turn to the authorities with this problem, and sells his soul to the Devil, or more precisely, to Marlo, instead (after this, he is indebted to Marlo, and becomes his henchman, although initially he did not want this). To put a stop to the sexual abuse, and also perhaps in order to get revenge, he has to turn to vigilante enforcers on the wrong side of the law. And although Michael's stepfather is only a common drug addict, taking no part in the violence of the drug dealers, I suspect few spectators feel sorry for him when he suffers a very violent death.

This pattern of rape-revenge is not very prominent in *The Wire*. If we turn to another recent television series, *The Shield*, however, this picture changes. *The Shield* is a vigilante narrative – the main plot is about 'the Strike Team,' a group of police detectives in the most crime-ridden part of Los Angeles, fictional Farmington, who are allowed to do some pretty unconventional police work in order to hold at bay the rivalling gangs in the district, and the violence between them. The Strike Team leader Vic Mackey refrains from nothing to keep his power in the district, and his crimes include murder – even of fellow police officers. As the series' seven seasons progress, the plot

Crossing the Line   129

slowly spirals downwards as Vic and the Strike Team are entangled in their own web of crimes, and forced to face the consequences. As a narrative about the Strong Man taking the law into his own hands, what is most interesting for my purposes here is the commonality of rape. While there were only a few instances of rape in *The Wire*, there is a lot of rape in *The Shield*. Again, this resonates with Cuklanz's study of older television series: The detective's revenge for rape figures prominently in the basic plot portrayals of rape. Cuklanz writes that

> the extreme evil and brutality of rape also serve as a clear contrast to the detective's behavior and legitimize his use of force. In most episodes rapists are shot to death, verbally condemned, or physically beaten by outraged detectives. Although such violence is not always condoned by other characters, it is presented as understandable and is common enough to be considered a basic element of hegemonic masculinity as constructed in these programs.
>
> (Cuklanz 2000: 20)

The Shield seems to fit neatly into Cuklanz's description of basic plot depictions of rape,[10] perhaps deviating from it most prominently in the extreme vigilante nature of the policeman. What is important for my discussion here is again the clearly polarizing effect (basic plot) rape has narratively. Vic Mackey's methods are amoral and mostly self-serving, but every so often the TV series enhances sympathy with and acceptance of Mackey's methods, and encourages the spectator to see them as warranted; when it comes to rape and sexual abuse of women and children especially, our intuitive and emotional reaction seems to be that (almost) anything goes. We sympathize with the devil when his opponent is a rapist.

The two narrative functions of rape are also evident in the second season of *Sons of Anarchy*.[11] As mentioned in chapter 4, Gemma is a strong woman who is in no way blind to their criminal lifestyle, but embraces it, and who does not hesitate to use violence herself to remain in position. Initially, she is not altogether easy to like, as she is highly manipulative – but then on the other hand, the whole motorcycle gang are a brutish lot. However, in the second season a group of neo-Nazis are introduced to serve as contrast characters. The neo-Nazi group wants to squeeze the Sons of Anarchy out of business. The Nazi group kidnaps Gemma, and three of them gang rape her.[12] The rape is brutal and the portrayal of it is graphic. The narrative dwells on Gemma's emotional reaction to the rape and her difficulties in dealing with its aftermath. She refuses to tell her husband and her son what has happened. In their own words, the Nazis intend to get to the Sons of Anarchy by "destroying the matriarch" – they rely on her telling her husband about the rape, hoping that it will stir him into such a rage that he will want to retaliate immediately and walk right into the trap they have set for him. The function of rape again seems to be clear: the neo-Nazis come off as monstrous, clearly morally worse than the Sons of Anarchy. As spectators, we long to see the neo-Nazis punished. Gemma, however, refuses to give them what they want, and does not tell any of the Sons. Revenge is postponed, and suspense is generated by the spectator wondering whether the Sons will find out some way, and retaliate – or whether Gemma will find some way to avenge herself. Although the Sons of Anarchy are murderers, they are morally preferable to the neo-Nazis.

Figure 5.2 When Gemma is raped by a group of neo-Nazis, this makes the Sons of Anarchy morally preferable, and stirs up the spectator's desire for revenge (*Sons of Anarchy*, FX).

A fourth example of the revenge function of rape, and how it is used to make the antihero morally preferable, is found in *Banshee*'s first season. This antihero series begins with the unnamed antihero being released from prison. He seeks out his former lover and partner in crime Anastasia/Carrie, who now lives in the little town Banshee. When the sheriff in Banshee is killed, the antihero takes on his identity and becomes known as Lucas. Several characters are used to make Lucas morally preferable: Kai Proctor is the unscrupulous local villain who keeps this town in a stranglehold, and Rabbit is the crime boss from Lucas and Anastasia/Carrie's past who got Lucas imprisoned. Notably, in the third episode there is also a minor character who commits a monstrous act.[13] The prize-fighter Sanchez comes to town for an exhibition fight at the local casino. He picks up a local cocktail waitress, and while they have consensual sex he turns on her, beats her severely and rapes her. Lucas visits her at the hospital and is incensed. He goes to the casino, interrupts the celebration, and physically challenges the larger man and beats him to a pulp. The rape again justifies the violence exerted by the antihero, and makes Lucas appear morally preferable.

The most obvious conclusion to draw is that rape is one of the crimes that we perceive as most unsympathetic, and that arouses our desire for revenge most easily. There is a much-discussed instance of rape in *The Sopranos* that supports this too – the rape of Dr Melfi.[14] When she is brutally attacked and raped in a parking garage when leaving her office, the narrative arguably plays with our desire as spectators that she tell her patient Tony, the mobster boss, what has happened. The legal system is unable to deal with the perpetrator; although he is found and identified as the rapist, the police have to let him go because some legal bureaucratic rule was not followed during his arrest. Jessica Baldanzi points out that the complaints about the violence in *The Sopranos* in the press had never, up to that point, been as vociferous as after the airing of the episode in which Dr Melfi is raped (Baldanzi 2006). She speculates that this is because Dr Melfi is not part of the Mafia – thus, she does not 'deserve' what is coming her way, as the many other victims of violence, themselves violent mobsters, in the series arguably do. One could add that perhaps the audience was also frustrated because Dr Melfi finally refuses to tell Tony about the rapist, and we as spectators do not get the revenge that we desire.[15] In any case, rape is used narratively to ensure that the spectator desires revenge.

The Repulsive Rapist

To sum up, depiction of rape is a powerful narrative strategy to evoke feelings of antipathy, and stir up desire for revenge. This is not to suggest that narratives cannot depict rape with the intention that spectators will enjoy it, and that spectators may indeed enjoy it – such narratives would be controversial, however, and in all likelihood be judged as *obscene* because they encourage enjoyment of something we find not just morally wrong, but repulsive.[16] In the series I have discussed, it makes more sense to claim that rape is typically used to clearly mark some characters as all bad, and to make us dislike them so much that they can be dispensed with (sent to jail, or killed) all the while we enjoy their punishment – rather than primarily encouraging us to enjoy rape in a perverse manner. How come the antihero is often – indeed, typically – a murderer, but never – or rarely – a rapist? In addition to antihero series, video games are another example that comes to mind: shooting other characters in the game is quite common, and it would be strange to say that the players of these games do not enjoy this – but the few instances of rape in video games gave rise to massive player protests.[17] Various empirical studies of what video game players find acceptable and unacceptable also find that users are unwilling to tap a taboo, such as rape (e.g., Whitty et al. 2011, see also Hartmann 2013).

The observation that rape in particular stirs up feelings of antipathy is further supported in a study conducted by Arthur A. Raney. He investigated how different individuals' sense of moral judgment influences evaluation of, and enjoyment of, justice outcomes in crime drama (Raney 2002).

132   *Crossing the Line*

In so-called justice sequences in crime drama, justice is restored through punishment of a criminal who has caused an injustice. The crime-punishment dyad in the narrative, and the spectator's reaction to such dyads, can be read as a statement about what is considered fair and appropriate retribution. Raney's informants completed a survey intended to identify their attitudes towards social justice, specified as their attitudes toward vigilantism (how favourably the respondent evaluates retribution and punishment enacted by private citizens) and punitiveness (how severe the respondent thinks a punishment should be).[18] Then they were shown an edited portion of the film *Rob Roy* (Michael Caton-Jones, 1995). From this film, one group of respondents were shown the physical abuse of Rob Roy's wife Mary, and the burning and destruction of their home and livestock (no-rape condition). The other group of respondents were in addition shown a 30-second rape sequence from the original film (rape condition). For both groups, the retribution scene where Rob Roy kills the villain is included. The respondents' views on vigilantism and punishment predicted their enjoyment of the retribution in the no-rape condition – but not in the rape condition: "*All* viewers thought that the act was deplorable, thus eliminating any variance on the deservedness factor even between participants with quite different social-justice beliefs," Raney concludes (Raney 2002: 319). This empirical investigation does not compare attitudes towards rape and murder – to which I will soon turn – but still shows that at least compared to physical abuse alone, sexual abuse makes the spectator's condemnation of the crime, and enjoyment of the retribution, near universal, independently of his/her attitudes toward punishment and vigilante action.

The observation that rape plays this role more prominently than does physical violence and even murder raises a series of questions. Is the observation valid for all film and television fiction, or merely some types or genres of fiction, or fiction from some historical epochs? Does it merely reveal something about our attitudes towards rape in contemporary Western societies, or can one argue that the repulsiveness of rapists is a near universal trait of human moral psychology? And finally, a question-begging contrast is found between fiction and real life in this matter. Mittell describes rape as more taboo and emotionally volatile on screen than is murder. However, if one takes real-life law in Western societies into consideration, I believe murder is typically considered a graver crime than rape is – a murderer is typically punished harder than a rapist in our Western legal systems. I also assume that this reflects a real-world attitude; that we typically also think that murder is a worse crime than rape. In the fictional context, however, this seems to be reversed: as spectators, we seem to be willing to imagine ourselves in the shoes of a murderer, such as Tony Soprano – and not only willing to do so, but enjoying our doing so, as discussed in chapter 4. But we are not asked to sympathize with a rapist. Why the asymmetry between real life and fiction?

Crossing the Line   133

Although I will not be able to discuss – let alone answer – all of these questions here, I will try to delineate some suggestions. To start with the question of film and television history, a critic might point out that my claim that we are not asked to sympathize with rapists is not true without qualifications. Take such films as *A Clockwork Orange* (Stanley Kubrick, 1971) or *Happiness* (Todd Solondz, 1998) – are we not to feel, and indeed do feel, a slight trace of sympathy with these rapists? These films are indeed interesting cases that invite sympathy for a rapist. Nonetheless, as alternative films they are also intended to be disturbing – far from the comfort zone of most commercial films. So sympathy for rapists in the alternative film tradition is not necessarily the best counterargument to the observation that this is rare in commercial entertainment. Be that as it may, there may also be a few instances of main characters whom we are intended to sympathize with, but who rape, in commercial film – in *Once Upon a Time in America* (Sergio Leone, 1984), *High Planes Drifter* (Clint Eastwood, 1973) and *Straw Dogs* (Sam Peckinpah, 1971), for example.[19]

There is also a study of earlier American television series with notably different findings than Cuklanz' study of prime time series, and that is Elana Levine's study of daytime soap opera in the mid-1960s and 1970s (Levine 2007).[20] As the title of her book reveals, daytime soap operas in the 70s were wallowing in sex, and as part of this, there was also a virtual explosion of rape plots. Levine suggests that because daytime soap opera had such low cultural status, it "managed to address one of the more disturbing matters raised in the post-sexual revolution society with a degree of complexity and ambiguity difficult to come by in the more high-profile world of prime-time" (Ibid., 251).

In her analysis of these rape plots, she identifies what she labels *the old fashioned rape plot*, where rape is motivated by lust or "the result of a tumultuous romantic relationship and the man's resulting intensity of feeling" (Levine 2007: 213). Further into the decade, rape plots were increasingly inflected by the feminist political discourse. Portrayals of rape changed to acts of violence, often combined with a political and pedagogical agenda to educate audiences about the crime. For my discussion here, it is interesting that in the old-fashioned rape plots, the rapists are not always portrayed as villainous. For example, the non-villainous character Mike Bauer rapes his wife in *The Guiding Light* (CBS, 1952–2009) in 1964 – but as marital rape was not yet illegal, this is not portrayed as a crime, but only something slightly shameful. And as Levine writes of other, similar cases:

> Like *The Guiding Light*'s Mike Bauer, the men who committed rape in these stories [including *Days of Our Lives* and *Love is a Many Splendored Thing*] were established and well-liked members of their on-screen communities and, as a result, the shows' writers had to build a justification for their actions into the stories. (...) [They] acted out of an overwhelming romantic attachment to the women they raped.
>
> (Levine 2007: 217)

134 *Crossing the Line*

An even more ambivalent – and the period's most infamous – instance of rape is found on *General Hospital* (ABC, 1963-present) in 1979. Luke rapes Laura – but a year later they have fallen in love and marry! Without going into details on this controversial example, it is, in Levine's words, depicted as a "disturbingly ambiguous act" (Ibid., 246), and elicited a range of viewer responses from rape fantasy-like enthusiasm from fans crying "Rape me, Luke! Rape me!" to actor Geary in Texas in 1980 (Ibid.), to abhorrence in fan letters such as one fan writing that "[t]he idea that [Laura feels] anything anything but repulsion for Luke, the man who raped her, is sickening" (quoted in Levine 2007: 248). The bottom line is that this case of falling in love with one's rapist was controversial. Nevertheless, Levine's study shows that before feminist and human-rights efforts had put marital and acquaintance rape on the agenda, and clearly defined this as rape, such acts could be portrayed ambiguously and without the clear-cut polarizing function that depictions of rape in American television mostly have now.

Nevertheless, there are also contemporary examples to be found similar to the ones Levine discusses. For example, one possibly similar case in a recent American television series is when young Daenerys Targaryen is married off to the barbarian Khal Drogo in the first season of *Game of Thrones*.[21] On the wedding night the bride weeps and is clearly opposed to them having sex, but he has his way with her.[22] When a slave woman teaches her how to seduce her husband, Daenerys turns things around, and later in the season she warms up to him. They are then presented as a couple very much in love with each other. In season 4 there is another controversial sequence where Jamie Lannister possibly rapes his twin sister Cercei.[23] This sequence is controversial because it is ambivalent; while some claim that the sex was consensual (the twins have had a love affair for years, producing offspring – a king, even), others point to the fact that Cercei clearly says no to Jamie's advances in this particular situation. The first instance of rape in *Game of Thrones*, however, poses more of a counterargument to my theory here than the second, as Khal Drogo is to become a sympathetic character, whereas Jamie is not portrayed as sympathetic: he is commonly referred to as The King Slayer, and thus mocked by other characters for his betrayal and butchering of a previous king on the Iron Throne to pave the way for the Lannister family. His incestuous relationship with his sister does not aid our sympathy either. Although we do get to know some of Jamie's more likable sides as the seasons progress (such as his bonding with, and saving the life of, Brienne of Tarth), forcing himself on his sister can also be said to corroborate an already dark portrayal of this character.

Despite these counterexamples, portrayals of rape do overall seem to have changed on American television. The *Game of Thrones* examples are controversial also because they stand out as deviant portrayals because the rapists in *Game of Thrones* are not clearly portrayed as antipathetic; in contrast, typically across American prime-time drama, the rapist is clearly condemned. Another study of current American TV series, namely Susan Berridge's study of the portrayal of rape in teen drama series *Buffy the Vampire Slayer* (WB Network 1997–2000, UPN 2001–2003), *Veronica Mars* (UPN, 2004–2006, CW, 2006–2007) and *Life Unexpected* (CW, 2010–2011) also confirms this: "sexual violence is typically presented as the domain of an individual 'baddie' across the genre" (Berridge 2014: 477). In the female heroine teen drama series Berridge studies, central male characters can be presented as rapists, but they are indeed portrayed as villainous.[24] Thus there is a cultural and historical dimension to our perception of rape – especially perhaps what kind of force or pressure in what kind of relation counts as rape. For example, in the case of Mike Bauer, his act was not at that time in history unequivocally defined as rape, but it now is.

So there are examples of commercial films and television series with sympathetic main characters who rape. Does this not point to rape being (more) acceptable in some historical epochs? Is it not the case, then, that the polarizing function I point to is a phenomenon specific to our contemporary television culture? Indeed, perhaps I should limit my discussion to our attitudes in present time Western societies here, and assume that one can only make some generalizations about "us" in this cultural context. The attitudes towards rape in Western societies can be said to have improved, as for example Steven Pinker argues in his analysis of the Rights Revolution (Pinker 2011: 394ff). Pinker argues that our condemnation of rape is due to an increased awareness of rape as a heinous crime first and foremost because of the lack of respect for the autonomy of the female victim.[25]

Nonetheless, Cuklanz also points out that rape convictions were traditionally severe, and that the fear of false accusations has "been linked historically with the idea that rape is a horrendous crime that could ruin a man's reputation forever" (Cuklanz 2000: 43). In the feminist critique, punishment for rape has traditionally been severe because rape is seen as a violation of a man's property. Another way to see this is that traditionally convictions for rape have been severe because rape has negative consequences not just for the woman being raped, but also for the relations she has to others in her family or group. Indeed, as evolutionary psychologists Thornhill and Palmer argue, in-group rape has been punished in all known societies (Thornhill and Palmer 2000: 173, 195). Thornhill and Palmer argue that this universal condemnation (of at least some types of rape under some circumstances) makes sense from an evolutionary perspective: rape has negative consequences for reproductive success. Among the reasons they point to, is that rape reduces the woman's choice of a suitable father for her offspring and that this may influence negatively her parental effort for the child; rape may influence negatively her ability to pair-bond with her partner, again influencing negatively her and his care for the child; and rape decreases the woman's partner's parental certainty, again influencing negatively his care for the child (Ibid., 85–6). Although other aspects of Thornhill and Palmer's evolutionary psychological account of rape are controversial – and it is beyond the present chapter to discuss this thoroughly – it is nonetheless relevant to note that these evolutionary psychologists point to the condemnation of rape universally.

136 *Crossing the Line*

My point in bringing this up here is to suggest that the discourse on rape needs to acknowledge that rules against rape are not only recent inventions of Western societies, but that from an evolutionary perspective it makes sense that some form of abhorrence towards rape will have been instilled in humans – akin to the disgust towards incest – because in the evolution of mankind, rape of in-group members has not been an evolutionary advantage.

Those opposed to this kind of evolutionary explanation might object at this point, and argue that the reason that murder is more common in American film and television than rape is, is only because sex is more taboo in American culture than is violence. Furthermore, adding to cultural explanations for the taboo on rape one could argue that Western societies are in a state of moral panic about rape due to specific reasons in our historical context. Joanna Bourke, for example, argues that the fear of rape is not proportionate with actual risk, and that the fear of rape "masked other fears about inner-city degeneration and anxiety about change more generally" (Bourke 2006: 335). However, I do not think we need to choose between evolutionary and cultural explanations here. In fact they point in the same direction, namely on rape as taboo – and the causes of the taboo on rape may be many and complex.

I will thus move on to and concentrate only on the third question listed above, addressing the seeming asymmetry between fiction and real life in this matter: why do we in Western societies[26] accept murder but not rape in fictional narratives, when murder is considered a graver crime than is rape when considering legal sanctions? In order to propose an explanation, I will first suggest that rape is considered morally disgusting, while murder need not be. Again I will argue that this points to us navigating through these fictional contexts with an intuitive moral compass, whereas our real life Western laws are the result of very deliberate, rational evaluations. In the case of murder versus rape, it seems that what we might find acceptable emotionally (such as murder being acceptable with some important qualifications) is different from how we see things when asked to evaluate deliberately (murder is never acceptable). While we might agree that murder is perhaps the greatest violation of another human being rationally, emotionally speaking rape seems to be perhaps just as – or more – disturbing: rape seems not to be acceptable at all, not even in fictional contexts with qualifications. Feelings of moral disgust seem not to be open for negotiation. Thus, when relying on moral intuitions and emotions, we find rape unacceptable. This is what I will suggest that the narrative function of rape in these series points to.

Rape and Moral Disgust

In order to narrow in on feelings of moral disgust, let us return to the CAD hypothesis originally proposed by anthropologist Richard Shweder, as introduced briefly in the first chapter. Building on this hypothesis Paul Rozin,

Crossing the Line 137

Jonathan Haidt, Jesse Prinz and others have developed a theory about (real-life) *moral disgust* that may shed light on the narrative role of rape (Haidt, Koller, and Dias 1993; Rozin, Haidt and McCauley 1993; Rozin, Lowery, Imada and Haidt 1999; Shweder 1990; Prinz 2007). According to this theory, morality builds on basic emotions that are cultivated and expanded to include trespassing of moral rules. Three basic emotions give rise to three different kinds of moral emotions, each to a different kind of moral trespass. To reiterate, the three basic emotions are contempt, anger and disgust (CAD). Feelings of contempt point to virtues such as respect, duty and hierarchy being violated in an ethics of community; feelings of anger arise when individual rights and autonomy are violated according to an ethics of autonomy; and finally, feelings of disgust are prompted when the perceived natural order is violated. I follow Jesse Prinz here, as according to Shweder's original theory, disgust belongs to an ethics of divinity, and arises when what is perceived as divine or pure is violated. Prinz suggests that "[v]iolations of divine nature elicit disgust because they are violations against nature, not conversely. Such violations are first, and foremost, unnatural acts" (Prinz 2007: 73). Feelings of moral disgust thus signal that something is perceived as an unnatural act – morally disgusting acts are violations against nature. It is this latter category I wish to look at more closely.

The basic emotion of disgust, or core disgust, originates in food rejection, and protects us from bacteria and infections by making contaminated food repulsive. Spoiled food, faeces, vomit, bodily fluids and decaying bodies are commonly found disgusting. These researchers point out that we do not restrict the label disgusting to these things, but can also say, for example, that we find incest disgusting. A more cultivated emotional response, labelled moral disgust, is derived from core disgust and includes violations of moral norms with only an associative link to core disgust. Jesse Prinz writes:

> Sexual mores are obvious candidates for moral disgust because sex is a carnal act that saliently involves the transfer of bodily fluids. Since these things can elicit disgust on their own, it is unsurprising that violations of sexual rules are regarded as disgusting. Moral disgust is also directed at mass murderers, perhaps because they are associated with mutilation and death, which are primitive elicitors of disgust (Ibid., 71).

Rozin and colleagues have a related explanation of moral disgust: we find morally disgusting what reminds us that we are animals (Rozin et al.1993).[27] They write that "[i]nsofar as humans behave like animals, the distinction between humans and animals is blurred, and we see ourselves as lowered, debased, and (perhaps most critically), mortal" (Ibid., 584–5). They also tie this theory to anthropologist Mary Douglas's theory about pollution as violation of accepted categories (see Douglas 2003) and point out that this can explain our moral disgust towards deviant sex acts, for example.

138 *Crossing the Line*

Based on these different proposals, I suggest that we find morally disgusting those trespasses where we find that the perpetrator behaves sub-humanly, where we perceive the perpetrator's acts to be unnatural and impure in some way, and where the moral trespass has an associative link to some of the things that elicit core disgust. Jonathan Haidt argues in a similar manner: we feel moral disgust when someone does something that seems "monstrous – lacking in some basic human sentiment" (Haidt 2012: 104). We would commonly say of a rapist that he is 'an animal'.[28] Having sex against someone's will is perceived as unnatural, as the natural way to have sex is consensual. Rape is not just a violation of someone's autonomy, triggering anger, but is also perceived as an unnatural act. We find the rapist disgusting. This is echoed in what Bourgois writes about his unwillingness to report about his crack dealing informants in New York: he is worried that portrayals of rape will make the reader "too *disgusted* and angry with the crack dealers and deny them a human face" (Bourgois 2003: 207, my emphasis). This is also mirrored in Cuklanz's choice of words, when she writes that "[in the basic rape plot, rape] is the result of *sick*, perverted, and even psychopathic individuals" (Cuklanz 2000: 69, my emphasis).[29]

Let us now turn to murder. According to the criteria for moral disgust outlined above, a gory murder could surely be seen as morally disgusting because we find the flesh and blood of human bodies disgusting and the murderer as sub-human and violating nature. This is in line with what Torben Grodal suggests in a similar analysis of crime fiction drawing on the CAD model (Grodal 2010). Grodal writes that mutilation of bodies is morally disgusting. However, he also points to the prominence of sex crimes in eliciting moral disgust. If comparing the feelings of moral disgust elicited by murder and rape respectively, it seems clear that we do not necessarily see all murderers as morally disgusting to the same degree as rapists. An example demonstrating the difference between murder and rape when it comes to moral disgust is perhaps the splatter film. The Norwegian *Dead Snow* (Tommy Wirkola, 2009) is an enjoyable example with zombie Nazis. In splatter films the attraction is precisely the gore that ordinarily is a candidate for disgust. Nevertheless, arguably even gory killings appear less morally disgusting than rape. It is more difficult to imagine a comedy genre playfully portraying rape as a laughing matter. Rape seems thus to evoke moral disgust more prominently than even very gory murders.

Let us look at one example in greater detail. Grodal points to the mutilation of bodies as morally disgusting, and Prinz to mass murderers eliciting moral disgust. How about the serial killer Dexter Morgan in the television series *Dexter*? Dexter surely enjoys his killings, and the spectator enjoys *Dexter*.[30] Should not this series be perceived as perverse and sickening – indeed, as morally disgusting? As mentioned previously, for most spectators I would indeed suspect that the moment when Dexter kills is slightly unpleasant – a reality check even. However, as explained in the first chapter also, a high degree of very careful stage setting is used to make us as spectators go along

Crossing the Line   139

with this narrative set-up and accompany Dexter right up until the point when he kills; e.g., he only kills other serial killers.

Furthermore, the burlesque style of the series and its black humour is important for us as spectators to accept its basic premise – sympathy with a serial killer. In the opening sequence of the series, a quirky, childish Tivoli tune-like music accompanies Dexter's humdrum morning ritual turned grotesque in close-up pictures of a sharp knife cutting through a squirting orange, and hands tightening around shoelaces as if about to strangle someone. The opening sequence sets the tone through which the spectator is supposed to engage this series – namely black humour. Never has making breakfast been so wonderfully grotesque – the flesh of the bacon being cut, the gore of the eggs being cracked, the cafetiere plunger pressed down so brutally. It would be strange to deny that it is exactly disgust that is being put into play here. The opening sequence invites an aestheticized gaze, however. The spectator is encouraged to find sensual pleasure in these little acts of (seeming) cruelty – just as the series will later invite the spectator to take part in Dexter's pleasure in killings.[31] *Dexter* is not mere realism; the series is burlesque and playful. Throughout every episode, we hear Dexter commenting on himself in an extensive use of voice-over. Typically, he views himself with pitch-black humour, ironically pointing out his own monstrosity to the spectator, personalizing the murderer within him as 'the dark passenger'. Humour is a well-known distancing technique, and in this context it facilitates our engagement with this serial killer.

Another narrative technique used to encourage sympathy for Dexter is that we learn of his childhood trauma of seeing his mother being slaughtered in a veritable bloodbath. His stepfather Harry taught him to channel his fascination in death and killing (animals) to what Harry sees as the greater good, namely vigilante killings of serial killers. It is thus suggested that the dark passenger was planted in Dexter at a young age, and coached by the Code of Harry until adulthood. Dexter's awareness of the monstrosity of this dark passenger is troubling for him, and almost seems like an aspect of his personality for which he is not fully responsible. Dexter struggles with his dark side. This also adds to our sympathy for him.

Finally and most importantly, as Mittell rightfully points out in the interview quoted above, it is hard to imagine us accepting Dexter raping his victims. This corroborates the point that when it comes to what is morally disgusting, rape is perceived as worse even than serial murderers. Dexter himself encounters a group of men who rape, torture and kill women in the series' fifth season. Although these men are not only rapists, their torture rape, recorded by themselves, disgusts Dexter – and the series' spectators probably with him. Struggling with his own dark passenger, these serial rapists remind him what monstrosity really is. "Despite having considered myself a monster for as long as I can remember, it still comes as a shock when I'm confronted with the depth of evil that exists in this world," he reflects in voice-over.[32] Rape is one of the primary elicitors of moral disgust even in this series.

140 *Crossing the Line*

With some narrative stage setting, a fictional television series can make a murder appear as legitimate and emotionally acceptable (the Mafioso or serial killer deserves it; he is part of the game; the victim is morally worse than the murderer, etc.). When Tony Soprano kills a competing mobster or an unruly subordinate, or Dexter kills another serial killer – who does not, like Dexter, have a moral code – we do not find these acts as morally disgusting (unnatural, perverse and sick) as we would if Tony or Dexter had raped people. Managed within the narrative frame, these murders can appear as legitimate – the victims merely had it coming – and they do not seem to trigger moral disgust to the same degree as rape does. It seems more difficult to manipulate the spectator to see rape as deserved – or rather, whether or not the victim were to 'deserve' it, in a way akin to how murder is legitimated in a fictional context by thinking that the unruly mobster or ruthless killer deserved what was coming his way, this would not make the rapist less suspect: taking pleasure in sexual violence would still, I propose, be perceived as disgusting.[33] This can explain why antiheroes do not rape, and why rape is used to clearly mark some characters as unsympathetic.

Indeed, this is supported by a series of studies on moral disgust compared to anger conducted by Pascale Sophie Russell and Roger Giner-Sorolla (Russell and Giner-Sorolla 2011a; 2011b; 2011c; 2013). They find that moral disgust is an inflexible emotion – less open to adjustments and justification than anger. They write that

> [o]ne key feature of bodily moral disgust [disgust triggered by moral transgressions where a violation of the body is involved] is that it is categorical. A person who committed a disgusting act is tainted in the eyes of others, who do not consider consequences, excuses, or justifications for the act. The act is just disgusting, and by extension the person as well. On the other hand, for anger, the social context is more likely to be involved in generating the emotion beforehand and reasoning about it after the fact. In short, the cognitions surrounding core disgust and bodily moral disgust are simple, basic, concrete and hard to change with mere thought: the cognitions surrounding anger are more abstract, complex, and amenable to change by thought and reappraisal.
>
> (Russell and Giner-Sorolla 2013: 339)

This can explain why we are willing and able to justify murder in a fictional context, as the anger first and foremost triggered by a murder is open to justifications. Anger is more context-sensitive than is disgust. We are more able to make exceptions to moral violations triggering anger than we are to violations evoking disgust: a murder can appear legitimate depending on consequences and circumstances. Moral disgust triggered by rape makes the rapist categorically repulsive. It is thus probably not coincidental that the empirical evidence for moral dumbfounding referred to in chapter 1 (and to which

Crossing the Line   141

I will return in the next chapter) is tied to feelings of moral disgust specifically: we find it more difficult to give reasons for moral disgust than for anger.

Moral disgust plays a special role in establishing who the proper villains in a story are. Without exploring the rapist as morally disgusting specifically, Carl Plantinga also points out that disgust is often used in film to create antipathy toward and promote condemnation of antagonists (Plantinga 2006; 2009: 198ff).[34] Murder is also commonly seen as evoking feelings of anger due to the violation of someone's autonomy, but we are able and willing to turn a blind eye to this when we know the perpetrator well. We are thus prone to be partial to the antihero's reasons for killing someone (again, in a fictional context). Feelings of moral disgust are harder for us as spectators to counteract. This is one explanation for why these series typically do not encourage sympathy with rapists.

On the Asymmetry Between Fiction and Real Life

We are now narrowing in on the asymmetry question. To recapitulate, why do antihero series not encourage sympathy for rapists when we are encouraged to sympathize with murderers, and murder is considered a graver moral trespass in real life? The asymmetry between fiction and real life in this case suggests that the moral system activated by fiction may not be activated in the same way as in real life. I suggest that rape is perceived as a graver moral trespass than is murder in a fictional context because we evaluate trespasses in fictional contexts based on moral emotions. Let us again reiterate the terrain of moral theory introduced in chapter 1.

In Western societies, our real-world laws build on reason-based moral evaluation. As Jonathan Haidt and Selin Kesebir point out, the dominating moral theories in our Western societies (after the Enlightenment) have in common

> an emphasis on parsimony (ethics can be derived from a single rule), an insistence that moral decisions must be reasoned (by logic or calculation) rather than felt or intuited, and a focus on the abstract and universal, rather than the concrete and particular.
>
> (Haidt and Kesebir 2010: 798)

This is true both of Kantian deontology and Millian consequentialism, to mention only briefly the two most important moral theories coming out of the Enlightenment. By defining morality as reasoning about abstract principles of right and wrong, however, the dominant moral philosophies of Western societies may define morality in such a way that it excludes other societies' moral systems. Haidt and Kesebir label the emphasis on reason, impartiality and universalism the great narrowing in moral theory, and argue for a new synthesis in moral psychology that builds on evolutionary psychology.

142   *Crossing the Line*

We have evolved in much smaller groups than our current big Western societies; we have evolved some *moral foundations* to secure cooperation (Ibid., 814ff, see also Haidt and Joseph 2004; Haidt and Graham 2009). These foundations are found to some degree in all human societies and are seen as innate – but which moral foundations or taste buds are activated in what way varies between cultures. Haidt argues that in Western societies, we have narrowed down what counts as moral questions to merely two of our six moral foundations (harm and fairness), which is why we might fail to understand that people in other societies may see respect for hierarchy, or purity, for example, as moral questions too (Haidt 2012). These are moral foundations (authority, sanctity/purity) that are downplayed in Western societies.

For simplicity, and in order to explain my argument, I will stick to the CAD (contempt, anger and disgust) hypothesis, and not the more complex six-foundations model that theory Haidt develops later (the Moral Foundations Theory) in order to explain my argument here. Haidt and his colleagues wanted to investigate cultural differences in moral assessment, building on the CAD hypothesis. They presented to respondents in the U.S. and Brazil a series of harmless taboo violations, offensive stories intended to produce a flash of disgust although no humans are actually harmed. One of these stories reads as follows:

> A man goes to the supermarket once a week and buys a dead chicken. But before cooking the chicken, he has sexual intercourse with it. Then he cooks it and eats it.
>
> (Haidt, Koller and Dias 1993: 617)

Is what the man does morally wrong? When investigating how the respondents reason about this case, Haidt and his colleagues found cultural differences. To take the two groups with the greatest difference, respondents high in socioeconomic resources in the U.S. would reason that as long as it does not harm anyone, it is not *morally* wrong. Were some societies to regard this as acceptable behaviour – who are we to criticize?, they might reason. Respondents low in socioeconomic resources in Brazil, however, would say that it is indeed morally wrong, because it is repulsive. For Haidt and his colleagues there was also a surprising class effect on the responses to the harmless taboo violation – educated, urban Brazilians were more similar to educated, urban Americans than to their rural, lower-class neighbours (and likewise in the U.S.). The respondents high in socioeconomic resources demonstrate the kind of reasoning typical for moral questions in the moral philosophies of Western societies: restricting a moral question to issues of harm. If it violates no one's autonomy or individual rights, it is not a moral violation. The second group demonstrates a different view of what counts as a moral violation: finding something disgusting, perceiving it as a violation of the natural order, makes it morally wrong. Restricting morality only to

Crossing the Line 143

questions of harm and fairness may be an educated response, most typical perhaps for a specific group in Western societies.[35]

The reason for returning to Haidt's research here is that it suggests that morality can be dependent on emotions and intuitions in relation to various moral domains, and need not only be based in reasoning about abstract principles relating only to harm and fairness. I suggest that even in our Western societies, where at least our laws have been made through deliberate reasoning about abstract principles about harm and fairness – definitely a case of using the manual setting of our morality, as in Greene's metaphor – an intuitive and automated, emotion-based morality is sometimes activated. These moral feelings in other moral domains are not something we have left behind altogether; rather, depending on the situation in which we find ourselves, we might allow ourselves to navigate by use of the automatic settings of our morality, to stick to the metaphor that Greene uses. I propose that engagement in fiction is one such instance.

Although a Westerner high in socioeconomic resources might not report eating a chicken carcass one has just used for masturbation as morally wrong *on reflection*, while engaging with fiction, portraying a character as doing just that is probably an effective way of blocking sympathy for that character.[36] It is hard to imagine any of the antiheroes in recent American television series masturbating with, and then eating, a dead chicken. Tony Soprano would not, neither would Dexter Morgan nor D'Angelo Barksdale. While we do not find it morally wrong on reflection, intuitively we too will probably feel there is something genuinely wrong with such a character, and this keeps feelings of sympathy towards or moral allegiance with such a character from arising. One matter is whether we see this as a moral violation while reasoning why; another is what we intuitively feel when we are not encouraged to reflect.

Thus, whereas to some degree we are not encouraged to think of morality in terms of purity in Western societies, for example, finding incest and rape disgusting does suggest that even in our Western moral psychological makeup, evaluations relating to purity and a perceived threat of the natural order give rise to feelings other than mere anger (as violations of a person's autonomy triggers). Whereas Haidt emphasizes how moral intuitions in Western societies are shaped socially (and, one might add, through education) to be restricted to questions of harm and fairness, I would argue that the research on moral disgust referred to above supports the idea that when we react intuitively, other criteria for morality are activated too. Moral disgust is triggered when something is considered a violation of the natural order. In real life, we might feel we should be able to give fully rational arguments relating only to harm and fairness to explain why a moral trespass is more or less grave. When we engage in fiction, however, we relieve ourselves of this perceived obligation, and rely much more intuitively on moral emotions. Feelings of disgust as morally relevant become more obvious when relating to fiction, because we do not feel that we must evaluate a fiction's morality rationally and deliberately according to principles relating only to harm and fairness.

144   *Crossing the Line*

When rationally considering a moral violation solely in relation to the harm it causes, it makes sense that taking someone's life is among the worst crimes one can commit. We would probably all agree with this principle in real life. Emotionally speaking, however, I think rape is just as disturbing because in addition to the harm it causes the victim, it is morally disgusting (as already discussed), and this makes the rapist repulsive. The repulsion felt towards the rapist is evident in our engagement with fiction.

There is one additional line of research that may back up the claim that rape is just as emotionally disturbing as is murder, namely studies of our tendency to blame rape victims in real life. One gets the impression from public debates that we have a far greater tendency to blame rape victims than to blame murder victims (or victims of other violent crimes). A critic may indeed use this to argue against my theory about rape and moral disgust in this chapter: if it is the case that rape is perhaps just as or more emotionally disturbing than is murder, why are rape victims so commonly blamed for their own misfortune? Why are public debates about rape typically much more muddled than our views on murder (e.g., murder victims are hardly ever said to have 'asked for it')? However, instead of being seen as a counter-argument to my theory, I think these observations actually support my view. Martin Lerner and colleagues (Lerner and Simmons 1966; Lerner and Miller 1978) proposed the so-called Just-World Theory to explain our tendency to blame victims.[37] The reasoning behind the theory is simple: in order for us to co-operate, we need to believe that the world is just and that people get what they deserve. Victims of misfortunes that are not objectively speaking their fault threaten this basic worldview. We typically protect ourselves from this threat by blaming the victims, finding reasons for why the misfortune really is the victim's own fault. This restores our much-needed belief that the world is just and makes us feel safe. This tendency has received much support in empirical investigations, and among the most typical cases used to investigate this are indeed rape victims (see e.g., Carli 1999; Bieneck and Krahé 2011; Janoff-Bulman, Timko and Carli 1985). In one of these experiments the participants read two identical stories where only the final outcome varied: the story either ended with a rape or with a marriage proposal (Carli 1999).[38] It was found that the participants saw both the rape and the marriage proposal as a result of the female character's behaviour – in hindsight, the victim's behaviour was seen as causally linked to the outcome (although the stories were identical – so if one were to say that the female character deserved to be raped, she just as much deserved to get married!). This biased perception of rape victims can be tied to the Just-World bias as well in that if in hindsight we see whatever a woman does prior to a rape as leading up to that rape, we might, of course, see the rape as deserved. The Just-World Theory points to a cognitive bias – a pattern of judgment that we typically make use of, although it is not rational of us to do so. Indeed, the Just-World bias can be seen as only one type of attributional bias that contributes to blaming victims.[39] The robust body of literature documenting the many

Crossing the Line   145

heuristics and biases to which we are prone attest to some of our mind's automatic settings at work (cf. Kahneman 2011). Furthermore, this also demonstrates that although it might once have been useful for mankind to rely on these automatic settings in order to secure co-operation and facilitate trust in a group (clinging to hope that our world is a just one might have been important in order to facilitate group trust and collaboration), in our present times we should see this specific bias – the Just-World bias – for what it is: an outdated survival mechanism that does more harm than good, but rather prevents society from putting the blame for a heinous crime such as rape where it belongs – namely, on the perpetrator. Be that as it may, most important for my discussion here is that the tendency to blame rape victims in real life does suggest that this is a crime we perceive as very emotionally disturbing; in fact, so disturbing that this is one of the crimes that we seem to feel the need to protect ourselves against the most by thinking that the victim had it coming. The Just-World bias seems most prominently to be activated in relation to rape victims, and indirectly this also adds support to my suggestion that emotionally speaking, rape is perceived as a horrendous crime – a real threat to our sense of justice and security.

When blaming rape victims we do, in fact, rely on some notoriously unreliable biases in real life. Here is one case, then, where our morality in real life is heavily influenced by our mind's automatic settings. This further demonstrates that arguing that something is intuitive does not mean that it is more true, accurate or right than what we hold as right rationally; on the contrary, in this case what we perceive intuitively is manifestly wrong from a rational point of view. Neither is it the case that moral intuitions are always wrong – concerning partiality, for example, most people would also agree rationally that I do have a special obligation to help my own family over complete strangers, in line with what I feel intuitively (as discussed in chapter 2). And one can certainly argue that the disgust felt towards the rapist demonstrates that rape is a heinous crime that should be taken very seriously by society. This is thus not a return to the now seemingly outdated view that emotions are irrational *per se*.[40] However, there is no easy solution to when we can and should rely on our moral emotions, and when we should not, and in any case this question is beyond my scope in this book.[41]

To return to the Just-World Theory, an intriguing question is why these biases are then not even more evident when we engage with fiction? If we take for granted my theory about us relying on moral intuitions and emotions when we engage with fiction, should it not be predicted that these kinds of biases are clearly evident when we engage in fiction? Should not my theory predict that we blame rape victims in fictional stories even more easily than in real life? Perhaps the repulsiveness that the rapist evokes takes priority when we engage with fiction. Or, as the perpetrator is usually punished in fictional worlds, perhaps we have less need to activate the Just-World bias when we engage with fiction: we can usually rely on the guilty party being

146 *Crossing the Line*

punished, and our belief in the world as just is therefore restored anyway. Only in the real world do rapists typically get away with it. A third reason might be that the Just-World bias is not triggered, or triggered only to a lesser degree, by fiction, and triggered fully only by real life events: for example, in one experiment testing the Just-World bias the researchers found that it was activated when the subjects were informed that they were actually witnessing a suffering victim (a person receiving electrical shocks), but not when they were informed that the victim they were witnessing was merely someone pretending to suffer (Simons and Piliavin 1972; see Lerner and Goldberg 1999: 637).[42] Perhaps we somehow feel less threatened by victims in fiction and thus feel less need to protect ourselves by blaming the victim. What remains is the simple observation that as spectators of fiction we seem more willing to empathize and sympathize with murderers than with rapists. I have concentrated on the depiction of the rapist here; more work is needed to settle how the rape victim is portrayed in current American television series.

To sum up, there seems to be an asymmetry between our reluctance to engage imaginatively with rapists onscreen but not murderers, even though murder is seen as a graver crime in real life than is rape. The asymmetry can be explained by proposing that we depend on moral intuitions when engaging with fiction. We thus bracket the moral reasoning about abstract principles that we would probably feel mandated to activate in real life – at least if making universal and abstract laws. Repulsion toward the rapist is probably something we feel in real life, too. I do not argue that our moral emotions in relation to fiction and in real life are different; rather, I argue that our moral emotions become more evident when we engage in fiction. Although I have concentrated on rape here, this conclusion can probably be extended to include other morally disgusting acts as well – moral disgust can be expected to trigger strong feelings of antipathy toward a character.

In the next chapter we shall turn to a very different kind of villain in the antihero narrative – much more subtly and sneakily, many spectators find that they cannot stand the antihero's wife. Rationally speaking, she should rightly be seen as morally preferable; this, however, is not how many spectators perceive her.

Notes

1. After spending a year in the Baltimore police homicide department Simon also wrote *Homicide: A Year on the Killing Streets*, published in 1991 (Simon 2009). *Homicide* was also fictionalized as the television series *Homicide: Life on the Street* (NBC, 1993–99).
2. See also Horeck (2004: 91ff) for a discussion of *The Accused* (Jonathan Kaplan, 1988) and on how the fictionalized narrative changed the victim's ethnic background from Portuguese-American, as was the case in the real case on which this fiction film draws (known in the media as 'Big Dan's rape case'), to a white Anglo-American victim, played by Jodie Foster. In recent American television series one exception is found in *Treme* (HBO, 2010–2013), also created

by David Simon in collaboration with Eric Overmyer, where one of the main African-American characters is raped in the second season and where the narrative does give access to the stress and trauma she experiences afterwards.

3. *The Wire*, "Lessons", season 1, episode 8.

4. *The Wire*, "Game Day", season 1, episode 9.

5. Projansky (2001) emphasizes the versatility of rape in fiction film historically: however, her analysis seems also implicitly to confirm that despite variation in terms of who rapes, the rapist is indeed typically the villain.

6. See Cuklanz (2000: 28ff) on how depictions of rape in her material changed – in late 70s and early 80s, basic plot depictions of rape dominated almost completely, while acquaintance and date rapes where increasingly put into focus in rape depictions throughout the later 80s and the 90s.

7. *The Wire*, "Alliances", season 4, episode 5.

8. *The Wire*, "Margin of error", season 4, episode 6.

9. See also Dan Hassler-Forest's analysis of *The Walking Dead* (AMC, 2010-present) (Hassler-Forest 2014).

10. This is not to say that there are not deviating portrayals of rape in *The Shield* – for example, one of the lead male police officers is raped, and rape of male characters is rare on American prime-time television (see Cuklanz 2000: 132–5).

11. There is also a rape in season 1 that fulfils the revenge function well: a 13-year-old girl is raped, and the Sons of Anarchy are drafted in to get revenge. Again, this storyline is used to make us feel more sympathetic toward them. *Sons of Anarchy*, "Fun Town", season 1, episode 3.

12. *Sons of Anarchy*, "Albification", season 2, episode 1.

13. *Banshee*, "Meet the New Boss", season 1, episode 3.

14. *The Sopranos*, "Employee of the Month", season 3, episode 4.

15. See also my analysis of this in Vaage (2013).

16. See Kieran (2002) for an analysis of obscenity along these lines.

17. See Pinker (2011: 401). Thanks to Francis X. Shen for discussions about this observation.

18. These definitions are from Raney and Bryant (2002).

19. Thanks to Dan Hassler-Forest for these counterexamples. See also Anne Eaton's careful discussion of *Talk to Her* (Pedro Almodovar, 2002) (Eaton 2009).

20. Thanks to Jason Mittell for pointing me to this study.

21. Although *Game of Thrones* is not an antihero series strictly speaking, as in *The Wire* there are antiheroes in the huge ensemble cast.

22. *Game of Thrones*, "Winter is Coming", season 1, episode 1.

23. *Game of Thrones*, "Breaker of Chains", season 4, episode 3.

24. Another important finding in this study worth mentioning is that whereas series with male protagonists (e.g., most of the antihero series I investigate here) typically focus on one single sexual violence plotline at a time, these series with female protagonists often explore multiple plotlines at the same time. Berridge argues that this may establish connections between individual instances of sexualized violence that potentially could be seen as "complicating the individualised understandings of sexual violence privileged by male-fronted and ensemble cast teen drama series" (Berridge 2014: 484). Thanks to Tanya Horeck for pointing me to this study.

25. And not, as in earlier times, because rape of a woman shows disrespect toward the father, husband or brother, whose 'woman it is', see also Brownmiller (1975).

148 *Crossing the Line*

26. I remind the reader that when I write about 'us', 'we' and 'the spectator', this refers to general tendencies in Western societies as it is beyond my scope here to explore cultural and individual differences.

27. In the current theoretical landscape, this view may increasingly seem dated, as animal morality is now hotly debated. Thanks to Rikke Schubart for pointing this out. For an overview of research on animal morality or pro-morality, see e.g., Bekoff and Pierce (2009) and de Waal (1996).

28. See also Rozin et al. (1999: 584–5).

29. However, Cuklanz criticizes basic plot portrayal of rape for not depicting rape as connected to structural elements such as socialization and patriarchy.

30. For an empirical investigation of engagement with Dexter, see Tan, Timmers, Segijn and Bartholomé (unpublished manuscript).

31. On this and other title sequences in Quality TV, see Fahlenbrach and Flueckiger (2014).

32. *Dexter*, "In the beginning", season 5, episode 10. Finally, to add to the suggestions offered already, an additional explanation for the taboo on rape is perhaps that it is typically portrayed as violence against women, and this is more culturally condemned than violence against men. Thanks to Anne Gjelsvik for pointing this out, and see Gjelsvik (2013). Thus, one could also predict that *Dexter* would be more uncomfortable to watch if Dexter killed women (he does in fact mostly kill men).

33. Again, there are counterexamples: in *The Girl With a Dragon Tattoo* (Nils Arden Oplev 2009, and in the remake with the same title by David Fincher, 2011), for example, Lisbeth Salander takes revenge on her rapist by brutally raping him back. The degradation and violence involved in the first rape scene, where Salander is raped, does arguably prepare the spectator to enjoy the revenge of the second rape scene (rape of the rapist). I would suspect most spectators find both rape scenes emotionally disturbing – but Salander hardly comes off as monstrous in the same way as her rapist does.

34. See also how feelings of disgust are elicited in relation to the rapist in Hitchcock's *Frenzy* in Elliott (2011: 103ff). On a different yet related note, for a discussion of how racialized disgust can prevent whites from engaging with black characters in films such as *12 Years a Slave* (Steve McQueen, 2013), see Flory (2015). Also, the study mentioned in chapter 2 on ratings of heroes and villains according to the domains of the Moral Foundations Theory (Eden et al. 2015) found that although villains were rated as violating the purity domain less than other moral domains, they found that violation of purity was nonetheless a strong predictor for the perception of the villain, and conclude that violation of purity "can play a very strong role in perceptions of villains as good or bad people. Even small purity violations appear capable of having a strong effect on perceptions of villains" (Ibid., 203).

35. Indeed, it has been argued that it is a problem for moral psychology that most of the empirical research has been conducted on a narrow range of people in Western societies, as Western, Educated, Industrialized, Rich and Democratic (WEIRD) societies are particularly unusual compared to the rest of the human species. See Henrich, Heine and Norenzayan (2010).

36. There is an intriguing line of research on the difference between moral judgments of acts and character that might illuminate this further: whereas we find harmful *acts* more morally wrong than non-harmful acts, when judging the perpetrator's *character* in relation to disgust the opposite is true – we find the one

Crossing the Line 149

who does something non-harmful but morally disgusting, such as masturbating with a dead chicken, as having a less moral character than someone doing something harmful (e.g., stealing something) (Uhlman & Zhu 2014). Assessments of moral disgust might seem especially important when judging someone's character (as compared to merely judging the act in its own right). Thanks to Roger Giner-Sorolla for pointing me to this research.

37. See also Furnham and Procter (1989), Hafer and Begue (2005) and Lerner and Goldberg (1999) for reviews of the literature, the latter being especially relevant for my discussion here as it also ties the Just-World Theory to dual-process models.

38. Carli does not discuss this in relation to the Just-World Theory, but sees these investigations more specifically as related to the Hindsight Bias – after an event we tend to see the event as determined by what happened prior to that event – and how our reconstructive memory contributes to this. However, her studies are often discussed in relation to Just-World Theory, see e.g., Lerner and Goldberg (1999: 633).

39. Other biases pulling in the same direction are, for example, fundamental attribution error and optimism bias; for a popular account see e.g., Britt (2007).

40. Rather, in cognitive psychology most would now hold that emotions have an important function for us, cf. a functional theory of emotions; see e.g., Frijda (1986) and Plutchik (1994).

41. Though Greene has a suggestion: when it comes to mechanisms securing co-operation within a group (Me vs. Us), our moral intuitions and emotions are more trustworthy than when it comes to questions of Us vs. Them (my group's moral values versus another group's values). Our moral intuitions and emotions were not developed to secure co-operation between groups. In our globalized world, only a switch to manual, rational moral deliberation can solve the moral conflicts that come with cultural differences (Greene 2013).

42. However, this experiment may have little bearing on our engagement with fiction, as watching someone merely pretending to suffer is not the same as watching a fictional story in which someone is pretending to suffer (i.e., watching fiction is more than watching actors merely pretending to do things).

6 The Antihero's Wife

On Hating Skyler White, and on the Rare Female Antihero

In the previous chapter, I investigated the function played by villains in the antihero series – something is needed in order to make the antihero morally and emotionally preferable. In blogs and discussion forums online, however, a (un)fair amount of antipathy is often directed at the antihero's wife. Whereas antipathy toward raping psychopaths is easier to explain theoretically, the antihero's wife seems to fulfil the function of villain for some – or even many – spectators. As the TV critic Alan Sepinwall sums it up:

> Because the revolutionary dramas were mostly about men, and male anti-heroes at that, and because viewers tend to bond most with the main character of a show, there was a side effect to the era, where characters who on paper should be the sympathetic ones become hated by viewers for opposing the protagonist. And the greatest vitriol has been unfortunately saved for wives like Skyler White, Corrine Mackey, Carmela Soprano, and Betty Draper, who are viewed by some viewers as irredeemable bitches, no matter how poorly they're treated by their husbands.
>
> (Sepinwall 2012: 359)

There is an important gender aspect to the antihero series – its main character, the antihero, is typically male.[1] Amanda Lotz confirms the dominance of male protagonists in current American television series on cable (Lotz 2014). She labels this as the male-centred serial. In the first part of this chapter I investigate how the antihero's wife is portrayed in recent American television series, with a special focus on Walter White's wife Skyler in *Breaking Bad*. Discussing feelings of antipathy toward Skyler gives me the opportunity to sum up several of the debates I have visited in this book, and review my position once again. Furthermore, in order to shed more light on the portrayal of women in the antihero series, I also discuss female antiheroes in the latter half of the chapter. The portrayal of women in these series is linked in interesting ways to the portrayal of home and family, and I propose that there is a movement away from the home in the antihero series – arguably part of a resistance to melodramatic and soapy connotations.

The negative opinions about Skyler in *Breaking Bad* were so excessive that online discussions about her infamously turned into what has been called an Internet hate-fest. The actress playing Skyler, Anna Gunn, sums up the "vitriolic response" toward the fictional character she played as hateful, and writes that "[t]he consensus among the haters was clear: Skyler was a ball-and-chain, a drag, a shrew, an 'annoying bitch wife'" (Gunn 2013). She notes how other "complex TV wives" such as Carmela Soprano and Betty Draper have also inspired similar feelings, and concludes that the hateful response has to do with the spectators' perception of women and wives. "Because Skyler didn't conform to a comfortable ideal of the archetypical female, she had become a kind of Rorschach test for society, a measure of our attitudes toward gender", she concludes (Ibid.). Downright misogynistic responses seem to have been stirred up by this series, at least in a segment of the audience.

However, it is also worth asking whether the response toward Skyler is encouraged by *Breaking Bad*. The series' narration should be put under critical scrutiny. Analysing how *Breaking Bad* encourages antipathy toward Skyler surely does not exonerate the mad death threats toward the actress playing her, nor does it excuse the excessive online hate-fest. The death threats toward Gunn ("Could somebody tell me where I can find Anna Gunn so I can kill her?") should rightly be seen as Internet trolling, and it is beyond the scope of the present study to full explore the causal explanations for these online responses. I will concentrate only on how *Breaking Bad* encourages antipathy toward Skyler. The conclusion I draw is slightly different from Gunn's: I do not think the primary reason for the hateful response toward Skyler is that she does not conform to a comfortable ideal of the archetypical female. Rather, I think her problem, narratively speaking, is that she is holding her husband back from what the audience perceive as enjoyable transgressions. However, Gunn's point might explain why there are so few female antiheroes. I will return to this later in the chapter, and resonating with Gunn's observations about the antihero series as a measure of our attitudes toward gender, the few female antiheroes we do find in series such as *Banshee*, *Nurse Jackie*, *Weeds* (Showtime, 2005–2012) and *Orange is the New Black* (Netflix, 2013-present) are typically less transgressive, and their husbands (if they have one) are portrayed more sympathetically than is the male antihero's wife. This testifies to it still being perceived as less acceptable to portray non-conformist, difficult and transgressive female characters on-screen. Portrayal of female characters in antihero series is typically conventional, despite the oft-celebrated innovative nature of these series; women in these stories are either expected to be morally good and play the traditional roles of mother or daughter,[2] or play 'fallen' and sexually alluring women as strippers, prostitutes or lovers. However, at the very end of the chapter I turn to one prominent counterexample to this diagnosis: Patty Hewes in *Damages* (FX 2007–2010, Audience Network 2011–2012).

152 *The Antihero's Wife*

Quality TV and the Feminine Sphere

Michael Newman and Elena Levine criticize the very notion Quality TV (Newman and Levine 2012). They see the notion as part of a process of legitimation by distancing some television programmes from regular TV (illustrated perhaps most clearly by the HBO slogan "It's not TV. It's HBO"). To compare it to its perhaps closest cousin, the heavily serialized Quality TV series is presented (by its creators) and perceived (in critical reception) as radically different from the traditional form of serialized narration on TV, namely soap opera. Soaps are regular TV; appealing mostly to women of lower classes, they have had low cultural status. Soap opera portrays the home, family and personal relations. Newman and Levine argue that regular TV is seen as tied to the feminine sphere. With increased segmentation of the audience came the TV channels' quest to capture new audiences that were not traditionally attracted to fiction on prime-time TV – affluent, highly educated male spectators were seen as particularly important. In order to appeal to them, the new trend of TV series distanced itself from regular TV, seen as feminized and of lesser value. Newman and Levine argue that the mere label Quality TV naturalizes this hierarchy of taste.

This argument is controversial. Taking an aesthetic approach to television, both Ted Nannicelli and Sarah Cardwell disagree that discussing television as art entails such a denigration of certain parts of the audience (Cardwell 2013, 2014; Nannicelli 2012, forthcoming). I will not engage this discussion about the evaluation of television here. Rather, I am interested in one smaller, specific claim that Newman and Levine make in their discussion of Quality TV as gendered masculine, namely that Quality TV tends to "avoid, reject or de-emphasize the very subject matter of soaps – that of domestic family drama and romance" (Newman and Levine 2012: 96). They argue that *The Sopranos*, for example, "spends quite a bit of narrative time resisting its status as soapy TV", and illustrate this by arguing that

> Tony is at once an object of ridicule and a site of identification for the masculinized viewing subject, to be mocked but also pitied for his failure to live up to the masculine ideal of the cinematic gangster, padding around his house in his underwear and raiding his well-stocked suburban refrigerator for leftover lasagna.
>
> (Newman and Levine 2012: 95)

Newman and Levine hold that Tony appears comical and pathetic in his suburban home – it is outside of this home that he is the exciting gangster. The soapy connotations given by Tony's family life are ridiculed and resisted.[3] This can be seen as one way to appeal to male viewers in particular and to prop up the series' status.

Others disagree with this view of the use of the soap genre in *The Sopranos*. Robin Nelson, for example, argues that because American Quality TV and other high-end television programmes are "a hybrid of one kind or another,

The Antihero's Wife   153

it may be that viewers socially constructed by tradition into gender and other social segments (...) might ultimately be reconstructed" (Nelson 2007: 181). *Pace* Newman and Levine, Nelson sees *The Sopranos* as a proper mix of the gangster genre and a soap opera; indeed, such hybridity and genre mix is typical for high end television, he argues. Dana Polan sees both sides of the question, and argues that

> there might be moments that mock the soap opera, in keeping with that genre's widespread reputation as a low, kitsch form: for example, when Uncle Junior is put under house arrest in the second season and has to find ways to occupy himself, it is considered one mark of how this once-violent Mafia bigwig has fallen when he becomes glued to his television set and, in particular, shows himself to be obsessed by daytime soap operas. However, whatever local jokes it may make at the expense of an ostensibly superficial television low culture (thereby seemingly to proclaim its superiority over it), *The Sopranos* adopts many of the conventions of the soap opera.
>
> (Polan 2009: 42)

Quality TV's relation to soap is a hotly debated issue, and I will not try to settle this question here.[4] What I will do, however, is to argue that the portrayal of the antihero's wife supports Newman and Levine's argument in one specific sense – the portrayal of home and family is typically fairly negative in antihero series. In fact, the trend they point toward has possibly become more outspoken after *The Sopranos*. Without having the space here to elaborate on this claim, one can argue against Newman and Levine that the domestic drama in *The Sopranos* is not only given equal weight narratively, but also that the female characters in *The Sopranos* are often portrayed as powerful, as Cindy Donatelli and Sharon Alward point out in their comparison of the strong women in *The Sopranos* to their by far weaker cinematic counterparts in films such as *The Godfather* (Donatelli and Alward 2002). Similarly, Kim Akass and Janet McCabe note that women in *The Sopranos* – Carmela and Dr Melfi in particular – negotiate what and who Tony is through traditional television mode such as confessions, gossip and focus on inter-personal communication (Akass and McCabe 2002). Both Carmela and Dr Melfi thus serve important functions and are powerful – in their own way – in this narrative. Furthermore, as Merri Lisa Johnson also convincingly argues about the episode "University", centring on a storyline about the stripper Tracee and her boyfriend Ralph, one of Tony's subordinates (discussed in chapter 4 also), *The Sopranos* does give proper access to the difficulties female characters face. In this particular episode, Tracee has a utopian and naïve dream about a family life with Ralph, but Ralph offers little else than humiliation and violence – he beats her to death. Johnson argues that

> *The Sopranos* reenacts a widespread cultural wrestling match with the "miscarriage" of family, home, and the American dream. This popular

154   *The Antihero's Wife*

> subgenre characteristic of HBO original series – the "it's not TV" of family drama – produces a paradoxically utopian relief from empty master narratives of family values. "University" mobilizes this contrast between utopian and dystopian visions of home in the service of Tracee's complex characterization as fallen woman with class-driven aspirations to redeem herself in the eyes of her gangster boss and boyfriend, thereby gaining access to the good life.
>
> It is in fact a commonplace of the feminist movement against domestic violence that classism is responsible for the misleading idea of home as a safe retreat from the dangers of the public world.
>
> (Johnson 2007: 272)

However, as I will go on to show, although there is much critical potential in the antihero series' portrayal of the domestic sphere as anything but safe, and also to depict the challenges faced by the female characters in these dramas, in later antihero series such as *Breaking Bad* there is a tendency to cast not just the domestic sphere, but everything feminine, in a negative light, and to give little access to its female characters. Increasingly, the antihero series has emphasized how the male can live a transgressive and exciting life if only he breaks free from the home, restricted as it is by a traditionally feminine sphere portrayed as boring. So although I disagree with Newman and Levine's claims about *The Sopranos*, I do think they have a point in relation to several other antihero series.

Whereas Newman and Levine discuss this in relation to soaps, another way to explore the antihero series' relation to the feminine sphere is to address its relation to melodrama. Linda Williams investigates melodrama as a mode of storytelling that is foundational to American film (Williams 1998).[5] I will not discuss the antihero series' melodramatic features fully here, but merely focus of one of Williams' five characteristics, namely that a melodrama begins, and wants to end, in a space of innocence – which is typically the home. A melodrama is typically about a victim-hero who loses his home and struggles to return to it, to re-establish this place of innocence. *Gladiator* (Ridley Scott, 2000) is a good example from American film – Maximus is the victim-hero who loses his much-loved home and family, portrayed as a near heavenly place of peace and happiness to which he desperately wishes to return. Maximus' sorrow over losing this home is emphasized both narratively and stylistically in the pathos typical for the melodramatic mode.

Although the portrayal of the antihero's home and family is complex, it seems fair to say that his home is not unequivocally portrayed as innocent, happy and peaceful in the antihero series. Lotz observes that the main character's family life is important in the trend of male-centred serials (Lotz 2014). Indeed, she argues that the "presence of and attention to domestic affairs is one of the primary distinctions of the male-centered serial, which features considerable thematic consistency in depicting the men's home lives" (Lotz 2014:

The Antihero's Wife   155

68). She contends that this marks the male-centred serial off from other episodic series centring on male characters on American television, where the men are often childless and single. Lotz's main argument is that

> the male-centered serial [is] a narrative form that conspicuously enables the examination of aspects of men's lives such as the intersection of work and family in a manner different from other narrative forms.
>
> (Ibid., 69)

It would thus be wrong to say that family and home is unimportant for the antihero series. However, as Lotz also points out, first and foremost these series explore the importance of being a father. The main character values fatherhood, and it is construed as central to men's identity. The male character's relation to his wife, however, is typically portrayed as more problematic: "unstable marital relationships are by far the norm, and in most cases, the cumulative narratives of the series chart the uncoupling, negotiations, and in some cases recoupling of the men and their spouses" (Ibid., 68). She adds to this that

> [i]n contrast to this emphasis on men engaged with paternal duties, marital bonds are depicted as fragile and permeable, and these relationships provide much of the personal dramatic tension of the series.
>
> (Ibid., 70)

This important perspective, however, is not fully explored in her otherwise compelling and careful analysis. When analysing the series' implicit argument about masculinity, for example, she states that "[w]omen, wives, and feminism are never constructed as in any way responsible for the situations with which the men contend" (Lotz 2014: 84). Although my aim here is not to investigate these series in relation to hegemonic masculinity, I think there are good reasons to dwell on the negative portrayal of the antihero's wife. Lotz is right in pointing out that the male character sees his role as father and provider for his family as important, and that caring for his family is typically the male character's starting point (though it often goes wrong because he wants to provide for them through illegal means).[6] Also, as argued in chapter 2 and 4 initially the antihero claims he does it all for his family, and this moral code is important in order to legitimize his actions for spectators: he is a good man, basically, because he loves his family and wants to provide for them and protect them. However, there is much more tension in the antihero series' portrayal of home and family that this analysis suggests. My exploration of the portrayal of the antihero's wife might be taken to imply that she is at least partly blamed for the disempowered and humiliated state in which the antihero finds himself at home, to which his immoral transgressions offer an enjoyable relief. Furthermore, the antihero's family background is often also portrayed as a drawback – from

156 *The Antihero's Wife*

Tony's wicked mother Livia to Ray's selfish father Mick in *Ray Donovan* and Patty's brutal father in *Damages*, familial relations are typically portrayed as difficult and sometimes also menacing in the antihero series. I will now focus on how the antihero generally also wants to break free from the home, not return to it, as the home is in some sense also restricting and disempowering. In the antihero series there is typically a movement away from the home, not back toward it: the home is not where the heart is in the antihero series. Although loyalty toward the family is used as an excuse initially, ultimately family life is portrayed as restricting. The antihero's wife gets a raw deal in these narratives, where everything (traditionally) seen as masculine seems to be celebrated at the expense of everything (traditionally) tied to the feminine sphere. The best example is perhaps *Breaking Bad*.

Preventing Sympathy with Skyler White

Let us return to the intervention in the Talking Pillow sequence in the first season of *Breaking Bad*, a sequence I started discussing in chapter 3.[7]

Figure 6.1 "I have the talking pillow now": the portrayal of Skyler is intrinsically linked to the claustrophobic atmosphere of the Whites' home (*Breaking Bad*, AMC).

I argued that we as spectators are invited to see the intervention as humiliating, as this is how Walter sees it. Skyler has been portrayed as humiliating Walter before. In the pilot episode, for example, we see her unenthusiastically masturbating Walter all the while being more engaged in an online auction and her confronting Walter for charging a purchase on the wrong credit card. In the Talking Pillow sequence, as will be remembered, Skyler has called on their family in order to confront Walter, aimed at changing his

The Antihero's Wife   157

mind about not getting treatment for cancer. The claustrophobic atmosphere in the living room is emphasized by the characters' long, awkward silences and efforts to avoid eye contact. Furthermore, I also suggested that Skyler is portrayed as unsympathetic when she breaks her own rules. At the beginning of the intervention, she takes the Talking Pillow in her lap and explains that whoever has the pillow is allowed to air his or her concerns openly and uninterruptedly. However, when Marie, her sister, disagrees with her and supports Walter, Skyler is infuriated and scolds her for clearly not understanding what the intervention is about. One is left with the impression that it is not about the family coming together in an open conversation about their emotions related to Walter's illness. Rather, Skyler has staged it in order to make Walter listen. In chapter 3, I contrasted family sequences such as this one to suspenseful sequences where Walter tends to his criminal career, and argued that the latter offer an attractive relief. Here I will continue exploring how sequences such as this one triggers antipathy toward Skyler.

The portrayal of Skyler in *Breaking Bad* is intrinsically linked to the portrayal of the Whites' home. It is not a particularly happy or appealing one. It is not stylish, but looks like a regular middle class bungalow, with a collection of oldish furniture. From the very beginning of the series, their home is brewing with discontent. Both Skyler and Walter seem to have had talent and prospects at a younger age. Skyler had aspirations to be an author of fiction, Walter was an innovative researcher in the successful company Grey Matter – a company he created with two colleagues but chose to withdraw from at quite a loss to himself. Their lives have now stagnated in a dull, uneventful, disempowered everyday life where they struggle to make ends meet. Theirs is a home of broken dreams. From the very beginning we are most prominently aligned with Walter, and as we saw in chapter 3, his escape from the common life they live is suspenseful and enjoyable. Although Skyler takes up a new position in an office, and even has an affair in later seasons (for which she is roundly condemned by some spectators, as we shall see), Skyler cannot escape their home as does Walter. She remains – traditionally – tied to it, and everything that is unappealing about it latches onto her.

This is typical of the portrayal of the antihero's wife in recent American television series. From Carmela in *The Sopranos*, to Betty in *Mad Men*, to Skyler in *Breaking Bad* and Abby in *Ray Donovan*, the antihero's wife (typically blond, white, middle-aged) is trapped in her suburban kitchen, resentfully sneering at her husband as he makes his escape to the far more suspenseful and rewarding outside world. The antihero's wife is the unhappy homemaker, where the home represents everything that is dull about everyday life – like the very incarnation of what causes a (male, presumably) midlife crisis. A regular trope in the antihero genre is found at the moment when, faced with her husband's incessant lying, deception and cheating, she hisses the question at him: who *are* you?[8] He is, of course, something by far more exciting than his regular appearance as father and husband in this suburban setting would suggest. The antihero lives an exciting double existence, where his role in the family home is the least appealing.

158 *The Antihero's Wife*

Figure 6.2 "Who are you, Ray?" asks the antihero's wife Abby Donovan (*Ray Donovan*, Showtime).

There is little attraction to be found in engaging in the perspective of the antihero's wife. (Female) fans of melodrama and soaps may object, and surely viewers do traditionally find the suffering victim-hero appealing. However, as I will go on to argue, the lack of attention given to the antihero's wife works a long way to block such melodramatic effects and pleasures. One *can* feel sorry for her and wish for her escape from this dreary situation. Typically, however, her point of view is not emphasized. Furthermore, for the spectator, engaging in her husband's escapades is by far more rewarding. As pointed out already, the first wives in the American antihero narratives were more sympathetically portrayed than is Skyler.[9] For example, Carmela Soprano is a more active character than is Skyler; temperamentally, she reciprocates Tony's anger and is fully aware of what her husband does all along; we are aligned with and given access to her to a greater degree than to Skyler. Although Carmela has a guilty conscience, she sometimes takes advantage of her powerful situation. I will return to this line of argument later and suggest that the wife who takes part in her husband's transgressions fares better than the wife who tries to stop her husband from breaking the law.

Nonetheless, as pointed out by Sepinwall, for example, online discussions reveal that some spectators disliked Carmela, too. Perhaps the creators of the antihero narrative slowly discovered the potential for fuelling the spectator's (and perhaps in particular the male spectator's) sympathy for the antihero through this emotionally subtle – and politically incorrect – mode: contrasting the enjoyable male antihero with his wife, who is a drag. Case in point: even when Skyler becomes an accomplice to Walter's crimes from season 4, she is portrayed not as living on the wild side,

The Antihero's Wife   159

as is Walter, but planning their cover stories carefully and meticulously. She makes up a story about Walter being a notorious gambler in order to explain the money they suddenly have at their disposal. She writes several pages of dialogue, insisting that they practice before going to visit Hank and Marie where their little scheme will play out; planning each and every detail such as where it might be appropriate to cry a little in order to make the story convincing.[10] Walter clearly signals that he finds her plan pedantic and tedious. When Walter has planned something in detail, we merely see him set it in motion – often learning only after the fact that Walter had planned the whole thing in advance. When Skyler is in on it, however, we have to rehearse every step of it with her (as surely Walter must have carefully planned his many elaborate schemes as well!). The result is that she looks obsessive, cynical even, and most certainly dull, whereas Walter comes off as cooler and more fun.

In addition to representing the dullness of everyday life, antipathy toward the antihero's wife is enhanced by several other factors. Primary among these is arguably the fact that she is often portrayed as hypocritical. She is typically portrayed as being deeply ambivalent and resentful toward her husband's illegal line of work, and her accusing him of destroying her and their children's lives would again be a typical trope in the antihero genre. Nevertheless, she is also typically shown as embracing the material comfort, wealth and glamorous lifestyle that her husband's crimes bring them. Carmela, for example, loves the expensive furniture she can buy with her husband's blood money; Abby Donovan is also portrayed as loving her expensive wardrobe and being taken to top-notch restaurants. She wants to enjoy their wealth without dealing with the consequences – which is another way of saying having her cake and eating it too. When she continually blames her husband for this deep-seated ambivalence, she comes about as a hypocrite. Emotionally, I think the spectator punishes her for this. She is like a freeloader, in on the enjoyable part of the ride but not ready to pay the price. Her husband, although usually also ambivalent to some degree, embraces this criminal lifestyle more fully, so he appears more consistent.[11]

What can then appear as unfair is how Skyler is perhaps judged most severely of all the antiheroes' wives, as she never enjoys the money that Walter brings in. First she is unaware of his crimes, and then shocked and repulsed when she finds out. She consistently accuses him of putting their family in danger. She only helps him whitewash his earnings to protect their children from ever finding out what their father is up to, and she suffers in her role as accomplice. However, there are also sequences that make Skyler appear either hypocritical, or incomprehensible at best. For example, at the very end of season 2 Skyler asks Walter to move out because she has confirmed that he is lying to her. As season 3 begins, Walter lives in another flat, and Skyler has approached a lawyer in order to get a divorce. Notably, she refuses to tell anyone why she has thrown Walter out. Their son, Walter Jr., vehemently blames her for this and continues to either yell at her or give

160 *The Antihero's Wife*

her the silent treatment. In response to her sister Marie's inquiries, she icily insists that it is none of her business. Even her boss, Mr Beneke, asks her what went wrong between her and Walter (this is when she has an affair with him). Importantly, because Skyler refuses to tell anyone how she is feeling and what she is thinking, the narrative misses out on these opportunities to give the spectator access to her. Furthermore, instead of potentially seeing other characters in this fictional world sympathize with Skyler, we see them judge her harshly. Their feelings toward her can be said to influence us – and it arguably has influenced some spectators when they argue that *she* is breaking their family apart (see the following).

Against my interpretation of the effects of these sequences one could argue that perhaps Skyler is made to appear more sympathetic here, not less, in that we are invited to feel sorry for her as the spectator knows why she has left Walter – yet in the story world nobody understands her plight and she is being unfairly judged. However, interestingly, in episode 3 Skyler finally does tell her lawyer, who is bound by the lawyer-client privilege. In a thin voice, Skyler explains that she does not want her children to know that their father is a criminal. He has terminal cancer, so she is hoping that, as she puts it, "things will resolve themselves" without her having to lay this on her family. The lawyer, however, immediately advises Skyler to move out and inform the police of her husband's crimes, and she adds that their children finding out may not be up to her – "drug manufacturers have a way of getting caught." This is a rare opportunity to hear exactly what Skyler feels and why she behaves as she does. But how easy is it to understand Skyler's decision not to inform the police? Is it credible that she would choose not to tell anyone in order to protect the children, all the while allowing Walter to continue to put them in danger? The lawyer's reaction adds to Skyler's choice being hard to understand. The one person Skyler opens up to immediately points to the flaws in Skyler's strategy, arguably making it harder to sympathize with and understand Skyler, not easier.

A similar example is found in an episode where Skyler is worried that Walter might be in danger. She suggests he was scared the previous night; that he is in over his head.[12] This throws Walter into a tantrum, infamously yelling at her: "I am the danger! I am the one who knocks!" He refers to an earlier worry aired by Skyler that one day someone will want to hurt both Walter and his family; someone will come knock at their door. The spectator can only imagine what Skyler must be feeling. She looks shocked and then abruptly leaves. The spectator is not aligned with her directly after this event and not given access to what must be going through her mind. It is the first glimpse she gets of what her husband is turning into: it is not the case that he only cooks a little meth, as she has been thinking. His speech reveals that he considers himself a major player in the drug underworld – a man with power, whom others fear. The next we see of her later in the same episode, she has driven to the Four Corners Monument (where New Mexico, Colorado, Utah and Arizona meet). She walks over to the monument and flips a coin. It lands on Colorado, suggesting that she should leave

The Antihero's Wife   161

(as Albuquerque is in New Mexico). Skyler, however, picks it up and flips it again, suggesting that she does not want to leave. The coin again lands in Colorado. In a close-up of her foot, we see her step on the coin and slowly drag it down into New Mexico, again seemingly stubbornly insisting that she will not leave. This is all we see of what she is going through. We see her foot. It must be an emotional ordeal for her – but we can only imagine. This is yet another missed opportunity to understand Skyler. When she returns she seems at first afraid, and then accusative – but it appears inconsistent of her, as the narrative suggests she wanted to stay.

The series makes it difficult to empathize with Skyler. We are often not aligned with her, and given little access to her. As Skyler is growing increasingly angry with and resentful toward Walter, the narrative does typically linger on close-ups of her face. One would think this gives the spectator ample opportunity to empathize with her. In an interview, however, Anna Gunn reveals how she was instructed to play Skyler:

> [Vince Gilligan, the series' creator] didn't want her to be a hand-wringing, weak sort of person who sat and cried all the time. He would really caution me, because, personally, I'm a big crier and I'm emotional, so he really had to remind me a lot, "She's not that, she's not as in touch with her emotions and she's not able to necessarily access that".
> (Gunn quoted in Paskin 2012)

By not allowing the actress to fully portray Skyler's devastation in these situations, Gilligan also affected the spectator's opportunity to empathize with her. Not that one *cannot* empathize with her – as I will soon argue, one can do so by making an imaginative effort – but the narrative does not facilitate low-level, automatic empathy with her. Indeed, the added explanation that Gunn gives is telling. She says that

> if you lose your sympathy for Walt that early [in season 2] what are you going to do with the show? Much too early you would have been thinking, "This guy's horrible, look what he's doing to this poor woman" (Ibid.).

According to the line of reasoning here, it would have been important to give access to Skyler's frustration and pain toward the end of the series. However, increasingly the close-ups of Skyler's face show her stuck in a segmented passive-aggressive stare. She does not typically yell or cry or plead or threaten, but simply puts up with it, albeit hatefully. There are some sequences where she does yell and cry – arguably, these are relieving, and it is instantly easier to engage in her perspective. This suggests that the lack of traditional melodramatic techniques – pathos – is playing a role here; one can imagine the antihero series as a melodramatic story about a wife's suffering – but this is not the way this story is told. Giving Gunn freer rein to show the spectator what the character she is playing is going through would

162 *The Antihero's Wife*

have facilitated engagement with her – opening up the route to sympathy via empathy as explained previously in this book. It seems odd – hypocritical even – of Gilligan not to want to acknowledge having downplayed Skyler's emotional reactions in order to secure sympathy for Walter. I suspect this was done deliberately not only at the beginning of the series, but right toward the end of it. After all, a big part of the press that the series got was tied to the puzzling question of how come we as spectators keep sympathizing with him for as long as we did.

This links to an interesting distinction Mittell introduces. He asks whether the Skyler haters hate her as a fictional character (i.e., as one would dislike a real life person behaving like Skyler) or hate the way she is constructed as a character (i.e., that the character Skyler is not credible; that the character appears inconsistent and is thus badly written) (Mittell 2012).[13] Now, fans of complex TV are notoriously nit-picking when it comes to analysing their favourite TV shows – part of the phenomenon of *forensic fandom*, as Mittell labels it, where fans turn into amateur narratologists and engage in detailed analysis of narrative techniques of their favourite series (Mittell 2015: 288ff). One would think that fans would thus be able to pinpoint why they are made to dislike Skyler, if it is due to character construction. However, I think the emotional and moral effect of the narrative techniques in use in this series is quite difficult to pin down. I think a flawed character construction is the primary reason why many spectators do not feel more sympathy toward Skyler, yet many seem unaware of this underlying reason for their feelings toward her. For example, as already pointed out, we are not given an explanation for why she returns when she could have left. If she truly believes they are all in danger, would not leaving instantly be a better strategy in order to protect her children? Does she truly fear her husband? Is it credible that a woman like Skyler stays in this situation because she does not want her children to know that their father is a criminal (as is the only reason she initially gives)? As we shall see, Mittell describes her as a battered wife, and this could, of course, explain why she does not leave – she would then be too scared to leave. There are, however, narrative events that complicate such a view, and I will return to these shortly. I suspect these kinds of annoyances related to the construction of Skyler as a fictional character add to the spectator's impression of Skyler: she appears unlikable because she is not as carefully presented and constructed as is Walter. Answering Mittell's question, I think many spectators come to dislike her for aesthetic reasons – she is not a well-constructed, well-presented fictional character. As will be evident, I think irritation over the construction of the character Skyler has the spectator's disliking Skyler as a result – subconsciously, a collapse of the distinction between external and internal perspectives on the fiction. Rationally speaking, fans should complain about the writing of the series, but sometimes fail to identify that this is one of the reasons for their disliking Skyler.

Mittell, however, argues that Skyler is a battered wife (Mittell 2012). The best argument against Skyler being a battered wife is perhaps found

The Antihero's Wife   163

in one of the last episodes of the series.[14] Walter's house of cards is tumbling down, and he has also ended up in a physical fight with Skyler. After this confrontation, he leaves their house and takes their baby with him. Skyler is naturally devastated, and she alerts the police. Walter calls home, knowing that the police are listening in. In that telephone conversation, Walter presents himself as the abusive husband. Skyler is shocked at first, but then plays along with the ploy she understands that he is instigating: in an attempt to actually help her, he is presenting her as an innocent victim in his criminal enterprise. Rudely, he is verbally abusing her, trying to deceive the listening police officers into thinking that she is, indeed, a battered wife. It is portrayed as one truly selfless act (in a long row of egocentric ones, as Walter also finally admits). What is striking about this telephone conversation is that it also demonstrates that this is not the Walter we know. He may be many things, but he is not a wife beater. This is not an accurate representation of the story about Walter and Skyler.

In order to corroborate the claim that Skyler is a victim and deserves our sympathy, Mittell asks us to imagine their story from Skyler's point of view. She obviously deserves our sympathies, he argues:

> if we retell the series focusing primarily on Skyler's character's arc, *Breaking Bad* becomes a very different type of gendered tale, offering a melodramatic account of deception, adultery, and ultimately an abusive, dangerous marriage.
>
> (Mittell 2015: 254)

And despite my reservations against seeing her as a battered wife, imagining *Breaking Bad* from her point of view is an interesting thought experiment. When working on this chapter, I re-watched the entire series, and, as instructed by Mittell, paid special attention to how Skyler must feel. I must come clean and admit that on a first-time viewing I could not stand Skyler. However, by re-watching the series focusing on her point of view, it is easy to agree with Mittell's conclusion that she is a victim, and in consequence, that she is morally preferable.[15] (Merely reasoning about the series without re-watching it might bring similar results.) I now saw clearly how she finds herself in a horrible position. Continually reminding myself of how she must feel gave me such a different viewing experience from my first time viewing of *Breaking Bad* that it felt akin to an *aspect change*: to compare it with the famous duck-rabbit figure, in my first-time viewing I saw only the duck and now what appeared was the rabbit.[16] What I first did not notice was now obvious: I saw the narrative differently. Of course Mittell is right that Skyler deserves nothing but our sympathy. Mittell sums up the effect of this thought experiment in the following way:

> Of course, it is not Skyler's story. Walt is *Breaking Bad*'s protagonist, so we are invited to see his perspective on his marriage and share his

164 *The Antihero's Wife*

singular knowledge of his actions and motivations (...). [T]he series was promoted primarily as a crime drama, hyping Walt's dangerous exploits as an emerging drug kingpin far more than his familial drama or Skyler's emotional abuse. Yet Skyler's story is there, creeping toward the narrative center as the series progresses (...) Skyler's presence serves as an irritant for some viewers, but for others willing to consider her perspective, Skyler's experiences offer a vital critique of Walt's damaged masculinity. By considering Skyler's perspective, *Breaking Bad* functions in part as a "women's film" in reverse, told through the rationalizing perspective of the abusive spouse whom we only slowly grow to recognize as the villain.

(Mittell 2015: 256–7)

However, arguably it takes quite an effort from the spectator to see things this way. Deliberately focusing on Skyler's perspective one may come to see *Breaking Bad* as a critique of Walter, but this perspective seems to be very well hidden – so well hidden that it seems to me wrong to say that *Breaking Bad* may function as a women's film telling the story of an abused wife – even in reverse. It took a second viewing of the entire series for me to find it, and the perspective seems more like something I add than a perspective given by the series.

Importantly, something has changed in the way I engage with the series the second time. Turning back to Greene's writing, one can suggest that what I am now doing is truly evaluating the narrative rationally, using the manual mode of morality, explicitly reasoning about the narrative events. As will be remembered from chapter 1, Greene suggests that reasoning about morality is "conscious application of (...) rules" (Greene 2013: 136). When finding Skyler morally preferable, at least fuzzily and tentatively I am able to say what principle I am applying, for example, something like "Murder is a worse crime and moral trespass than accounting fraud and infidelity". I do defend this rule in general. As Greene points out, moral reasoning makes our moral judgments more consistent. I would not at the same time hold that murder is a worse crime than accounting fraud, and that Skyler is morally worse than Walter because she is guilty of accounting fraud while Walter is merely a murderer. Thus, when re-watching *Breaking Bad* with such a focus on moral issues, especially relating to Skyler's point of view, it becomes clear to me that I would surely not judge Skyler as harshly in real life. This realization is unpleasant, and I feel guilty: my prior feelings of antipathy toward Skyler now appear to be inconsistent with the moral principles I hold to be true. This is a reality check. I now see how narrative techniques make Skyler appear so unlikable. Relating this back to the discussion of bad fans in chapter 4, they never get this distinction, and instead of mulling over the construction of the character Skyler they write mean tweets about Anna Gunn. When evaluating the morality of *Breaking Bad* rationally, Skyler is morally preferable to Walt. Nevertheless, on a second viewing the choices the creators have taken in order to prevent sympathy with Skyler also stand out clearly.

The Antihero's Wife 165

However, when engaging with *Breaking Bad*, arguably most spectators allow themselves to navigate morally by use of emotions and intuitions, as did I on my first-time viewing. The second time around, I paid special attention to what her character is going through, but this requires an effort. It is surely more cognitively taxing than going with the narrative flow – and the narrative flow aligns us with, and enhances our sympathy for Walter, not her. Emotionally, we are not invited to feel with Skyler, but rather to see her as an annoying obstacle to everything fun. And as Raney has pointed out, when engaging in fiction, first and foremost we want to secure entertainment. As cognitive misers, sympathizing with Walter is by far easier than feeling with and for Skyler.

There have been a lot of discussions of Skyler online that may serve to illustrate the spectator's response toward Skyler. I will not attempt at analysing all these discussions thoroughly, but concentrate on merely a few of the 75 comments found in one such discussion here. Stephen Silver sums up *Breaking Bad* fans' critique of Skyler as her being unfaithful (having an affair with her boss while separated from Walt), hypocritical (changing her mind about divorcing him and dropping her disgust toward his criminal lifestyle and instead opting for cooperation), and emasculating (wanting to control Walt and criticizing him constantly) (Silver 2012). He then points out how unreasonable it is to judge her so harshly for this, when Walt has killed several people, lives a double life that involves lying to his wife and children, makes crystal meth that ruins people's lives and kills them; how he has set off a bomb in a nursing home, poisoned a little boy, and so on. The discussion that follows is interesting.

"Walter has his faults and can really act like an idiot sometimes, but Skylar [sic] is a cold, calculating person who consistently thinks that she is in the right regardless of the way that she is hurting other people", Becca writes. "'I'll prefer any drug producing murderer who loves his family above all and treats them with love and care over an accounting fraud accomplice who loves to break her family apart as viciously as possible", writes Jur. This last commenter seems to want to argue that accounting fraud is worse than producing drugs and killing people intentionally. Or according to the first commenter's line of reasoning, killing people is acting "like an idiot sometimes", but Skyler is cold and calculating, and that is morally worse. What is most striking about these comments is how unreasonable these spectators' defence of their antipathy toward Skyler is. Rationally speaking, it simply makes no sense to say that accounting fraud is worse than murder, and I very much doubt these spectators would defend such a view in principle. Earlier in this book I introduced the notion moral dumbfounding, taken from Jonathan Haidt's research, and the related notion of rationalization that Greene uses. As will be remembered from chapter 1, Haidt used this label about approximately a third of the respondents' persistent attempts at defending their moral evaluations rationally when feeling hypnotically induced disgust at neutral words. These respondents knew that they felt

166   The Antihero's Wife

Dan, the council representative, was doing something morally wrong when trying to organize an academic debate – and they tried to find rational arguments for why this is so. Haidt argues that moral dumbfounding shows that the moral evaluation is made intuitively, and rational arguments are simply invented afterwards in order to defend the verdict one has already reached. Greene, too, ties rationalization to arguments we come up with in order to defend the moral judgments already made intuitively.[17] One makes up "a rational-sounding justification for that feeling" (Greene 2013: 300). Notably, Greene separates between rational consideration of moral issues proper, and rationalization. When rationalizing, one merely generates justification. Truly considering a moral issue rationally demands putting feelings aside and deliberating according to principles, striving for consistency among principles.

From a rational point of view, it is easy to share actress Gunn's bewilderment in the following quote:

> It's interesting that people still continue to feel like, "Oh poor guy, he's doing the best he can, why doesn't she stop giving him a hard time?" It's funny to us because we've been scratching our heads and saying, "You do know that he's cooking crystal meth, and you do know that he's been killing people, and you do know that he's endangering his whole family, right?"
>
> (Gunn quoted in Paskin 2012)[18]

Those that seriously try to explain why Skyler is morally worse than Walter sound as if they are morally dumbfounded. However, quite a few other spectators in the same online discussion point to narrative techniques that increase antipathy toward Skyler – such as her being a wet blanket, a 'buzzkill', and that "the show has trained me to dislike them [the antihero's wife]". I think these spectators correctly pinpoint what is causing their antipathy toward Skyler. Through the narrative means already discussed, sympathy with Skyler is prevented, and as she is increasingly perceived as a drag, the spectator even comes to dislike her – indeed, to perceive her as morally worse than Walter. The antihero's wife is almost not recognized consciously as an antagonist – although that is the function she has emotionally in the narrative. This makes the antihero's wife a very special kind of villain, perceived as morally worse simply because she is not well-constructed as a character, and because she represents everything that is not fun in the narrative. She prevents or delays suspense and enjoyment. It is a subtle narrative technique, but morally murky.

The hateful response toward Skyler supports Carl Plantinga's point, first presented in chapter 1, about the rhetorical force of narratives (Plantinga 2010). Plantinga argues that because we tend not to be able to see how our moral evaluations are influenced by non-moral factors, narratives can have a strong rhetorical effect. Many see Skyler as morally worse than Walter, and

The Antihero's Wife   167

naturally presume that this evaluation has legitimate moral force. However, the main reason they see her as such is not because they have evaluated her morality rationally, but rather because the many non-moral factors in the narrative structure of the series have this effect. In line with this reasoning, the unsympathetic portrayal of this female character can be said to be an effect of the way suspense is distributed in the series, for example, as analysed in chapter 3: the series is simply more suspenseful and thus enjoyable when Walter engages in criminal activities outside of the home. The portrayal of Skyler is less appealing, and the tedious nature of the domestic affairs in which she is situated influences our moral evaluation of her. The series' affective structure can have a suspicious ideological effect, namely portraying the wife as an unsympathetic, nagging drag. This can, at least partly, explain the intense response the series stirred up. Another part of the explanation would be the persistently vociferous attacks on women online, which is beyond the topic of this book.

To return to the terminology introduced at the beginning of this book, the fictional reliefs that *Breaking Bad* invite entail enjoying Walt's criminal transgressions. As I have argued in chapter 4, an important part of the attraction of the antihero series is empathizing with the antihero (giving us some 'vicarious thrills', as it is so precisely formulated in *The Sopranos*). The pleasurable fictional relief that he offers is at the very core of what we have by now, in this cycle of stories, learned to expect and want from an antihero series. The enjoyable suspense found in his escapade as drug kingpin is the essential component in *Breaking Bad* as an antihero series. Skyler, however, is one long, persistent reality check, constantly wanting to remind Walter – and us in the audience – of the danger he puts his family in. There are other consequences she could have highlighted as well, such as the many victims of his crimes in the form of junkies. Skyler focuses on the safety of her family, and who can blame her for this? On the contrary, caring for one's family is something that would usually strengthen our sympathy for a character. However, by being such a 'wet blanket' on the suspenseful action, Skyler is constantly slowing this narrative down, almost bringing Walt's exciting character arc as transgressive to a halt. When being used throughout an antihero series as a reality check, Skyler carries a heavy burden. The reality check she represents is arguably intended to make us reflect critically on our own engagement with and enjoyment of the antihero. However, we might not be willing to admit to ourselves that through him, we enjoy serious moral transgressions vicariously.

One can also see Jesse as a character typically embodying reality checks: he suffers the consequences, and confronts Walter with this. Jesse is also a continual reminder of Walter's unsympathetic side – repeatedly Walter lets Jesse take the fall for their crimes, and he lures him back into their destructive partnership again and again although Jesse wants out. However, importantly, Jesse is in on the fun, suspenseful bits. Furthermore, where Skyler often holds back and where we are denied access to her reactions,

168 *The Antihero's Wife*

Jesse is typically allowed to cry out his pain while we watch. We are thus explicitly encouraged to feel sorry for him.

There are also other reality checks in this narrative, and I pointed to some in chapter 2, such as the small child in the junkies' house or Brock. Some of these other reality checks come in the form of characters we do not get to know and who do not play an important role in the narrative overall. Skyler, however, plays a major part in *Breaking Bad* from start to finish. As a character, for these reasons she is doing some heavy-duty lifting, so to say, in the form of inviting critical reflection. Although we might enjoy the puzzling effect the antihero series have overall, it seems that making one character carry the burden of distancing alone is too demanding – many come simply to dislike her. The reality checks in the antihero series must be distributed carefully.

It is interesting to compare Skyler to Dr Melfi in *The Sopranos* in this respect. I argued in chapter 2 that Dr Melfi also represents a reality check. However, Dr Melfi is more supportive of her mobster patient than Skyler is of her husband. Although Dr Melfi is sometimes disgusted and frightened by Tony, most typically his sessions with her plead for excuses: we mostly learn about Tony's weaker sides, and see Dr Melfi try to understand Tony and encourage him. Implicitly, she seems to condone his criminal lifestyle; she enjoys the vicarious thrills that he offers. Realizing that she has perhaps helped him become a more effective mobster does make her end treatment of him abruptly in the last season, and this is a massive reality check – part of an overall strategy to decrease sympathy with Tony in the last season. Be that as it may, the reality check that Skyler represents is much more persistent.

Perhaps one's feelings toward Skyler depend on how one feels about reality checks in fiction generally. One's tolerance for reality checks probably depends on many factors, one of them being genre preferences. *Breaking Bad* presents itself mainly as a suspenseful antihero series, and in this setting the reality checks can be perceived as an unpleasant obstacle to fun, as already argued. In the social realism of *The Wire*, for example, one would perhaps be more willing to let the reality checks induce the intended ethical and political reflections in their due course.[19] Furthermore, this is probably also a matter of personal taste. As I explore further elsewhere, my enjoyment of the character Omar Little in *The Wire* is also revealing (see Vaage 2013): admittedly, I prefer fictional reliefs to reality checks. On this, the taste of film theorists differ – in the critical tradition of so-called counter-cinema, for example, many film theorists would for normative and political reasons prefer and celebrate reality checks in their stronger, Brechtian form (cf. Wollen 2008 [1972]). However, I would hold that my taste is closer to the ordinary spectator in this regard: most spectators value fictional reliefs higher than reality checks. This is, of course, an empirical claim that could turn out to be incorrect; indirectly, however, looking at which films succeed in the box office is a simple test that corroborates my claim. Simple escapist

The Antihero's Wife   169

entertainment fare is by far more popular than films riddled with reality checks (such as in social realism or modernist fiction). It is first and foremost the critically minded academic or political activist who prefers reality checks in entertainment. Nevertheless, when considering the specific segment of the audience that the antihero series (or Quality TV in general) is tailored to appeal to, a case can be made for reality checks being more appealing to this segment (e.g., highly educated), as spectators in this group would want their entertainment to be perceived as thought-provoking and perhaps even provocative to a greater degree. This, however, is mere speculation, and although the spectators' responses vary both individually and across groups, this variation in reception falls outside of the scope of the present discussion. I merely point to some general tendencies in this book, which is admittedly a limitation inherent to the methodological approach I take. One fertile line of future research would be to investigate the appeal of the antihero series for various segments of the audience.[20]

When the Antihero's Wife is Enjoyable

Investigating the antihero's wife as a special case of villainy was the main purpose of this chapter. I have argued that the antihero's wife is a drag – one prolonged, lingering reality check offering little attraction amidst the enjoyable transgressions her husband offers. In order to corroborate my analysis of the portrayal of women in the antihero series, there are a few more issues I wish to highlight. First, I suggest that the antihero's wife is more enjoyable – we are given more reason to like her – when she joins forces with her transgressive husband instead of working against him.

Arguably the antihero's wife is at her most enjoyable when she escapes the conflicted role in which she finds herself trapped, and embraces the power her position as the antihero's wife actually gives her (or, even more enjoyably, ends her marriage altogether – although soon that will have the unfortunate effect that she becomes less important in the story). The antihero's wife becomes enjoyable the moment she steps out of her kitchen, and breaks with the restrictive role designated her as merely a good mother and wife. One such enjoyable moment is found in *The Sopranos'* second season.[21] Carmela wants a female lawyer she is acquainted with to write her daughter, Meadow, a letter of recommendation in order to ensure that Meadow is accepted at a good college, and gives her one of those infamous mobster offers one cannot refuse. One day, just as the lawyer's secretary is announcing that she has a visitor, Carmela paves her way into the office. She is armed with a ricotta pie she has made, as a gift. Smilingly, she is offering the lawyer the cake and explains that she would like her to write Meadow a letter of recommendation. The lawyer, however, says no. Carmela insists. Seemingly disarming and sweet, she repeats that she has brought a cake and would like to ask her to write a letter of recommendation for her daughter. Now the lawyer realizes that this is the mobster wife talking. The lawyer is well aware

170   The Antihero's Wife

of the power Carmela's husband has. Of course, Carmela gets that letter for Meadow. It is a remarkable sequence, with the unhappy homemaker stepping out of her suburban cage and fully embracing the power she in fact has as Tony's wife. This sequence is a very enjoyable display of Carmela's power.

A similar sequence is found in *Boardwalk Empire*'s season 3, when the antihero Enoch "Nucky" Thompson's wife Margaret Thompson makes use of her power when she practically frames a head doctor at the local hospital to launch a pre-natal women's clinic that she is passionate about – an idea the doctor has vehemently rejected earlier.[22] Margaret is an atypical antihero's wife in other respects; she too has a love affair in season 3, for example – an illicit pleasure usually only granted the notoriously unfaithful antihero (as is Nucky). Carmela, by contrast, lusts tremendously after Tony's henchman Furio, but never dares having an affair with him.[23] The strength and independence with which Margaret is portrayed makes her an attractive character – she is never presented as the victimized, resentful captive.

Another intriguing example of a transgressive wife is found in Gemma in *Sons of Anarchy*. Although Gemma is also in one sense a homemaker – cooking for the bikers sometimes, taking care of the home and having no official role in the motorcycle gang – she refuses the victimized position into which the antihero's wife often falls. Gemma takes Carmela's anger one notch forward. She interferes more actively in her husband and son's business dealings, and constantly keeps her ear to the ground as she figures out how she can pull the right strings in order to see her husband and son get what they want – and what she wants. Furthermore, Gemma is a violent woman. For example, she is literally hard-hitting towards one of her husband's younger mistresses – violently bashing her with a skateboard and seriously injuring her.[24] The antihero's infidelity is one of the things the antihero's wife typically has to put up with. Gemma, however, fights back more literally than does Carmela, who screams, shouts and throws things at her husband but never physically molests anyone. Gemma is portrayed as scary in a way that few of the other antihero's wives are. It makes her powerful and thus more enjoyable.

More recently, Claire Underwood in *House of Cards* is another transgressive wife – indeed, as Gemma, tending toward being a sidekick, female antihero. Nevertheless, Claire's potential has not been fully developed. In the first season, she has an affair with a former lover, suggesting that she is in fact craving another life, more authentic perhaps, that the Machiavellian partnership she has with her scheming politician husband Frank Underwood.[25] There are hints of her feeling guilty for what they do to other people – that she is melancholy and unhappy. We never see Frank suffer from a guilty conscience. Furthermore, in the second season she seems pretty much reduced to Frank's wife, now president of the United States, while initially she ran her own environmental non-profit organization. Claire is, however, fully in on her husband's ruthless political power

The Antihero's Wife   171

struggles, and plays the power game too whenever they can benefit from it. In an antihero narrative, this makes her more enjoyable.

There is also Alicia Florrick in *The Good Wife* (CBS, 2009-present). The series' starting point is intriguing in light of the trend of male antiheroes: what happens when the humiliated antihero's wife goes back to her daytime job in order to provide for her children while her husband serves time? Indeed, the pilot episode begins with her slapping her politician husband after a press conference – one is tempted to say that it is for all of those humiliated TV wives. The series investigates the challenges she faces as a middle-aged woman going back to work; a feministic agenda, one could argue, in stark contrast to most of the antihero series. Furthermore, it is interesting than one of the big three networks, CBS, chooses to tell this story from a wife's perspective – this demonstrates the audience appeal of this perspective, and suggests that the male-centredness of the antihero trend has more to do with status than audience appeal *per se*, as suggested above. However, I will have little to say about *The Good Wife* here as arguably Alicia Florrick is not an antihero – although she grows increasingly cynical, and sometimes puts the spectator's allegiance to the test, she never crosses the moral boundaries that is a defining feature of the antihero as I have used the notion in this study.

To sum up, it is not that there are no strong, morally complex and unconventional female characters in American antihero series. From the (admittedly restricted) survey I have done in this chapter, one can argue that it is first and foremost in her role as the homemaker that the antihero's wife is portrayed negatively. I have argued that this is because the home represents everything that the antihero needs to break free from in order to become enjoyably transgressive. This supports Newman and Levine's point about Quality TV distancing itself from what is considered traditionally feminine.

The Female Antihero

I have concentrated on male antiheroes up until now, and on the function played by his wife in the antihero narrative, where she is seen as traditionally tied to their home. Although the male antiheroes dominate, there are also female antiheroes to be found. Let us stick to a definition of an antihero defined by more than everyday, humdrum and all-too-human flaws. This would, for example, make Carrie Bradshaw in *Sex and The City* (HBO, 1998–2004), Hannah Horvath in *Girls* (HBO, 2012-present) and Carrie Mathison in *Homeland* (Showtime, 2011-present) antiheroes, too – and in some sense they are, as they are less than perfect, and not only clearly heroic. However, such a use of the term is too wide for my purposes, as I examine main characters whose moral transgressions are more severe. Concentrating on main female characters who break the law, there are such women as Jackie Peyton in *Nurse Jackie*, Nancy Botwin in *Weeds* and Piper Chatman in *Orange is the New Black*. Although a sidekick to the main, male antihero, Anastasia/Carrie

172 *The Antihero's Wife*

Hopewell is also a female antihero in *Banshee*. How is the female antihero portrayed, compared to her male counterpart, and what is her relation to her home and family?

In *Banshee* the female antihero Anastasia/Anna/Carrie is living incognito, so to say, as an ordinary, suburban mum, although she is actually an ex-criminal. Anna has a history with the male antihero Lucas, as the two worked as highbrow thieves together. However, as the series begins Anna has married a straight, law-abiding man. They live happily in the little town of Banshee, and she wants the antihero – her ex-partner both romantically as well as in crime – to leave her alone. However, as he is released from prison and seeks her out, she is pulled back into the criminal underworld. The topical antihero genre question is thus reversed between husband and wife when Anna's husband distrustfully and resentfully asks her: who *are* you?[26] It is she who is living a double life, and she who is deceiving him. In the first season finale, it is *him* that I as spectator see as a dull drag when he tries to hold her back from the final showdown. When he asks her not to go, it is against *his* better advice that I find myself silently coaching her to ignore him – as I have found myself coaching the male antihero to ignore his wife so many times.

In another episode, similarly it is she who uses her son's illness to legitimize one last heist (she needs the money to cover his medical expenses),[27] as we have heard Walter so many times legitimize his meth production as doing it for his family.

There is thus an intriguing reversal of familiar antihero tropes to be found in *Banshee*. This late antihero series can be said to be playfully aware of the

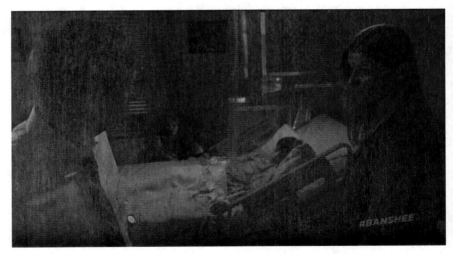

Figure 6.3 Gender relations are reversed when the female antihero Carrie Hopewell ventures out on one last heist in order to get the funding to save her son (*Banshee*, Cinemax).

conventions of the antihero series. In *Weeds*, too, there is some reversal of tropes to be found – one where Nancy, the weed-dealing suburban mother, threatens the next-door neighbour with a knife in her ticky-tacky suburban kitchen, for example – far removed from the conventional, resentful wives we have gotten used to seeing in that setting.[28] Nevertheless, in these two series the family and the home is to a much greater degree presented as desirable and happy than in many series with male antiheroes. In *Banshee*, Anna wants to preserve and protect her new life as an ordinary, suburban mother and wife – she is indeed happy in her new life. The male antihero who goes by the name Lucas is also portrayed as wanting a family life – wanting Anna back. In *Weeds*, Nancy Botwin's entire family is in on her drug-dealing escapade. There is not the same tension to be found between moral transgression and family life as is typically found in the series with a male antihero. Thus, although there are some reversals of tropes to be found, the female antihero's home is often happier and more attractive than the male antihero's.

Another difference between female and male antiheroes is that of the gravity of their moral transgressions. Only in *Banshee* do we find a female antihero who is also a murderer. The female antihero's transgressions are usually minor, relatively speaking – drug related, for example, as in *Nurse Jackie*, *Weeds* and *Orange is the New Black*. Thus we see nurse Jackie cheating on her husband with the hospital pharmacist in order to secure prescription drugs to feed her drug addiction. Jackie is an unfaithful, more or less well-functioning drug addict. Those are her crimes. The first thing to note is that compared to the bloody murders that the male antiheroes commit, Jackie is not awfully bad. In many ways Jackie is nothing short of a saint. While she makes a mess of her personal life, at least initially she is portrayed as a good, empathic nurse – taking the well-being of her patients seriously, and being the one who can comfort severely hurt or dying patients. So, as antiheroes go, there is more good in Jackie than there is bad, at least in the first seasons of the series.

Furthermore, she stars in a TV series made in the more comical and light-hearted half-hour sitcom format, and is thus not awarded the darker, full hour Quality TV series drama format. *Weeds* is also told in half-hour episodes, leaving us with only *Orange is The New Black* as the full hour drama series with a female antihero (and *Damages*, of which I will have more to say later). This does suggest that commercial television is less willing to portray seriously morally flawed female antiheroes in a more serious, darker setting.

One interesting way to shed more light on the male antihero's wife is to compare her to the female antihero's husband. There are some similarities between Jackie's husband Kevin and the prototypical antihero's wife that I have previously discussed. Kevin lives in their suburban home and is the main caretaker of their two children. However, he never quit his daytime, or rather, night-time job: he owns a bar and works there as

174 *The Antihero's Wife*

a bartender. Furthermore, he is never portrayed as the sneering captive as is so often the antihero's wife. He is first happily unaware of Jackie's transgressions, and perceives her only as a caring wife. Since he does not know, he cannot be a drag in the same way as is the antihero's wife. He never tries to talk her out of the transgressions that we as spectators find enjoyable. There is none of the hypocrisy that makes the antihero's wife unsympathetic, not the constant nagging and quarrelling, none of the guilt trips with which the antihero's wife typically showers her husband. In fact, Kevin is the one informing her that he has been unfaithful, and that causes their separation in season 3.[29] It is not until after they are separated that he learns about her infidelity and drug addiction. Then he is outraged and immediately files for divorce as well as custody of their children. The antihero's wife, as we have seen, typically wavers between wanting to leave her husband and staying with him throughout the series. Jackie's husband is thus presented as much more strong-willed and dignified.

This corroborates a critical, feminist analysis of the antihero's wife: when the gender roles are reversed, the antihero's husband is not portrayed as unsympathetically as is the antihero's wife. And when the antihero is female, she is morally better than the male antihero, or, in other words, less transgressive. Despite this, she can still be punished harshly for those relatively speaking minor transgressions – for example, the end of season 6 leaves Jackie alone, found out and humiliated at work, without any friends or a partner. As is typical for the antihero series, as the seasons progress our sympathy for the antihero is repeatedly put to the test, and the negative consequences for the antihero's family are emphasized. This is also clear in series with female antiheroes, such as *Nurse Jackie* and *Weeds*. In the series finale of *Weeds*, for example, Nancy has near lost her entire family due to her persistent favouring of the lure of illegal transgression. As she mourns the loss of their trust, her brother-in-law Andy tries to convince her that there is now "no-one to hold you back. Do the things that you want to do."[30] As the TV critic Drew Grant points out in a piece about *Weeds*, "there is a reason that guys like James Bond and Indiana Jones don't have families" (Grant 2011). The same tension thus remains between the female antihero's enjoyable transgressions and her family life as in series with male antiheroes, although the portrayal of the antihero's family is arguably more favourable in the former than the latter.

One Notable Exception: Patty Hewes

Before ending this chapter about the representation of women in the American antihero TV series trend, something must be said about one female character I have not so much ignored as saved, like a treat, until the very end: Patty Hewes in *Damages*.[31] Unusually, it is not clear whether

The Antihero's Wife   175

Patty is an antihero or a regular villain. Patty Hewes starts out as a proper villain: she is the high-profile litigator who must win her case, come hell and high water. She refrains from nothing to make this happen; the end certainly unscrupulously justifies the means for Patty. In the beginning of the series, we are aligned with a young, female lawyer, Ellen Parsons, as she first encounters Patty after graduating from law school. Ellen is emphatically told to stay away from Patty, and asked by a colleague to sign a card stating that she, Ellen Parsons, was duly warned: this woman is evil. The five following seasons all primarily revolve around one main suspenseful question: how evil is Patty Hewes really? Patty is clearly cynical. But is she psychopathic? Specifically, we as spectators want to know whether Patty actually tried to have Ellen killed in season 1. The special relation between Patty and Ellen that develops also poses the question of whether Ellen will follow in Patty's footsteps, and whether that would entail that Ellen, too, becomes pure, unadulterated evil.[32]

Undeniably, Patty is portrayed as unlikable in many ways. She is not, even in her own words, a good mother. She is neither empathic nor caring. She does not cherish family and friendship but rather seems consistently to want to refrain from forming any genuine personal relationships – one gets the impression that Patty works very hard to allow for personal relationships only to the degree that they are instrumental for her in some way or another. She uses those around her as she sees fit. She puts her work first.

In heightened, dramatic form, *Damages* can be said to explore the conflicts a career-minded woman encounters, as the sacrifices that are necessary for a truly ambitious career often seem incompatible with traditional expectations toward devoted mothers and daughters. For example, in the pilot episode Patty mocks Ellen for prioritizing her sister's wedding instead of a job interview with her. Patty comments on Ellen's commitments, and warns her that

> you try to lead by example, and they want you to lead – and they resent you for it. They put you on a pedestal, look up to you, and then blame you for the crick in their necks.[33]

Later in the series, too, Patty sarcastically remarks on Ellen wanting to attend a family dinner instead of being present to witness a dramatic turn in the case she is running. This time Patty's comment resonates with Ellen: the family brings her many worries, with a meth-selling sister and a bullying father, and she resolutely leaves her parents' living room and calls Patty to hear how their case is turning out.[34] Ellen's career is presented as offering protection against and escape from this family context, although her career surely also hurts her family, as it gets her fiancé killed. Ellen can thus be said to incarnate the conflict between career and family that a young female professional would face. The family context and

176 *The Antihero's Wife*

personal relations are to a degree portrayed as restrictive, as is typical for the antihero series.

Furthermore, although one can argue on the one hand that Patty is not particularly caring toward her family, on the other hand one can also argue that Patty's family is not particularly good to her. For example, Patty's son sends her a hand grenade in the mail as a prank and refuses to take responsibility for his own life. Her husband cheats on her. Patty grew up with an abusive father who eventually left her and her mother. The series' main suspenseful question of how evil Patty really is, and whether Ellen will follow in her steps, is thus mirrored in another, related question: what is most damaging, being willing to sacrifice everything for one's career, or the personal relations of a dysfunctional family? One interpretation of Patty is that she holds personal relations at bay and trusts no one, because her own personal relations have never offered much in return. Her family is portrayed as providing little support, and in line with the deep-seated ambivalence in the series, again it is unclear whether this is mainly Patty's fault or whether Patty's reactions can also, at least partially, be seen as warranted.

This portrayal of the family as damaging can be said to add sympathy for Patty. She can be seen as an antihero. Furthermore, she is portrayed as an excellent lawyer, for whom Ellen is increasingly full of awe – Ellen learns from Patty. Perhaps Ellen's awe and respect for what Patty can do as a lawyer also slowly latches on to us as spectators.

Patty is an interesting inversion of the traditional male antihero. As discussed in chapter 2, the male antihero's moral code is typically some sort of loyalty with his own group – he is basically doing it for his family (or so he claims). Patty, however, rejects most of the personal relations in her life, and she is loyal to none. She does what she needs to win. But in line with my suggestions in chapter 4, it is enjoyable to empathize with powerful characters. And Patty is surely powerful; she is portrayed as the one lawyer who takes on cases that no one else dare touch. She is feared. For female spectators in particular, it may be pleasurable to watch such a powerful female character – there are not that many of them in antihero series.

Adding to the pleasures of engaging with Patty is also the fact that she makes the series exciting, in line with my earlier suggestions about narrative desires and the important role that villainy plays in these. Also, aesthetic appreciation is part of the picture here, too, as Glenn Close gives a wonderful performance as Patty. Patty is the dominant personality never presented as a loud-mouthed, aggressive scare (as many villains in the gangster genre are, for example). Rather, she usually smiles disarmingly, seemingly a perfectly polite, mild and gentle woman – but there is a disturbing, menacing twist to it. When she gives someone (typically a powerful but guilty male) her signature stare, her smile is somewhere between a caring grandmother's and a crocodile eyeing its prey.[35]

Figure 6.4 The unscrupulous yet enjoyably powerful high-stake litigator Patty Hewes is smiling sweetly as she gives one of her targets her signature stare (*Damages*, FX).

Furthermore, through her line of work, Patty can be said to accomplish morally praiseworthy things. She takes on cases against huge companies and the most powerful of families in the U.S.: in season 1, billionaire Arthur Frobisher is guilty of insider trading leaving thousands of his employees without pensions and benefits; in season 2, Ultima National Resources CEO Walter Kendrick is guilty of using toxins in a chemical compound that have poisoned and killed both livestock and people in the area; in season 3, Patty takes on Louis Toben, who is responsible for the biggest investment fraud in Wall Street history; and in season 4 she faces the mercenary Howard Erickson, CEO of the paramilitary organization High Star. Patty is the one who dares take down the richest and most powerful of villains, those who, in reality, cause huge problems for society. Rationally speaking, the retribution against individual wrongdoers that an antihero like Dexter contributes with, for example, are small fish compared to the antagonists Patty takes on. However, the villains in *Damages* are not portrayed as psychopathic brutes, or disgusting and reprehensible perverts in the way that villains in the antihero series often are, leaving it to a greater degree up to us as spectators to assess who are morally worse – Patty or her targets. Patty seems to be willing to kill – or at the very least, undeniably she is willing to sacrifice a life – in order to win. Is this morally worse than what these CEOs are doing?

Without arguing that Patty is a utilitarian – Patty makes it clear that she is driven by mere anger toward her opponents, so suggesting that she is displaying concern for the greater good would be to give too much to

178   *The Antihero's Wife*

her – one could nevertheless possibly defend Patty by appeal to utilitarian principles. She is unscrupulous, literally prepared to sacrifice lives to win a case, but winning that case will always stop some truly corrupted and cynical criminals, who are effectively killing many more or destroying thousands of people's lives. In effect, Patty is willing to sacrifice a few innocent lives in order to save more. In the season finale of season 4, for example, Patty tries to convince Ellen to sacrifice her friend Chris Sanchez's life (but it was Ellen who initially put Chris in danger by pressuring him to witness, building up under the suspenseful plotline related to Ellen becoming like Patty). In the season finale, however, Ellen retracts, and Patty argues that "if you back down now, you will never have the power to win the cases you want to win. Erickson [CEO of High Star] is not a man to negotiate with – he is just a different kind of terrorist."[36] Ellen, however, now wants to save her friend's life, making her appear as more intuitively moral after all. One could, however, argue that Patty is right: in order to win over people who are willing to sacrifice lives, one cannot balk. However, to see Patty as morally right is demanding and controversial. Most people will probably see the sacrifices she is willing to make as unacceptable.

Furthermore, as an antihero who could be said to be morally preferable according to utilitarian principles, Patty is untypical. She never claims she does it for her family, and she is not loyal to those in her own group (indeed, at the end of the series she hardly belongs to any group at all – she has employees, that is all). However, again adding to our sympathy toward her, Patty does bond with Ellen. She claims that she simply needs Ellen for the various cases she is working on, but one can argue that increasingly Patty actually cares about Ellen. Patty is tortured by nightmares, suggesting that this one relation is beyond instrumental value for Patty. She actually truly wishes for Ellen's friendship and gratitude. By believing that this relation is merely valuable instrumentally to her, Patty seems to be deceiving herself. In the final season, Patty shows Ellen affection in the one way she is truly capable of – by trying to teach her all the tricks of the trade in order to groom Ellen into becoming a brilliant lawyer like her. In this season Patty takes on a case that is in many ways below her dignity, as the hacker McClaren is not like her usually vile opponents. She takes on the case in order to meet Ellen in court. Despite herself, Patty cares.

Nevertheless, ultimately Ellen chooses to start her own family – the series leaves Ellen happily walking down a street with her daughter after having quit law altogether.[37] Patty, however, is on her way to the office. The struggle between family and work is pessimistically portrayed as unsolvable – Ellen chooses one and Patty the other. The narrative suggests that Patty is disappointed about the loss of trust between her and Ellen. Her friendship with Ellen and the admiration of this young protégé has grown important to her: through subjective narration, we see her envision a reunion with Ellen.[38] In truth, Patty is all alone as she asks her driver to take her to the office. A long take lingers on Patty sitting in her car. Patty pays a high price for her transgressions. And the separation between the antihero's transgressions and family life is maintained. Those who would want to enjoy the antihero's transgressions further should follow Patty to the office. Staying with Ellen and her new life as a mother is an entirely different genre and a different story – surely offering many pleasures, but not primarily the transgressive ones typical for the antihero series. *Damages* gave us one of the most fascinatingly bad female characters in American antihero series. So I say, with Patty: take me to the office.

Notes

1. A good illustration of the male-centredness in the critical reception of these TV series is given by the title of the book *Difficult Men* (Martin 2013), a popularized account celebrating the success of the antihero series. The difficult men referred to in the title are primarily the main characters as antiheroes. The title also plays up to popular presentation of these series' difficult – and genial – male creators (e.g., David Chase of *The Sopranos*, David Simon of *The Wire*, David Milch of *Deadwood* and Vince Gilligan of *Breaking Bad*).
2. Lotz points out that it is actually rare in American television series that the main female characters are not working women – this is another trait marking the male-centered serials off from other American television series (Lotz 2014: 72). This also stands in stark contrast to the many female-centered dramas on American broadcast channels in the 1990s, depicting working women, e.g., *Ally McBeal* (Fox, 1997–2002) and *Judging Amy* (CBS, 1999–2005). See Lotz (2014: 61; 2006).
3. For a related point, namely that "*The Sopranos* implicitly critiques the 'televisionization' of the gangster genre", see (Creeber 2002: 125).
4. See e.g., the interview with Mittell in Ford (2010) and Mittell (2015: 233ff) for further discussion, and also Dunleavy (2009: 97ff).
5. She argues against understanding melodrama as a specific genre – known as Hollywood family melodrama, and tied closely to studies of "the woman's film" (for classic texts, see e.g., Elsaesser 1987; Mulvey 1987; Schatz 1981). More recently, Williams has also investigated how melodrama is used in *The Wire* (Williams 2014). I will not address this latter discussion here; arguably, the notion of melodrama used in this book is very wide, and I will stick to the narrower use of the notion found in earlier analysis. On how Quality drama was differentiated from prime time melodrama, see also Feuer (2005). For a general discussion of melodrama and what Mittell labels as complex TV, see Mittell's chapter on serial melodrama (Mittell 2015: 233ff). I must point out that I do not argue that there are no melodramatic features in antihero series – that would be wrong – but only that most antihero series break with the traditional portrayal of the home and family as a place of innocence in the melodramatic mode.
6. For a related analysis of Walter White's character arc, from almost a no-man in the pilot to representing hegemonic masculinity as *Breaking Bad* progresses, see also Weckerle (2014). She emphasises how being the provider is essential to hegemonic masculinity.
7. *Breaking Bad*, "Grey Matter", season 1, episode 5.

180 *The Antihero's Wife*

8. For a classical, straight-forward example of this trope in the antihero series, see *Ray Donovan*, "The Golem", season 1, episode 5; with a slight twist also in *Mad Men*, "The Gypsy and the Hobo", season 3, episode 11; and in *Breaking Bad*, it is posed by Walter and not by Skyler when he asks her "Who are you talking to right now?" in "Cornered", season 4, episode 6. On the prevalence of deception in these series, see also Smith (2014).

9. For a discussion of conflicted, but positive relations to the women in *The Sopranos* and Carmela in particular, see e.g., Akass and McCabe (2002).

10. *Breaking Bad*, "Bullet Points", season 4, episode 4.

11. Resenting the freeloader is also seen as one of the small intuitive pieces in our emotional moral machinery, securing co-operation in the group, as Joshua Green argues (see e.g., on how we are *pro-social punishers*, willing to punish freeloaders although no wrong has been done to us personally in Greene 2013: 57–8).

12. *Breaking Bad*, "Cornered", season 4, episode 6.

13. This mirrors the differentiation between F-emotions (fictional emotions) and A-emotions (artefact emotions) introduced in chapter 4 (cf. Tan1996: 81ff).

14. *Breaking Bad*, "Ozymandias", season 5, episode 14.

15. As mentioned in chapter 1, I have had the most to say about embodied empathy in this book, but his is a good example of imaginative empathy at work. See Vaage (2010).

16. On aspect change, an expression taken from Wittgenstein, see e.g., Addis (2010).

17. One of the disagreements between Greene and Haidt also becomes evident here. Haidt holds that we very seldom adjust our moral judgments due to moral reasoning, while Greene holds that we do so more often that Haidt wants to admit. While Haidt emphasizes how one-third of the hypnotically influenced respondents condemned Dan (cf. Wheatley and Haidt 2005), Paxton and Greene emphasize how the majority in fact did not: the latter group were able to adjust their intuitively felt moral judgments of Dan because it did not make sense to them rationally, they argue (Paxton and Greene 2010: 521).

18. For a sketch mocking this very response to *Breaking Bad*, see http://www.funnyordie.com/videos/c7f6feca3f/the-internet-s-problem-with-tv-wives.

19. For a discussion of the political argument and realism in *The Wire*, see e.g., Kinder (2008); Lavik (2012); McMillan (2009); Mittell (2009); Nannicelli (2009); Vaage (2013) and Williams (2011; 2014).

20. A promising approach is found in Joanne Lacey's study of British male spectators of *The Sopranos*, where she found that both young (18–19-year olds) and middle-aged male spectators enjoyed the fantasy of being a 'made guy' (Lacey 2002). These interviewees also clearly label *The Sopranos* as Quality, and to some degree tie this to its realism (in addition to other factors such as the series being well-written and well-crafted, etc.). However, there is not enough material here in order to conclude about these two groups' potential uptake of and reflection about what I label reality checks.

21. *The Sopranos*, "Full Leather Jacket", season 2, episode 8.

22. *Boardwalk Empire*, "Bone for Tuna", season 3, episode 3.

23. For an analysis of Carmela's attraction to Furio, see Akass and McCabe (2006: 48ff).

24. *Sons of Anarchy*, "AK-51", season 1, episode 6.

25. Interestingly, in the British original mini-series with the same title, she is a less central character, but more ruthless and wicked: she is the one who puts her husband up to some of his most sinister plans. See *House of Cards* (BBC, 1990).

The Antihero's Wife   181

26. *Banshee*, "Always the Cowboy", season 1, episode 9. However, in season 3 there is also a more traditional example of the male antihero's girlfriend asking Lucas: "Who the hell are you?", *Banshee*, "A fixer of sorts", season 3, episode 3.
27. *Banshee*, "Ways to Bury a Man", season 2, episode 7.
28. *Weeds*, "The Dark Time", season 3, episode 12. There is also an aesthetically pleasing cooking sequence to be found in *Weeds*, "MILF Money", season 2, episode 8 – pleasing because it is rare to see a woman in such a sequence.
29. *Nurse Jackie*, "… Deaf Blind Tumor Pee-Test", season 3, episode 12.
30. *Weeds*, "It's Time (Part 2)", season 8, episode 13.
31. Adding to my suggestion about the male-centeredness of Quality TV and status, and in spite of the critical praise for Glenn Close's performance as Patty Hewes, this series was cancelled by FX before it came to its end. *Damages* was taken up by the DirecTV channel Audience Network where it aired for the two final seasons.
32. As is the description of Patty by Frobisher, one of her targets, as an ideal villain in a wonderful meta-perspective on this series, as he is adapting his autobiography to film; see *Damages*, "All That Crap About Your Family", season 3, episode 11. With this plotline this series satirizes its own portrayal of the fascinating villain/antihero.
33. *Damages*, "Get Me A Lawyer", season 1, episode 1.
34. *Damages*, "Flight's at 11:08", season 3, episode 3.
35. The smile she gives at the end of the deposition in *Damages*, "Your Secrets Are Safe", season 3, episode 1 is one example.
36. *Damages,* "Failure Is Lonely", season 4, episode 10.
37. An interesting comparison to tease out the importance given to the antihero's family in individual series would perhaps be to analyze their ending – compare the family reunion in the series finales of *The Sopranos* and *Weeds*, for example, to the way *Breaking Bad* leaves Skyler and Walter, respectively.
38. *Damages*, "But You Don't Do That Anymore", season 5, episode 10.

7 Conclusion

Through the cycle of antihero series on American television the spectator has learned to expect certain things from these stories. Developing from the pivotal *The Sopranos*, through its various manifestations in series such as *Breaking Bad*, *Dexter* and *Sons of Anarchy*, the antihero series has established a set of narrative conventions. I will end this book by briefly exploring the TV series *Fargo* in order to sum up some of the antihero series conventions and also the pleasures these series offer the spectator.

Fargo is loosely based on the film with the same title (Joel and Ethan Cohen, 1996), and the first season tells the story of Lester Nygaard, a middle-aged man in the Midwest, who is henpecked by his wife. She is the dominant presence in their home and openly mocks Lester for not being man enough: she compares him unfavourably to his brother, who is rich and successful. Lester struggles in his job as an insurance salesman. The brute Sam Hess, who bullied Lester throughout high school, still bullies him. Lester is disempowered and humiliated.

However, while waiting at the local hospital for a doctor to tend to the broken nose with which an encounter with Sam Hess has left him, Lester makes an odd acquaintance.[1] Lorne Malvo strikes up a conversation, and when Lester confides in him, Lorne offers to kill Sam, plain and simple. And he does kill him, too. Lorne Malvo is a mysterious character in this story, who seems to stick around to wreak havoc and settle the score with whoever he sees as deserving such a fate in this small town. In particular, he engages in Lester's predicament. One day Lester's shortcomings as a man are further manifested in a broken washing machine in the basement – a machine Lester tries to repair, but fails. His wife will not allow this failure to pass unnoticed. Down there in the basement, with a broken washing machine and a spiteful wife, Lester has had it, and he kills her. And it is Lorne he calls in despair.

After this, Lester's life takes an upturn. Slowly he becomes a new man; toughened up and confident. He stands up to Sam Hess' widow and their two obnoxious sons, injuring them in order to gain respect. Upon seeing this his female co-worker immediately declares her love for him: "you're amazing!" Turning violent and powerful makes him more attractive to her.[2] And it is Lorne Malvo that gets this transformation going. Lester is thus the antihero, mirroring especially Walter White's transformation. When turning morally transgressive he becomes more attractive, offering those by now well-known

Conclusion   183

pleasures of power and revenge. Seeing him humiliated by his wife and by Hess is one of the primary pleas for excuses that make the spectator enjoy this transformation even more – although this particular story is untypical in that Lester actually kills his wife. As we have seen, the typical set-up is that the antihero's home is festering with discontent throughout the series. *Fargo* also deviates from the usual set-up in that the antihero typically claims that he does it all to provide and care for his family. Lester never claims such a thing – he kills his wife and frames his own brother as the killer. The selfishness of the American antihero takes centre stage in *Fargo* from the very beginning.

Furthermore, in this story the Janus-faced creature of the antihero is physically split in two – his bad, villainous sides incarnated in Malvo, and the human, everyday man represented by Lester. And even as Lester grows morally worse, he cannot compete with the flamboyant grandeur of the proper villain as he is found in Malvo, who like a devil seemingly enjoys toying with people and getting them to do bad things. In the first episode, he explains to Lester that he is more of a man for having (involuntarily) asked for the bully Sam to be killed:

> Your problem is you have spent your whole life thinking there are rules. There are not. We used to be gorillas. (...)
> It is a red tide, Lester. This life of ours. The shit they make us eat - day after day, the boss, the wife, *et cetera*. Wearing us down. If you do not stand up to it, let them know you are still an ape, deep down where it counts, you are just going to get washed away.

Once we were gorillas – you have to let them know that deep down you are still an ape. Living in a world with demanding moralities and complex legal systems, the antihero's villainous side tempts us with the allures of some intuitive responses that we might not even think we have in us. Seeking power is good; meting out punishment is good. Usually, the antihero also initially appears morally preferable simply because he cares about his own flock. Whereas the aesthetic strategies pushing these buttons may be worthy of admiration because they work so remarkably well, there is no reason to allow ourselves to be truly swayed by the antihero's own justifications. Rather, the morality he adheres to allows him to do horrible things. Through Lorne's character in *Fargo* these traits of our human psychology are depicted as anachronistic, like something re-appearing from another time – a mythical past perhaps. ("Maps used to say there would be dragons here. Now they do not. But that does not mean the dragons are not there.") Or Lorne is or has an animalistic residue that ever so easily resurfaces in his modern, human appearance. Toward the end of the series Lorne Malvo is severely hurt, watching a wolf in the snow outside of a cabin in which he is hiding. A policeman sneaks up on him and shoots him. Lorne Malvo tries to leap up, but is unable to. Wordlessly he dies with a bloody sneer, like an animal – as were he not human at all but more akin to the wolf outside. We sometimes see Tony Soprano's animal nature, too.

Conclusion

Figure 7.1 Lorne Malvo dies as spectacularly as this villainous character lived – with a bloody sneer as if he were a wolf like the one he was watching outside his window (*Fargo*, FX).

Furthermore, there is almost something supernatural about Lorne Malvo's powers: he seems to know exactly when to enter a room and when to make his escape without being seen, as if he senses what others are up to. Sometimes he may even vanish into thin air when threats are approaching. He is dead calm, always self-confident and fully in control. He wins every encounter, and knows he will. He is aesthetically pleasing and puzzling – putting up quite a display with his odd haircut and spectacular lines: the devil does, after all, always get the best tunes. Lorne Malvo magnificently represents why immorality is attractive on-screen: he gets the story in *Fargo* going, and he keeps making it both suspenseful and aesthetically pleasing.

As the immoral side of the antihero takes control in this antihero story Lester begins his trajectory – typically enjoyable up to a turning point when there is too much to remind the spectator of the consequences of his actions. Although the antihero's immorality offers some instant gratification, the antihero ultimately turns corrupted and selfish, and as the spectator is intended to increasingly question her sympathy for him and her enjoyment of the story about him, he is heading for what is usually some form of punishment in the series finale. In *Fargo*, too, both Lorne and Lester die. As already mentioned, Lorne dies spectacularly and enigmatically. As the everyday man that Lester really is, his death is less grand: running from the police over thin ice on a lake, the ice cracks and he falls through it. And then he is gone. Morality is restored in the small town of Bemidji.

We have seemingly reached a level of intertextual awareness that allows a series such as *Fargo* to appear a knowingly, playful homage to the antihero series. When Lester becomes salesman of the year and another character

Conclusion 185

asks him "Drugs?" this arguably makes *Breaking Bad* or *Weeds* spring to mind: what other association would make this the natural follow-up question? As shown in the previous chapter, other late antihero series, such as *Ray Donovan,* can also be seen as deliberately playing with expectations and conventions toward antihero series, such as the conventions tied to the portrayal of the nagging wife.

In *The Good Wife*, too, there are some wonderful asides to the dark material of current American television series: when Alicia Florrick is watching TV as relaxation (i.e., not watching TV news to catch up with some political scandal as part of her job), the series she watches is grim – supposedly a satire of *Low Winter Sun* (AMC, 2013), a story with the tagline "Good Man. Cop. Killer".[3] In one of these episodes Alicia witnesses the main character uttering the following over a dead corpse (which is attired in antlers, as it seems to be the trend among serial killers on American television nowadays to stage their victims thus):

> People just think there are black hats and white hats, but there are black hats with white linings. And white hats with black linings. And there are hats that change back and forth between white and black. And there are striped hats. Evil rests in the souls of all men.

This appears to be a satirical take on the moral complexity of the antihero – ridiculing the every finer lines between white and black on American Quality television. Depressed after the loss of a beloved friend, Alicia watches apathetically from her bed – but the images on screen are hardly uplifting.

By way of conclusion, I would like to point out that although it might be tempting to criticise these stories for appealing to our lower selves, so to say, the entertainment industry can also be seen as first and foremost producing content to satisfy our moral intuitive preferences (cf. Tamborini 2013). Through trial and error the entertainment industry will have figured out that when engaging with fiction, gut responses will tell us what is acceptable and enjoyable – and what is not. Criticising the antihero series would perhaps be a case of killing the messenger: these series remind us what our moral intuitions and emotions are, and also how easily these are manipulated narratively and stylistically. Instead of fearing that these stories will make us morally worse, can they perhaps help us face some facts about the way we work morally? As I have argued, whereas antihero series rely on the spectator navigating through these fictional worlds by use of moral intuitions and emotions – a response I have labelled fictional relief – an intended effect is also to take a step back at regular intervals and reflect rationally on what antihero series make us enjoy. Real-life morality demands so much more of us than does enjoyment of fiction, and through learning more about how easily our moral intuitions and emotions can be manipulated, the antihero series can be a learning experience, as Noël Carroll also argues. However, this suggestion trusts that the spectator will be both willing and able to

186 *Conclusion*

reflect on her engagement with these stories. Not all spectators are, as we have seen in the discussion of the bad fan.

Be that as it may, whether or not the antihero series is a learning experience for individual spectators, it has been a learning experience for me – an excellent case study for the theorist in order to tease out the moral psychology of fiction. Or so I have argued. A final conceivable counterargument to my hypothesis in this book is one of scope: is my theory about what characterizes our engagement with fiction restricted to my case study – the antihero series? Indeed, other genres of fiction can elicit other kinds of responses, such as social realism evoking very little fictional relief at all, but being more of a continual reality check; and other kinds of fiction being deliberately made to serve as a sort of moral puzzle that would primarily invite rational moral reflection, for example.[4] There are genre differences. Nevertheless, I hold that this study reveals much more about what is typical for our engagement with fiction overall than competing theories. We do typically rely on intuitions and emotions when engaging with fiction. In the case of the antihero series these intuitive responses stand in stark contrast to the principles we hold as morally right on reflection. If the contrast were not as great, the nature of our moral judgment would merely be less obvious.

Notes

1. *Fargo*, "The crocodile's dilemma", season 1, episode 1.
2. *Fargo*, "The heap", season 1, episode 8.
3. See Nussbaum (2014b), who makes the link between the series Alicia watches and *Low Winter Sun*. The sequence is found in *The Good Wife*, "A material world", season 5, episode 17.
4. See also Pizarro and Bloom (2003), who point out that the way the narratives in empirical explorations of morality are set up influences the activation of moral intuition vs. deliberate moral reasoning, respectively. This might be a starting point in order to explore genre differences.

References

Addis, M. (2010). Seeing As. In: Goldstein, E. B. (ed.). *Encyclopedia of Perception. Volume 2*. Thousand Oaks: Sage, pp. 877–878.

Akass, K., and McCabe, J. (2002). Beyond the Bada Bing: Negotiating Female Narrative Authority in *The Sopranos*. In: Lavery, D. (ed.), *This Thing of Ours: Investigating The Sopranos*. New York: Columbia University Press, pp. 146–161.

Akass, K., and McCabe, J. (2006). What Has Carmela Ever Done for Feminism? Carmela Soprano and the Post-Feminist Dilemma. In: Lavery, D. (ed.). *Reading The Sopranos. Hit TV From HBO*. London: I. B. Tauris, pp. 39–55.

Akass, K., and McCabe, J. (2007). Introduction: Debating Quality. In: Akass, K. and McCabe, J. (eds.). *Quality TV: Contemporary American Television and Beyond*. London: I.B. Tauris, pp. 1–11.

Allen, R. (2007). *Hitchcock's Romantic Irony*. New York: Columbia University Press.

Allen, R. and Smith, M. (1997). Introduction: Film Theory and Philosophy. In: Allen, R. and Smith, M. (eds.). *Film Theory and Philosophy*. Oxford: Clarendon Press, pp. 1–35.

Altmann, U., Bohrn, I. C., Lubrich, O., Menninghaus, W., and Jacobs, A. M. (2014). Fact vs Fiction – How Paratextual Information Shapes Our Reading Processes. *Social Cognitive and Affective Neuroscience*, 9(1), 22–29.

Alvarez, R. (2009). *The Wire. Truth Be Told*. Edinburgh: Canongate.

Anderson, C. (2008). Overview: Producing an Aristocracy of Culture in American Television. In: Edgerton, G. R. and Jones, J. P. (eds). *The Essential HBO Reader*. Lexington: The University Press of Kentucky, pp. 23–41.

Anderson, C., and Galinsky, A. D. (2006). Power, Optimism, and Risk-Taking. *European Journal of Social Psychology*, 36(4), 511–536.

Appiah, K. A. (2008). *Experiments in Ethics*. Cambridge, Mass.: Harvard University Press.

Austin, J.L. (1956–7): A Plea for Excuses: The Presidential Address. *Proceedings of the Aristotelian Society*, New Series, 57, 1–30.

Baldanzi, J. (2006). Bloodlust for the Common Man: *The Sopranos* Confronts Its Volatile American Audience. In: Lavery, D. (ed.). *Reading The Sopranos. Hit TV From HBO*. London: I. B. Tauris, pp. 79–89.

Bandura, A. (2002). Selective Moral Disengagement in the Exercise of Moral Agency. *Journal of Moral Education*, 3(2), 101–119.

Baron, A. S., and Banaji, M. R. (2006). The Development of Implicit Attitudes: Evidence of Race Evaluations From Ages 6 and 10 and Adulthood. *Psychological Science*, 17(1), 53–58.

Barratt, D. (2006). Tracing the Routes to Empathy: Association, Simulation, or Appraisal? *Film Studies: An International Review*, 8(1), 39–52.

188 References

Baudry, J.-L. (1974–5). Ideological Effects of the Basic Cinematographic Apparatus. *Film Quarterly*, 28(2), 39–47.

Bekoff, M., and Pierce, J. (2009). *Wild Justice. The Moral Lives of Animals.* Chicago: The University of Chicago Press.

Bennett, D. (2010).This Will Be On the Midterm. You Feel Me? Why So Many Colleges Are Teaching *The Wire. Slate* [online] 24. March. Available at: http://www.slate.com/id/2245788/ [Accessed 3. January 2015].

Bentham, J. ([1781] 1996). *An Introduction to the Principles of Morals and Legislation.* Oxford: Clarendon Press.

Berridge, S. (2013). Teen Heroine TV: Narrative Complexity and Sexual Violence in Female-Fronted Teen Drama Series. *New Review of Film and Television Studies*, 11(4), 477–496.

Bieneck, S., and Krahé, B. (2011). Blaming The Victim And Exonerating The Perpetrator In Cases Of Rape And Robbery: Is There A Double Standard?. *Journal of Interpersonal Violence*, 26(9), 1785–1797.

Blanchet, R., and Vaage, M. B. (2012). Don, Peggy and Other Fictional Friends? Engaging With Characters in Television Series, *Projections*, 6(2), 18–41.

Bloom, P. (2010). How Do Morals Change? *Nature*, 464, 490–490.

Booth, A.R. and Rowbottom, D. P. (eds.) (2014). *Intuitions.* Oxford: Oxford University Press.

Bordwell, D. (1979). The Art Cinema as a Mode of Film Practice. *Film Criticism* 4(1), 57–61.

Bordwell, D. (1985). *Narration in the Fiction Film.* London: Routledge.

Bordwell, D. (1996). Contemporary Film Studies and the Vicissitudes of Grand Theory. In: Bordwell, D. and Carroll, N. (eds.). *Post- Theory. Reconstructing Film Studies.* Madison: The University of Wisconsin Press, pp. 3–36.

Bornstein, R. (1989). Exposure and Affect: Overview and Meta-Analysis of Research, 1968–1987. *Psychological Bulletin*, 106(2), 265–289.

Bourgois, P. (2003). *In Search of Respect. Selling Crack in El Barrio.* 2nd Ed. Cambridge: Cambridge University Press.

Branigan, E. (1984). *Point of View in the Cinema. A Theory of Narration and Subjectivity in Classical Film.* Berlin: Mouton Publishers.

Branigan, E. (1992). *Narrative Comprehension and Film.* London: Routledge.

Britt, M. A. (2007). Episode 7: Blaming the Victim and Other Attribution Biases. *The Psych Files* [online], 11. March. Available at http://www.thepsychfiles.com/2007/03/episode-7-blaming-the-victim-and-other-biases/ [Accessed 1. April 2015].

Brombert, V. (1999). *In Praise of Antiheroes: Figures and Themes in Modern European Literatrue 1830–1980.* Chicago: The University of Chicago Press.

Brown, D. E. (1991). *Human Universals.* Philadelphia: Temple University Press.

Browne, N. (1975–6). The Spectator-in-the-Text: The Rhetoric of Stagecoach. *Film Quarterly*, 29(2), 26–38.

Brownmiller, S. (1975). *Against Our Will: Men, Women, and Rape.* New York: Simon and Schuster.

Bryant, J., and Miron, D. (2003). Excitation-Transfer Theory and Three-Factor Theory of Emotion. In: Bryant, J., Roskos-Ewoldsen, D., and Cantor, J. (eds.). *Communication and Emotion: Essays in Honor of Dolf Zillmann.* Mahwah, NJ: Lawrence Erlbaum, pp. 31–59.

Bryant, J., Raney, A. A., and Zillmann, D. (2002). Sports Television. In: Strauss, B., Kolb, M. and Lames, M. (eds.), *sport-goes-media.de: Zur Medialisierung des Sports.* Schorndorf: Hofmann, pp. 51–74.

References 189

Bryant, J., Thompson, S., and Finklea, B. W. (2013). *Fundamentals of Media Effects.* 2nd Ed. Long Grove: Waveland Press.

Bourke, J. (2006). *Fear. A Cultural History.* London: Virago.

Cardwell, S. (2006). Television Aesthetics. *Critical Studies in Television,* 1(1), 72–80.

Cardwell, S. (2007). Is Quality Television Any Good? In: Akass, K. and McCabe, J. (eds.). *Quality TV: Contemporary American Television and Beyond.* London: I.B. Tauris, pp. 19–34.

Cardwell, S. (2013). Television Aesthetics: Stylistic Analysis and Beyond. In: Jacobs, J. and Peacock, S. (eds.). *Television Aesthetics and Style.* London: Bloomsbury, pp. 23–44.

Cardwell, S. (2014). Television Amongst Friends: Medium, Art, Media. *Critical Studies in Television,* 9(3), 6–21.

Carli, L. L. (1999). Cognitive Reconstruction, Hindsight, And Reactions To Victims And Perpetrators. *Personality and Social Psychology Bulletin,* 25(8), 966–979.

Carroll, N. (1988). *Mystifying Movies. Fads and Fallacies in Contemporary Film Theory.* New York: Columbia University Press.

Carroll, N. (1990). *The Philosophy of Horror, or Paradoxes of the Heart.* New York: Routledge.

Carroll, N. (1996a). *Theorizing the Moving Image.* Cambridge: Cambridge University Press.

Carroll, N. (1996b). The Paradox of Suspense. In: Vorderer, P., Wulff, H. J., and Friedrichsen, M. (eds.). *Suspense: Conceptualizations, Theoretical Analyses, and Empirical Explorations.* Mahwah: Lawrence Erlbaum, pp. 71–91.

Carroll, N. (1998). *A Philosophy of Mass Art.* Oxford: Clarendon Press.

Carroll, N. (2003). *Engaging the Moving Image.* New Haven: Yale University Press.

Carroll, N. (2004). Sympathy For The Devil. In: Greene, R. and Vernezze, P. (eds.). *The Sopranos and Philosophy: I Kill Therefore I Am.* Chicago, Ill: Open Court Publishing, pp. 121–136.

Carroll, N. (2008). *The Philosophy of Motion Pictures.* Malden, MA: Blackwell.

Carroll, N. (2010). Movies, the Moral Emotions, and Sympathy. *Midwest Studies in Philosophy,* 34(1), 1–19.

Carroll, N. (2013). Rough Heroes: A Response to A.W. Eaton. *The Journal of Aesthetics and Art Criticism,* 71(4), 371–376.

Cashdan, E. (2003). Hormones and Competitive Aggression in Women. *Aggressive Behavior,* 29(2), 107–115.

Choi, J. (2005). Leaving It Up to the Imagination: POV Shots and Imagining from the Inside. *The Journal of Aesthetics and Art Criticism,* 63(1), 17–25.

Choi, J. K., and Bowles, S. (2007). The Coevolution of Parochial Altruism And War. *Science,* 318(5850), 636–640.

Cicchirillo, V., and Eastin, M. S. (2013). Effects from Violent Media, Short- and Long-Term. In: Eastin, M. S. (ed.). *Encyclopedia of Media Violence.* Thousand Oaks: Sage, pp. 127–130.

Cooke, B. (2014). Ethics and Fictive Imagining. *The Journal of Aesthetics and Art Criticism,* 72(3), 317–327.

Coplan, A. (2004). Empathic Engagement with Narrative Fictions. *The Journal of Aesthetics and Art Criticism,* 62(2), 141–152.

Coplan, A. (2006). Catching Characters' Emotions: Emotional Contagion Responses to Narrative Fiction Film. *Film Studies: An International Review,* 8(1), 26–38.

Coplan, A. (2009). Empathy and Character Engagement. In: Livingston, P. and Plantinga, C. (eds.), *The Routledge Companion to Philosophy and Film,* London: Routledge, pp. 97–110.

190 References

Coplan, A. (2011a). Understanding Empathy. In: Coplan, A. and Goldie, P. (eds.), *Empathy: Philosophical and Psychological Perspectives*. Oxford: Oxford University Press, pp. 3–18.

Coplan, A. (2011b). Will the Real Empathy Please Stand Up? A Case for a Narrow Conceptualization. *The Southern Journal of Philosophy*, 49(1), 40–65.

Creeber, G. (2002). "TV Ruined the Movies": Television, Tarantino, and the Intimate World of *The Sopranos*. In: Lavery, D. (ed.), *This Thing of Ours: Investigating The Sopranos*. New York: Columbia University Press, pp. 124–134.

Cuklanz, L. M. (2000). *Rape on Prime Time. Television, Masculinity, and Sexual Violence*. Philadelphia: University of Pennsylvania Press.

Currie, G. (1990). *The Nature of Fiction*. Cambridge: Cambridge University Press.

Currie, G. (1995). *Image and Mind: Film, Philosophy and Cognitive Science*. Cambridge: Cambridge University Press.

Currie, G. (1997). The Paradox of Caring: Fiction and the Philosophy of Mind. In: Hjort, M. and Laver, S. (eds.). *Emotion and the Art*. New York: Oxford University Press, pp. 63–77.

Currie, G. (1999). Narrative Desire. In: Plantinga, C. and Smith, G. M. (eds.). *Passionate Views. Film, Cognition, and Emotion*. Baltimore: The Johns Hopkins University Press, pp. 183–99.

Currie, G. (2004). *Arts and Minds*. Oxford: Clarendon Press.

Currie, G. (2010). *Narratives and Narrators: A Philosophy of Stories*. Oxford: Oxford University Press.

Dalakas, V., and Langenderfer, J. (2007). Consumer Satisfaction with Television Viewing: Insight for the Entertainment Industry. *Services Marketing Quarterly*, 29(1), 47–59.

Darwin, C. R. (1871). *The Descent of Man, and Selection in Relation to Sex*. London: John Murray.

De Dreu, C. K. W., et al. (2010). The Neuropeptide Oxytocin Regulates Parochial Altruism in Intergroup Conflict Among Humans. *Science*, 328(5984), 1408–1411.

De Dreu, C. K. W., Greer, L. L., Van Kleef, G. A., Shalvi, S., and Handgraaf, M. J. J. (2011). Oxytocin Promotes Human Ethnocentrism. *Proceedings of the National Academy of Sciences of the United States of America*, 108(4), 1262–1266.

De Fino, D. J. (2014). *The HBO Effect*. Bloomsbury: New York.

DePaul, M. R., and Ramsey, W. (eds.) (1998). *Rethinking Intuition: The Psychology of Intuition and Its Role in Philosophical Inquiry*. Lanham, MD: Rowman and Littlefield.

Donatelli, C., and Alward, S. (2002). "I Dread You"?: Married to the Mob in *The Godfather, Goodfellas*, and *The Sopranos*. In: Lavery, D. (ed.), *This Thing of Ours: Investigating The Sopranos*. New York: Columbia University Press, pp. 60–71.

Douglas, M. (2003 [1966]). *Purity and Danger: An Analysis of Concepts of Pollution and Taboo*. London: Routledge.

Dunleavy, T. (2009). *Television Drama: Form, Agency, Innovation*. London: Palgrave Macmillan.

Eaton, A. W. (2009). Almodóvar's Immoralism. In: Eaton, A. W. (ed.), *Talk to Her*. Abington: Routledge, pp. 11–26.

Eaton, A. W. (2012). Robust Immoralism. *The Journal of Aesthetics and Art Criticism*, 70(3), 281–292.

Eaton, A. W. (2013). Reply to Carroll: The Artistic Value of a Particular Kind of Moral Flaw. *The Journal of Aesthetics and Art Criticism*, 71(4), 376–380.

References 191

Eden, A., Oliver, M. B., Tamborini, R. Limperos, A. and Woolley, J. (2015). Perceptions of Moral Violations and Personality Traits Among Heroes and Villains. *Mass Communication and Society*, 18(2), 186–208.

Eder, J. (2006). Ways of Being Close to Characters. *Film Studies: An International Review*, 8(1), 68–80.

Eder, J. (2010). Understanding Characters. *Projections*, 4(1), 16–40.

Eder, J., Jannidis, F., and Schneider, R. (2010). *Characters in Fictional Worlds: Understanding Imaginary Beings in Literature, Film, and Other Media*. Berlin: de Gruyter.

Elliott, P. (2011). *Hitchcock and The Cinema of Sensations. Embodied Film Theory and Cinematic Reception*. London: I.B. Tauris.

Elsaesser, T. (1987). Tales of Sound and Fury: Observations on the Family Melodrama. In: Gledhill, C. (ed.), *Home is Where the Heart Is: Studies in Melodrama and Woman's Film*. London: BFI, pp. 43–69.

Fahlenbrach, K., and Flueckiger, B. (2014). Immersive Entryways Into Televisual Worlds: Affective and Aesthetic Functions of Title Sequences in Quality Series. *Projections*, 8(1), 83–104.

Fast, N. J., Sivanathan, N., Mayer, N. D., and Galinsky, A. D. (2012). Power and Overconfident Decision-Making. *Organizational Behavior and Human Decision Processes*, 117(2), 249–260.

Fehr, E., and Gächter, S. (2002). Altruistic Punishment In Humans. *Nature*, 415(6868), 137–140.

Feltham, B., and Cottingham, J. (eds.). (2010). *Partiality and Impartiality: Morality, Special Relationships, and the Wider World*. Oxford: Oxford University Press.

Ferguson, C. J., and Savage, J. (2012). Have Recent Studies Addressed Methodological Issues Raised by Five Decades of Television Violence Research? A Critical Review. *Aggression and Violent Behavior*, 17(2), 129–139.

Feuer, J. (2005). The Lack of Influence of thirtysomething. In: Hammond, M. and Mazdon, L. (eds.). *The Contemporary Television Series*. Edinburgh: Edinburgh University Press, pp. 27–36.

Flory, D. (2008). *Philosophy, Black Film, Film Noir*. University Park: The Pennsylvania State University Press.

Flory, D. (2013). Race and Imaginative Resistance in James Cameron's *Avatar*. *Projections*, 7(2), 41–63.

Flory, D. (2015). Imaginative Resistance, Racialized Disgust, and *12 Years a Slave*. *Film and Philosophy*, 19, 75–95.

Ford, S. (2010): Perspective: Scholar Jason Mittell on the Ties between Daytime and Primetime Serials (Based on an Interview by Sam Ford). In: Ford, S., De Kosnik, A. and Harrington, C. L. (eds.), *The Survival of Soap Opera: Transformations for a New Media Era*. Jackson: University Press of Mississippi, pp. 133–139.

Friend, S. (2011). Fictive Utterance and Imagining II. *Aristotelian Society Supplementary Volume*, 85(1), 163–80.

Friend, S. (2012). Fiction as a Genre. *Proceedings of the Aristotelian Society*, 112(2), 179–209.

Frijda, N. H. (1986). *The Emotions*. Cambridge, Mass.: Cambridge University Press.

Furnham, A., and Procter, E. (1989). Belief In A Just World: Review and Critique of the Individual Difference Literature. *British Journal of Social Psychology*, 28(4), 365–384.

192 References

Gallese, V., and Guerra, M. (2012). Embodying Movies: Embodied Simulation and Film Studies. *Cinema: Journal of Philosophy and the Moving Image*, 3, 183–210.

Galinsky, A. D., Gruenfeld, D. H., and Magee, J. C. (2003). From Power to Action. *Journal of Personality and Social Psychology*, 85(3), 453–466.

García, A. N. Moral Emotions, Antiheroes and the Limits of Allegiance. Unpublished manuscript.

Gaut, B. (2007). *Art, Emotion and Ethics*. Oxford: Oxford University Press.

Gendler, T. S. (2000). The Puzzle of Imaginative Resistance. *Journal of Philosophy*, 97(2), 55–81.

Gendler, T. S. (2006). Imaginative Resistance Revisited. In: Nichols, S., (ed.). *The Architecture of the Imagination: New Essays on Pretense, Possibility, and Fiction*. Oxford: Oxford University Press, pp. 149–173.

Gilovich, T., Griffin, D., and Kahneman, D. (eds.). (2002). *Heuristics and Biases: The Psychology of Intuitive Judgment*. Cambridge: Cambridge University Press.

Gjelsvik, A. (2013). What Novels Can Tell That Movies Can't Show. In: Bruhn, J., Gjelsvik, A. and Hanssen, E. F. (eds.). *Adaptation Studies: New Challenges, New Directions*. London: Bloomsbury, pp. 245–264.

Goldman, A. (2006). *Simulating Minds. The Philosophy, Psychology, and Neuroscience of Mindreading*. New York: Oxford University Press.

Grant, D. (2011). Nancy Botwin, TV's Worst Mom? *Salon* [online], 19. July. Available at: http://www.salon.com/2011/07/19/nancy_botwin_weeds/ [Accessed 27. March 2015].

Greene, J. (2013). *Moral Tribes: Emotion, Reason, and the Gap Between Us and Them*. New York: Penguin.

Greene, J. D., Sommerville, R. B., Nystrom, L. E., Darley, J. M., and Cohen, J. D. (2001). An fMRI Investigation of Emotional Engagement In Moral Judgment. *Science*, 293(5537), 2105–2108.

Greenwald, A. G., McGhee, D. E., and Schwartz, J. L. K. (1998). Measuring Individual Differences in Implicit Cognition: The Implicit Association Test. *Journal of Personality and Social Psychology*, 74(6), 1464–1480.

Gripsrud, J. (1995). *The Dynasty years: Hollywood Television and Critical Media Studies*. London: Routledge.

Grodal, T. (1997). *Moving Pictures: A New Theory of Film Genres, Feelings, and Cognition*, Oxford: Clarendon Press.

Grodal, T. (2010). High on Crime Fiction and Detection. *Projections*, 4(2), 64–85.

Gunn, A. (2013). I have a Character Issue. *New York Times* [online], 23. August. Available at: http://www.nytimes.com/2013/08/24/opinion/i-have-a-character-issue.html?_r=0 [Accessed 27. March 2015].

Hafer, C. L., and Bègue, L. (2005). Experimental Research On Just-World theory: Problems, Developments, And Future Challenges. *Psychological Bulletin*, 131(1), 128–167.

Haidt, J. (2001). The Emotional Dog and Its Rational Tail: A Social Intuitionist Approach to Moral Judgment. *Psychological Review*, 108(4), 814–834.

Haidt, J. (2012). *The Righteous Mind: Why Good People Are Divided By Politics And Religion*. London: Allen Lane.

Haidt, J., and Graham, J. (2007). When Morality Opposes Justice: Conservatives Have Moral Intuitions That Liberals May Not Recognize. *Social Justice Research*, 20(1), 98–116.

Haidt, J., and Graham, J. (2009). Planet of the Durkheimians: Where Community, Authority, and Sacredness Are Foundations of Morality. In Jost, J. T., Kay, A. C.

References   193

and Thorisdottir, H. (eds.). *Social and Psychological Bases of Ideology And System Justification*. New York: Oxford, pp. 371–401.

Haidt, J., and Joseph, C. (2004). Intuitive Ethics: How Innately Prepared Intuitions Generate Culturally Variable Virtues. *Daedalus*, 133(4), 55–66.

Haidt, J., Koller, S. H., and Dias, M. G. (1993). Affect, Culture, and Morality, Or Is It Wrong To Eat Your Dog? *Journal of Personality and Social Psychology*, 65(4), 613–628.

Haidt, J., and Kesebir, S. (2010). Morality. In: Fiske, S. T., Gilbert, D. T. and G. Lindzey, G. (eds.). *Handbook of Social Psychology, Volume 2, 5th Edition*. Hoboken, NJ: Wiley, pp. 797–832.

Hartmann, T. (2013). Moral Disengagement During Exposure to Media Violence: Would It Feel Right to Shoot an Innocent Civilian in a Video Game?. In: Tamborini, R. (ed.). *Media and the Moral Mind*. New York: Routledge, pp. 109–131.

Hassler-Forest, D. (2014). *The Walking Dead*: Quality Television, Transmedia Serialization and Zombies. In: Allen, R. and van den Berg, T. (eds.). *Serialization in Popular Culture*. New York: Routledge, pp. 91–105.

Hauser, M., Cushman, F., Young, L., Kang-Xing Jin, R., and Mikhail, J. (2007). A Dissociation Between Moral Judgments and Justifications. *Mind and Language*, 22(1), 1–21.

Hazlett, A. (2009). How to Defend Response Moralism. *British Journal of Aesthetics*, 49(3), 241–55.

Helm, B. (2013). Friendship. In: *The Stanford Encyclopedia of Philosophy* (Fall 2013 Edition), [online] Edward N. Zalta (ed.). Available at: http://plato.stanford.edu/archives/fall2013/entries/friendship/ [Accessed 20. April 2015].

Henrich, J., Heine, S. J., and Norenzayan, A. (2010). The Weirdest People In The World?. *Behavioral and Brain Sciences*, 33(2–3), 61–83.

Hjort, M., and Laver, S. (eds.). (1997). *Emotion and the Arts*. New York: Oxford University Press.

Horeck, T. (2004). *Public Rape. Representing Violation in Fiction and Film*. London: Routledge.

Howard, D. (2006). Tasting Brylcreem: Law, Disorder and the FBI. In: Lavery, D. (ed.). *Reading the Sopranos: Hit TV from HBO*. London: I.B. Tauris, pp. 163–78.

Hume, D. (1987). Of the Standard of Taste. In: Miller, E. F. (ed.). Essays Moral, Political, and Literary. Indianapolis: Liberty Classics, pp. 226–250.

Inesi, M. E. (2010). Power and Loss Aversion. *Organizational Behavior and Human Decision Processes*, 112(1), 58–69.

Iseminger, G. (1981). Aesthetic Appreciation. *The Journal of Aesthetics and Art Criticism*, 39(4), 389–397.

Iseminger, G. (2004). *The Aesthetic Function of Art*. Ithaca: Cornell University Press.

Janoff-Bulman, R., Timko, C., and Carli, L. L. (1985). Cognitive Biases In Blaming The Victim. *Journal of Experimental Social Psychology*, 21(2), 161–177.

Johnson, M., and Nado, J. (2014). Moderate Intuitionism: A Metasemantic Account. In: Booth, A.R. and Rowbottom, D. P. (eds.). *Intuitions*. Oxford: Oxford University Press, pp. 68–90.

Johnson, M. L. (2007). Gangster Feminism: The Feminist Cultural Work of HBO's 'The Sopranos'. *Feminist Studies*, 33(2), 269–296.

Jones, W. E. (2011). Transgressive Comedy and Partiality: Making Sense of Our Amusement at *His Girl Friday*. In: Jones, W. E. and Vice, S. (eds.). *Ethics at the Cinema*. Oxford: Oxford University Press, pp. 91–113.

194 References

Kahneman, D. (2011). *Thinking, Fast and Slow*. London: Allen Lane.

Keltner, D., Gruenfeld, D. H., and Anderson, C. (2003). Power, Approach, and Inhibition. *Psychological review*, 110(2), 265–284.

Kieran, M. (2002). On Obscenity: The Thrill and Repulsion of the Morally Prohibited. *Philosophy and Phenomenological Research*, 64(1), 31–55.

Kinder, M. (2008). Re-Wiring Baltimore: The Emotive Power of Systemics, Seriality, and The City. *Film Quarterly*, 62(2), 50–57.

Kinzler, K. D., Dupoux, E., and Spelke, E. S. (2007). The Native Language of Social Cognition. *Proceedings of the National Academy of Sciences of the United States of America*, 104(30), 12577–12580.

Knobloch-Westerwick, S., and Keplinger, C. (2007). Thrilling News: —Factors Generating Suspense During News Exposure. *Media Psychology*, 9(1), 193–210.

Kohlberg, L. (1968). The Child as a Moral Philosopher. *Psychology Today*, 2(4), 25–30.

Kohlberg, L. (1969). *Stage and Sequence: The Cognitive-Developmental Approach to Socialization*. In: Goslin, D. A. (ed.). *Handbook of Socialization Theory and Research*. Chicago: Rand McNally, pp. 347–380.

Krakowiak, K. M., and Tsay, M. (2011). The Role Of Moral Disengagement in the Enjoyment of Real and Fictional Characters *International Journal of Arts and Technology*, 4(1), 90–101.

Lacey, J. (2002). One For the Boys? *The Sopranos* and Its Male, British Audience. In: Lavery, D. (ed.), *This Thing of Ours: Investigating The Sopranos*. New York: Columbia University Press, pp. 95–108.

Lamarque, P., and Olsen, S. H. (1994). *Truth, Fiction, and Literature. A Philosophical Perspective*. Oxford: Clarendon Press.

Lavik, E. (2012). Style in *The Wire*. [online], 30. March. Available at: https://vimeo.com/39768998 [Accessed 27. March 2015].

Lerner, M. J., and Goldberg, J. H. (1999). When Do Decent People Blame Victims?: The Differing Effects of the Explicit/Rational and Implicit/Experiential Cognitive Systems. In: Chaiken, S. and Trope, Y. (eds.). *Dual-Process Theories in Social Psychology*. New York: Guilford Press, pp. 627–640.

Lerner, M. J., and Miller, D. T. (1978). Just World Research and the Attribution Process: Looking Back and Ahead. *Psychological Bulletin*, 85(5), 1030–1051.

Lerner, M. J., and Simmons, C. H. (1966). Observer's Reaction to the "Innocent Victim": Compassion or Rejection? *Journal of Personality and Social Psychology*, 4(2), 203–210.

Levine, E. (2007). *Wallowing in Sex. The New Sexual Culture of 1970s American Television*. Durham: Duke University Press.

Livingston, P. (2005). *Art and Intention. A Philosophical Study*. Oxford: Clarendon Press.

Livingston, P. (2009). *Cinema, Philosophy, Bergman. On Film as Philosophy*. Oxford: Oxford University Press.

Livingston, P. (2013). Du Bos' Paradox. *The British Journal of Aesthetics*, 53(4), 393–406.

Loehlin, J. 1997. "Top of the World, Ma": *Richard III* and Cinematic Convention. In: Boose, L. B. and Burt, R. *Shakespeare, the movie II: Popularizing the Plays on Film, TV, and Video*. New York: Routledge, pp. 68–80.

Lotz, A. D. (2006). *Redesigning Women: Television After the Network Era*. Urbana: University of Illinois Press.

References   195

Lotz, A. D. (2014). *Cable Guys: Television and Masculinities in the 21st Century.* New York: New York University Press.

Maibom, H. L. (2014a). Introduction: (Almost) Everything You Ever Wanted To Know About Empathy. In: Maibom, H. L. (ed.). *Empathy and Morality.* New York: Oxford University Press, pp. 1–40.

Maibom, H. L. (ed.) (2014b). *Empathy and Morality.* New York: Oxford University Press.

Marlowe, F. W., et al. (2008). More 'Altruistic' Punishment in Larger Societies. *Proceedings of the Royal Society B: Biological Sciences,* 275(1634), 587–592.

Marshall, C.W., and Potter, T. (2009)."I am the American Dream": Modern Urban Tragedy and the Borders of Fiction. In: Marshall, C. W. and Potter, T. (eds.), The Wire. *Urban Decay and American Television,* New York: Continuum, pp. 1–14.

Martin, B. (2013). *Difficult Men. Behind the Scenes of a Creative Revolution: From* The Sopranos *and* The Wire *to* Mad Men *and* Breaking Bad. New York: Penguin.

Matravers, D. (2010). Why We Should Give Up On the Imagination. *Midwest Studies in Philosophy,* 34(1), 190–199.

Matravers, D. (2014). *Fiction and Narrative.* Oxford: Oxford University Press.

Mazur, A., Booth, A., and Dabbs Jr, J. M. (1992). Testosterone and Chess Competition. *Social Psychology Quarterly,* 55(1), 70–77.

McMillan, A. (2008). Dramatizing Individuation: Institutions, Assemblages, and *The Wire. Cinephile,* 4(1), 42–50.

McMillan, A. (2009). Heroism, Institutions, and the Police Procedural. In: Potter, T. and Marshall, C.W. (eds.). *The Wire. Urban Decay and American Television.* New York: Continuum, pp. 50–63.

Mikhail, J. (2011). *Elements of Moral Cognition: Rawls' Linguistic Analogy and the Cognitive Science of Moral and Legal Judgment.* Cambridge: Cambridge University Press.

Mill, J. S. (1865). *On Liberty.* London: Longmans, Green, and Co.

Milligan, B. (2012). Traverse City National Writers Series: Vince Gilligan (Breaking Bad). *MyNorth* [online], 3. February. Available at: http://www.mynorth.com/My-North/February-2012/Traverse-City-National-Writers-Series-Vince-Gilligan-Breaking-Bad/ [Accessed 23. April 2015].

Mittell, Jason (2009). All in the Game: *The Wire,* Serial Storytelling and Procedural Logic. In: Harrigan, P. and Wardrip-Fruin, N. (eds.). *Third Person: Authoring and Exploring Vast Narratives.* Cambridge, Mass.: MIT Press, pp. 429–438.

Mittell, J. (2010). Previously On: Prime Time Serials and the Mechanics of Memory. In: Grishakova, M., and Ryan, M.-L. (eds). *Intermediality and Storytelling.* Berlin: De Gruyter, pp. 78–98.

Mittell, J. (2012). Skyler's story. *Just TV* [online], 7. August. Available at https://justtv.wordpress.com/2012/08/07/skylers-story/ [Accessed 27. March 2015].

Mittell, J. (2015). *Complex TV: The Poetics of Contemporary Television Storytelling.* New York: New York University Press.

Mulvey, L. (1987). Notes on Sirk and Melodrama. In: Gledhill, C. (ed.). *Home is Where the Heart Is: Studies in Melodrama and the Woman's Film.* London: BFI, pp. 75–79.

Monin, B., Pizarro, D. A., and Beer, J. S. (2007). Deciding Versus Reacting: Conceptions of Moral Judgment and the Reason-Affect Debate. *Review of General Psychology,* 11(2), 99–111.

196 References

Moreland, R. L., and Beach, S. R. (1992). Exposure Effects in the Classroom: The Development of Affinity among Students. *Journal of Experimental Social Psychology,* 28(3), 255–276.

Morton, A. (2011). Empathy for the Devil. In: In: Coplan, A., and Goldie, P. (eds.), *Empathy: Philosophical and Psychological Perspectives.* Oxford: Oxford University Press, pp. 318–330.

Nannicelli, T. (2009). It's All Connected: Televisual Narrative Complexity. In: Marshall, C. W. and Potter, T. (eds.), The Wire. *Urban Decay and American Television,* New York: Continuum, pp. 190–202.

Nannicelli, T. (2012). Ontology, Intentionality and Television Aesthetics. *Screen,* 53(2), 164–179.

Nannicelli, T. (2014). Cognitive Film Theory. In: Gabbard, K. (ed.), *Oxford Bibliographies: Cinema and Media Studies.* Oxford, United Kingdom: Oxford University Press, pp. 1–2.

Nannicelli, T. *Appreciating the Art of Television: A Philosophical Perspective,* forthcoming.

Nannicelli, T., and Taberham, P. (2014). Introduction: Contemporary Cognitive Media Theory. In: Nannicelli, T. and Taberham, P. (eds.), *Cognitive media theory.* New York: Routledge, pp. 1–23.

Nelson, R. (2007). *State of Play: Contemporary "High-End" TV Drama.* Manchester: Manchester University Press.

Newman, M. Z., and Levine, E. (2012). *Legitimating Television: Media Convergence and Cultural Studies.* New York: Routledge.

Nochimson, M. P. (2003). Tony's Options: *The Sopranos* and the Televisuality of the Gangster Genre. *Senses of Cinema,* 29 [online]. Available at: http://sensesofcinema.com/2003/feature-articles/sopranos_televisuality/ [Accessed 5. January 2015].

Nussbaum, E. (2014a). The Great Divide: Norman Lear, Archie Bunker, and the Rise of the Bad Fan. *The New Yorker,* [online] 7. April. Available at: http://www.newyorker.com/magazine/2014/04/07/the-great-divide-3 [Accessed 10. January 2015].

Nussbaum, E. (2014b). Shredding Her Skin. "The Good Wife"'s thrilling transformation. *The New Yorker* [online] 13. October. Available at: http://www.newyorker.com/magazine/2014/10/13/shedding-skin [Accessed 15. April 2015].

Oliver, M. B., and Bartsch, A. (2010). Appreciation as Audience Response: Exploring Entertainment Gratifications Beyond Hedonism. *Human Communication Research,* 36(1), 53–81.

O'Neill, P., and Petrinovich, L. (1998). A Preliminary Cross-Cultural Study of Moral Intuitions. *Evolution and Human Behavior,* 19(6), 349–367.

Paskin, W. (2012). "Breaking Bad's" Anna Gunn: Skyler might kill Walt. *Salon* [online], 26. August. Available at: http://www.salon.com/2012/08/26/breaking_bads_anna_gunn_skyler_might_kill_walt/ [Accessed 27. March 2015].

Paxton, J. M., and Greene, J. D. (2010). Moral Reasoning: Hints and Allegations. *Topics in Cognitive Science,* 2(3), 511–527.

Petrinovich, L., O'Neill, P., and Jorgensen, M. (1993). An Empirical Study of Moral Intuitions: Toward an Evolutionary Ethics. *Journal of Personality and Social Psychology,* 64(3), 467–478.

Piaget, J. (1932). *The Moral Development of the Child.* London: Kegan Paul.

Pinker, S. (2011). *The Better Angels of Our Nature. The Decline of Violence in History and Its Causes.* London: Allen Lane.

Pizarro, D. A., and Bloom, P. (2003). The Intelligence of the Moral Intuitions: Comment on Haidt (2001). *Psychological Review*, 110(1), 193–196.

Plantinga, C. (1987). Defining Documentary: Fiction, Non-Fiction, and Projected Worlds. *Persistence of Vision*, 5, 44–54.

Plantinga, C. (1996). Moving Pictures and the Rhetoric of Nonfiction Film: Two Approaches. In: Bordwell, D. and Carroll, N. (eds.). *Post-Theory. Reconstructing Film Studies*, Madison: The University of Wisconsin Press, pp. 307–324.

Plantinga, C. (1997). *Rhetoric and Representation in Nonfiction Film*. Cambridge: Cambridge University Press.

Plantinga, C. (1999). The Scene of Empathy and the Human Face on Film. In: Plantinga, C. and Smith, G. M. (eds.). *Passionate Views. Film, Cognition, and Emotion*. Baltimore: The Johns Hopkins University Press, pp. 239–255.

Plantinga, C. (2006). Disgusted at the Movies. *Film Studies: An International Review*, 8(1), 81–92.

Plantinga, C. (2009). *Moving Viewers. American Film and The Spectator's Experience*. Berkeley: University of California Press.

Plantinga, C. (2010). "I Followed the Rules, and They All Loved You More": Moral Judgment and Attitudes toward Fictional Characters in Film. *Midwest Studies in Philosophy*, 34(1), 34–51.

Plourde, B. (2006). Eve of Destruction: Dr. Melfi as Reader of *The Sopranos*. In: Lavery, D. (ed.). *Reading the Sopranos: Hit TV from HBO*. London: I.B. Tauris, pp. 69–78.

Plutchik, R. (1994). *The Psychology and Biology Of Emotion*. New York: HarperCollins College Publishers.

Polan, D. (2009). *The Sopranos*. Durham: Duke University Press.

Polichak, J. W., and Gerrig, R. J. (2002). Get Up and Win! Participatory Responses to Narrative. In: Green, M., Strange, J. J. and Brock, T. C. (eds.). *Narrative Impact: Social and Cognitive Foundations*. Mahwah, NJ: Erlbaum, pp. 71–95.

Prentice, D. A., and Gerrig, R. J. (1999). Exploring the Boundary between Fiction and Reality. In: Chaiken, S. and Trope, Y. (eds.). *Dual-Process Theories in Social Psychology*. New York: Guilford Press, pp. 529–546.

Prinz, J. J. (2007). *The Emotional Construction of Morals*. Oxford: Oxford University Press.

Projansky, S. (2001). *Watching Rape. Film and Television in Postfeminist Culture*. New York: New York University Press.

Pruessner, J. C. et al. (2005). Self-Esteem, Locus of Control, Hippocampal Volume, and Cortisol Regulation in Young and Old Adulthood. *NeuroImage*, 28(4), 815–826.

Pust, J. (2014). Intuition. *The Stanford Encyclopedia of Philosophy* (Fall 2014 Edition) [online], Edward N. Zalta (ed.). Available at: http://plato.stanford.edu/archives/fall2014/entries/intuition/ [Accessed 22. April 2015].

Raney, A. A. (2002). Moral Judgement as a Predictor of Enjoyment of Crime Drama. *Media Psychology*, 4 (4), pp. 305–322.

Raney, A. A. (2004). Expanding Disposition Theory: Reconsidering Character Liking, Moral Evaluations, and Enjoyment. *Communication Theory*, 14(4), 348–369.

Raney, A. A. (2005). Punishing Media Criminals and Moral Judgment: The Impact on Enjoyment. *Media Psychology* 7(2), 145–163.

198 References

Raney, A. A. (2006). The Psychology of Disposition-Based Theories of Media Enjoyment. In: Bryant, J. and Vorderer, P. (eds.). *Psychology of Entertainment.* Mahway, NJ: Lawrence Erlbaum. pp. 137–150.

Raney, A. A. (2011). The Role of Morality in Emotional Reactions to and Enjoyment of Media Entertainment. *Journal of Media Psychology,* 23(1), 18–23.

Raney, A. A., and Bryant, J. (2002). Moral Judgment and Crime Drama: An Integrated Theory of Enjoyment. *Journal of Communication,* 52(2), 402–415.

Raney, A. A., and Janicke, S. H. (2013). How We Enjoy and Why We Seek Out Morally Complex Characters in Media Entertainment. In: Tamborini, R. (ed.). *Media and the Moral Mind.* New York: Routledge, pp. 152–169.

Robertson, I. (2012). *The Winner Effect: The Science of Success and How to Use It.* London: Bloomsbury Publishing.

Rozin, P., Haidt, J., and McCauley, C. R. (1993). Disgust. In: Lewis, M. and Haviland, J. M. (eds.). *Handbook of Emotions.* New York: The Guilford Press, pp. 575–594.

Rozin, P., Lowery, P., Imada, S., and Haidt, J. (1999). The CAD Triad Hypothesis: A Mapping Between Three Moral Emotions (Contempt, Anger, Disgust) and Three Moral Codes (Community, Autonomy, Divinity). *Journal of Personality and Social Psychology,* 76(4), 574–586.

Russell, P.S., and Giner-Sorolla, R. (2011a). Moral Anger, but Not Moral Disgust, Responds to Intentionality. *Emotion,* 11(2), 233–240.

Russell, P.S., and Giner-Sorolla, R. (2011b). Moral Anger Is More Flexible Than Moral Disgust. *Social Psychological and Personality Science,* 2(4), 360–364.

Russell, P.S., and Giner-Sorolla, R. (2011c). Social Justifications for Moral Emotions: When Reasons for Disgust Are Less Elaborated Than for Anger. *Emotion,* 11(3), 637–646.

Russell, P. S., and Giner-Sorolla, R. (2013). Bodily Moral Disgust: What It Is, How It Is Different From Anger, and Why It Is an Unreasoned Emotion. *Psychological Bulletin,* 139(2), 328–351.

Saegert, S., Swap, W., and Zajonc, R. B. (1973). Exposure, Context, and Interpersonal Attraction. *Journal of Personality and Social Psychology,* 25(2), 234–242.

Salamon, L. B. 2000. "Looking for Richard" in History: Postmodern Villainy in *Richard III* and *Scarface. Journal of popular Film and Television,* 28(2), 54–63.

Schatz, T. (1981). *Hollywood Genres: Formulas, Filmmaking, and the Studio System.* New York: Random House.

Sepinwall, A. (2012). *The Revolution Was Televised: The Cops, Crooks, Slingers, and Slayers Who Changed TV Drama Forever.*

Shafer, D. M., and Raney, A. A. (2012). Exploring How We Enjoy Antihero Narratives. *Journal of Communication,* 62, 1028–1046.

Shweder, R. A. (1990). In Defense of Moral Realism: Reply to Gabennesch. *Child Development,* 61(6), 2060–2067.

Shweder, R. A., Much, N. C., Mahapatra, M., and Park, L. (1997). The 'Big Three' of Morality (Autonomy, Community, and Divinity), and the 'Big Three' Explanations of Suffering. In: Brandt, A. and Rozin, P. (eds.). *Morality and Health.* New York: Routledge, pp. 119–69.

Silver, S. (2012). "Skyler is Such a Bitch!," And Other Unfair Breaking Bad Observations, *Technology Tell* [online], 13. July. Available at: http://www.technologytell.com/entertainment/3659/essay-skyler-is-such-a-bitch-and-other-unfair-breaking-bad-observations/ [Accessed 27. March 2015].

Simon, D. (2009): *Homicide: A Year on the Killing Streets.* Edinburgh: Canongate.

References   199

Simon, D., and Burns, E. (2010). *The Corner. A Year in the Life of an Inner-City Neighbourhood.* Edinburgh: Canongate.

Simons, C. W., and Piliavin, J. A. (1972). Effect Of Deception On Reactions To A Victim. *Journal of Personality and Social Psychology,* 21(1), 56–60.

Smith, G. M. (2003). *Film Structure and the Emotion System.* Cambridge: Cambridge University Press.

Smith, M. (1995). *Engaging Characters. Fiction, Emotion, and the Cinema.* Oxford: Clarendon Press.

Smith, M. (1996). The Logic and Legacy of Brechtianism. In: Bordwell, D. and Carroll, N. (eds.). *Post-Theory. Reconstructing Film Studies,* Madison: The University of Wisconsin Press, pp. 130–48.

Smith, M. (1997). Imagining from the Inside. In: Allen, R. and Smith, M. (eds.). *Film Theory and Philosophy,* Oxford: Clarendon Press, pp. 412–30.

Smith, M. (1999). Gangsters, Cannibals, Aesthetes, or Apparently Perverse Allegiances. In: Plantinga, C. and Smith, G. M. (eds.). *Passionate Views. Film, Cognition, and Emotion.* Baltimore: The Johns Hopkins University Press, pp. 217–238.

Smith, M. (2011a). Just What Is It That Makes Tony Soprano Such An Appealing, Attractive Murderer? In: Jones, W. E. and Vice, S. (eds.). *Ethics at the Cinema.* Oxford: Oxford University Press, pp. 66–90.

Smith, M. (2011b). Empathy, Expansionism, and the Extended Mind. In: Coplan, A., and Goldie, P. (eds.), *Empathy: Philosophical and Psychological Perspectives.* Oxford: Oxford University Press, pp. 99–117.

Smith, M. (2014). Mad, Bad and Dangerous to Know: TV's Anti-Heroes. *Times Higher Education* [online], 17. July. Available at: http://www.timeshigher-education.co.uk/features/culture/mad-bad-and-dangerous-to-know-tvs-anti-heroes/2014483.article [Accessed 27. March 2015].

Smith, S. (2000). *Hitchcock: Suspense, Humour and Tone.* London: BFI/Palgrave Macmillan.

Smuts, A. (2013). The Ethics of Singing Along: The Case of "Mind of a Lunatic". *The Journal of Aesthetics and Art Criticism,* 71(1), 121–129.

Stanfield, P. (2015). *The Cool and the Crazy: Pop Fifties Cinema.* New Jersey: Rutgers University Press.

Stock, K. (2011). Fictive Utterance and Imagining I. *Aristotelian Society Supplementary Volume,* 85(1), 145–161.

Sturm, R. E., and Antonakis, J. (2015). Interpersonal Power: A Review, Critique, and Research Agenda. *Journal of Management,* 41(1), 136–163.

Swain, S., Alexander, J., and Weinberg, J. M. (2008). The Instability of Philosophical Intuitions: Running Hot and Cold on Truetemp. *Philosophy and Phenomenological Research,* 76(1), 138–155.

Tamborini, R. (2013). A Model of Intuitive Morality and Exemplars. In: Tamborini, R. (ed.) *Media and the Moral Mind.* New York: Routledge pp. 43–74.

Tan, E. S. (1996). *Emotion and the Structure of Narrative Film. Film as an Emotion Machine.* Mahwah, NJ: Lawrence Erlbaum.

Tan, E. S. (2008). Entertainment is Emotion: The Functional Architecture of the Entertainment Experience. *Media Psychology,* 11(1), 28–51.

Tan, E. S. (2013). The Empathic Animal Meets the Inquisitive Animal in the Cinema: Notes on a Psychocinematics of Mind Reading. In: Shiamura, A. P. (ed.). *Psychocinematics: Exploring Cognition at the Movies.* Oxford: Oxford University Press, pp. 337–368.

200 References

Tan, E. S. (2014). Engaged and Detached Film Viewing: Exploring Film Viewers' Emotional Action Readiness. In: Nannicelli, T. and Taberham, P. (eds.). *Cognitive Media Theory*. New York: Routledge, pp. 106–123.

Tan, E. S., Timmers, M, Segijn, C., and Bartholomé, A. Does Dexter Morally Entertain His Viewers?. Unpublished manuscript.

Taylor, A. The Light-Bringer's Homecoming: Immorality, Shadows and Reconciliation. Unpublished manuscript.

Taylor, A. (2007). Twilight of the Idols: Performance, Melodramatic Villainy, and *Sunset Boulevard. Journal of Film and Video*, 59(2), 13–31.

Taylor, A. (2014). A Cannibal's Sermon: Hannibal Lecter, Sympathetic Villainy and Moral Revaluation. *Cinema: Journal of Philosophy and the Moving Image*, 4, 184–207.

Thomson, J. J. (1985). The Trolley Problem. *Yale Law Journal*, 94(6), 1395–1415.

Thompson, K. (2003). *Storytelling in Film and Television*. Cambridge, Mass.: Harvard University Press.

Thompson, R. J. (1997). *Television's Second Golden Age: From "Hill St. Blues" to "ER"*. New York: Syracuse University Press.

Thornhill, R., and Palmer, C. T. (2000). *A Natural History of Rape. Biological Bases of Sexual Coercion*. Cambridge, Mass.: The MIT Press.

Truffaut, F. (1983). *Hitchcock. Revised Edition*. New York: Simon & Schuster.

Turiel, E. (1983). *The Development of Social Knowledge: Morality and Convention*. Cambridge: Cambridge University Press.

Uhlmann, E.L., and Zhu, L. (2014). Acts, Persons, And Intuitions: Person-Centered Cues And Gut Reactions to Harmless Transgressions. *Social Psychological and Personality Science*, 5(3), 279–285.

Vaage, M. B. (2006). The Empathic Film Spectator in Analytic Philosophy and Naturalized Phenomenology. *Film and Philosophy*, 10, 21–38.

Vaage, M. B. (2009). The Role of Empathy in Gregory Currie's Philosophy of Film. *British Journal of Aesthetics* 49:2, 109–128.

Vaage, M. B. (2010). Fiction Film and the Varieties of Empathic Engagement. *Midwest Studies in Philosophy*, 34(1), 158–179.

Vaage, M. B. (2013). Fictional Reliefs and Reality Checks. *Screen*, 54(2), 218–237.

Vaage, M. B. (2014). Point of View. In: Branigan, E. and Buckland, W. (eds.). *The Routledge Encyclopedia of Film Theory*, London: Routledge, pp. 371–75.

Vaage, M. B. (2014). Blinded by Familiarity: Partiality, Morality, and Engagement in Television Series. In: Nannicelli, T. and Taberham, P. (eds.). *Cognitive Media Theory*. New York: Routledge, pp. 268–284.

Vernezze, P. (2004). Tony Soprano in Hell: Chase's Mob in Dante's Inferno. In: Greene, R., and Vernezze, P. (eds.). *The Sopranos and Philosophy: I Kill Therefore I Am*. Chicago, Ill: Open Court Publishing, pp. 185–194.

Vorderer, P., Klimmt, C., and Ritterfeld, U. (2004). Enjoyment: At the Heart of Media Entertainment. *Communication Theory*, 14(4), 388–408.

de Waal, F. B. M. (1996). *Good Natured. The Origins of Right and Wrong in Humans and Other Animals*. Cambridge, Mass.: Harvard University Press.

Walton, K. L. (1990). *Mimesis as Make-Believe. On the Foundations of the Representational Arts*. Cambridge, Mass.: Harvard University Press.

Walton, K. L. (1994). Morals in Fiction and Fictional Morality. *Proceedings of the Aristotelian Society Supplementary Volumes*, 68, 27–66.

Warshow, R. (2001). *The Immediate Experience. Movies, Comics, Theatre and Other Aspects of Popular Culture*. Cambridge, Mass.: Harvard University Press.

References 201

Weckerle, L. (2014). *Breaking Bad* and Blending Boundaries: Revisioning the Myths of Masculinity and the Superhero. In: Whitt, D. and Perlich, J. (eds.). *Myth in the Modern World: Essays on Intersections with Ideology and Culture*. Jefferson: MacFarland Publishing, pp. 7–31.

Wheatley, T., and Haidt, J. (2005). Hypnotic Disgust Makes Moral Judgments More Severe. *Psychological Science*, 16(10), 780–784.

Whitty, M. T., Young, G., and Goodings, L. (2011). What I Won't Do In Pixels: Examining the Limits of Taboo Violation in MMORPGs. *Computers in Human Behavior*, 27(1), 268–275.

Williams, L. (1998). Melodrama Revised. In: Browne, N. (ed.), *Refiguring American Film Genres. History and Theory*. Berkeley: University of California Press, pp. 42–88.

Williams, L. (2011). Ethnographic Imaginary: The Genesis and Genius of *The Wire*. *Critical Inquiry*, 38(1), 208–226.

Williams, L. (2014). On *The Wire*. Durham: Duke University Press.

Wilson, R. A., and Foglia, L. (2011). Embodied Cognition. In: *The Stanford Encyclopedia of Philosophy*. [online] (Fall 2011 Edition), Edward N. Zalta (ed.). Available at: http://plato.stanford.edu/entries/embodied-cognition/#MorCog [Accessed 6. January 2015].

Wollen, P. (2008 [1972]). Godard's Cinema and Counter Cinema: Vent D'est. In: Rosen, P. (ed.) *Narrative, Apparatus, Ideology: A Film Theory Reader*. New York: Columbia University Press, pp. 120–29.

Zacks, J. (2014). *Flicker: Your Brain on Movies*. New York: Oxford University Press.

Zajonc, R. (1968). Attitudinal Effects of Mere Exposure. *Journal of Personality and Social Psychology Monograph Supplement*, 9(2), 1–27.

Zeller-Jacques, M. (2014). Don't Stop Believing: Textual Excess and Discourses of Satisfaction in the Finale of *The Sopranos*. In: Stewart, M. (ed.). *Melodrama in Contemporary Film and Television*. Basingstoke: Palgrave Macmillan, pp. 114–134.

Zillmann, D. (1983). Transfer of Excitation in Emotional Behavior. In: Cacioppo, J. T. and Petty, R. E. (eds.). *Social Psychophysiology: A Sourcebook*. New York: Guilford Press, pp. 215–240.

Zillmann, D. (1996). The Psychology of Suspense in Dramatic Exposition. In: Vorderer, P., Wulff, H. J., and Friedrichsen, M. (eds.). *Suspense: Conceptualizations, Theoretical analyses, and Empirical Explorations*. Mahwah: Lawrence Erlbaum, pp. 199–231.

Zillmann, D. (2000). Basal Morality in Drama Appreciation: In: Bondebjerg, I. (ed.). *Moving Images, Culture and the Mind*. Luton: University of Luton Press, pp. 53–63.

Zillmann, D. (2003). Theory Of Affective Dynamics: Emotions And Moods. In: Bryant, J., Roskos-Ewoldsen, D. and Cantor, J. (eds.). *Communication and Emotion: Essays in Honour of Dolf Zillmann*. Mahwah, NJ: Lawrence Erlbaum, pp. 533–567.

Zillmann, D. (2006). Dramaturgy For Emotions From Fictional Narration. In: Bryant, J. and Vorderer, P. (eds.). *Psychology of Entertainment*. Mahwah, NJ: Lawrence Erlbaum, pp. 215–238.

Zillmann, D. (2013). Moral Monitoring and Emotionality in Responding to Fiction, Sports, and the News. In: Tamborini, R. (ed.) *Media and the Moral Mind*. New York: Routledge, pp. 132–151.

202 References

Zillmann, D., and Bryant, J. (1975). Viewer's Moral Sanction of Retribution in the Appreciation of Dramatic Presentations. *Journal of Experimental Social Psychology*, 11(6), 572–582.

Zillmann, D., and Cantor, J. (1977). Affective Responses to the Emotions of a Protagonist. *Journal of Experimental Social Psychology*, 13(2), 155–165.

Zillmann, D., and Jennings, B. (1975). Viewer's Moral Sanction of Retribution in the Appreciation of Dramatic Presentations. *Journal of Experimental Social Psychology*, 11(6), 572–582.

Zillmann, D., and Knobloch, S. (2001). Emotional Reactions to Narratives About the Fortunes of Personae in the News Theater. *Poetics*, 29(3), 189–206.

Zwaan, R. A. (1994). Effect of Genre Expectations On Text Comprehension. *Journal of Experimental Psychology: Learning, Memory, and Cognition*, 20(4), 920–933.

Index

Page references in italics indicate illustrations.

Abby Donovan *(Ray Donovan)*
157–9, *158*
accomplices, antiheroes' wives as
158–9, 169, 170–1
The Accused 146n.2
A Clockwork Orange 133
actor, expressivity of 89n.12
Adriana La Cerva *(The Sopranos)* 39,
50–2, *51*, 62n.22
ADT (affective disposition theory) 8–9,
11, 13, 59, 60, 66; and fiction *vs.* non-
fiction 26–7; Raney's critique of 12–14
advantageous comparisons 11, 14.
See also antihero: moral
preferability of
A-emotions 89n.14, 108, 180n.13
aesthetics: analytical 27; and
appreciation of antiheroes xviii, 91;
augmenting tests of sympathy 110;
fiction's appeal to 34; of morally
flawed art 111; operational, of
complex TV 108
affect: discordant 8 *(see also* antipathy*)*;
effects on, of having power 99–100;
primacy of 43
Affective Disposition Theory
(Zillmann) 8–9
affective mimicry 36n.9, 73
affective primacy 44
aggression, audience's, and exposure to
media violence 101, 118n.16
Anthony Jr. *(The Sopranos)* 54, *55*
Alicia *(Notorious)* 73
Alicia Florrick *(The Good Wife)*
171, 185
alienation effect xvi
alien nature of antihero 94
alignment 5–7; and allegiance 44–5,
46, 47; epistemological 70; narrative

mechanisms of, and knowledge of
fictional characters 42
allegiance 4, 5–7; and alignment 44–5,
46, 47; operational 109; partial 55,
95; perverse 93, 95; renewal of, after
reality check 58; sympathetic 65, 74;
vs. sympathy and liking 10–11, 64
Allen, Richard xvii, 67, 68–9
alloy. *See* characters: morally complex
allure of the transgressive 7, 96
Ally McBeal 179n.2
Altman, Ulrike 30
altruism: parochial 41–2; in
punishment 97–8 *(see also* pro-social
punishment*)*
Alvarez, Raphael 121
Alward, Sharon 153
amoral fascination 93–4, 95
Anastasia/Anna/Carrie *(Banshee)* xix,
130, 171–3, *172*
anger: Carmela reciprocates Tony's
(The Sopranos) 158; cognitions
surrounding 140; at violations of
autonomy 16, 136, 142
animal morality 148n.27
antagonists: disgust used to create
antipathy towards 141; FBI as 39,
50–3; Livia *(The Sopranos)* as 39;
rapist, as evil and subhuman 14; with
some virtues, fostering suspense 67
(see also villains*)*
antihero: alien nature of 93; beyond
Quality TV 117n.1; defined xvi;
dislike of xvi, 90, 91; double
existence of 157, 165; female
(see female antiheroes*)*; as gangster
genre convention in film xiv; on
hero-villain continuum 40; liking
of *(see* liking: of antiheroes*)*; moral

204 *Index*

code of xvii; moral preferability
of 24, 30, 47, 90, 120, 127, 131
(*see also* advantageous comparisons);
powerful 98–102, 107; punished at
end of series 112, 184; on Quality
TV xii–xiii; reasons for killing
viewed with favouritism 141;
selfishness, vicariously enjoyed
98; unstable marital relationships
of 155, 159–60 (*see also* wives of
antiheroes). *See also* rough hero
antihero series xv; as case studies in
moral philosophy of fiction xiii;
as learning experiences 185; moral
disengagement techniques in 14
(*see also* moral disengagement);
negative portrayals of home and
family in (*see* home: and family);
proliferation of 107–12; reality
checks in 23, 26; self-referential
within genre 173, 185; spectator
sympathy 39 (*see also* sympathy);
unstable/dynamic moral structure
within 92
antipathy: emotions triggered by
103 (*see also* disliking); narrative
techniques fostering 166; prompted
by moral disgust 124, 131–2, 146;
towards villain 107, 120
Appiah, Kwame Anthony 41, 47
appraisal theory 88n.8
appreciation 107–8, 116
a-rational moral evaluation 12, 13
art: morally flawed, aesthetics of 111,
117; representational, and alleviation
of boredom 102
Arthur Frobisher (*Damages*) 177,
181n.32
aspect change 163
asymmetry: of knowledge, in cognitive
film theory 70; between real life and
fiction 141–6
audience segmentation 115
authorities and hierarchies, respect for
16, 40, 142
Austin, J.L. 47
"auto mode" of moral evaluation
19–20, 35, 143, 145
Avon Barksdale (*The Wire*) 124–5, 126

bad fans xv, 91, 112–17, 164, 186
Badger (*Breaking Bad*) 82, 85
Bal, Mieke 44
Baldanzi, Jessica 131

Bandura, Albert 14, 27–8
Banshee xi, xix, 151, 171–3, *172*
Barratt, Daniel 71, 73, 88n.8
"basically good" flawed characters
119n.31
behavioral effects of having power
99–100
belief: blameworthy 115; formation of,
in engagement with fiction *vs.* non-
fiction 29, 32; *vs.* imagining 27, 28
benevolence 10–11
Bentham, Jeremy 21
Berridge, Susan 124, 134–5, 147n.24
betrayal, of Tony Soprano by Livia
48–9
Betty Draper (*Mad Men*) 91, 150,
151, 157
biases 18–19, 73; and the bad fan
113–14; Just-World 146
black humour 139
blameworthy belief 115
blaming the rape victim 144–5
Blanchet, Robert 42–3
Bloodline 104–5
Boardwalk Empire xi, 99, 105–6,
112, 170
bodily fluids, disgust at transfer of 137
body, violations of, and moral
disgust 140
Booth, Wayne 44
Bordwell, David xxn.5
boredom, relief from 37n.23, 102
Bourgois, Philippe 122, 138
Bourke, Joanna 136
bracketing, of rational moral evaluation
14, *55*, 146
brain, human: damage to, and
utilitarian bridge-problem answer
22; DLPFC area 22, 26; VMPFC area
22, 24
Brandon (*The Wire*) 126
Breaking Bad xi, xvi, xvii, xviii, xix
185; and bad fans 113; as complex
TV 108; deception and identity in
180n.8; ending, treatment of family
in 181n.37; feminine space of, in
negative light 154, *156*, 156–7;
intermittent suspense and dysphoria
in 83–7; moral inversion of suspense
in 77–80; post-hoc ethical discussions
about 107; reality checks in 114–15;
Skyler becomes Walter's accomplice
158–9; structure of sympathy in
56–8; suspense structure in 80–3

Index   205

bridge problem 20–2
Brienne of Tarth *(Game of Thrones)* 134
Brock *(Breaking Bad)* 56–7
Bryant, Jennings 9
Buffy the Vampire Slayer 135
burlesque and black humour 139
Burns, Ed 121

"cable guys" xii–xiii, 40
CAD model, of morality 16, 17, 136–7, 138, 142
camera angles, strange 89n.16
camera metaphor, Greene's 19–20
"can-do" orientation 99, 100–1
Cantor, Joanne 9
Cardwell, Sarah 152
care: as moral domain 40; for one's family, and feeling of power 99
Carli, L.L. 149n.38
Carmela Soprano *(The Sopranos)* 48, 54, 111, 113, 150, 151, 153, 157, 158, 159; display of power by 169–70
Carrie *(Banshee). See* Anastasia/Anna/ Carrie
Carrie Mathison *(Homeland)* 171
Carrie Bradshaw *(Sex and the City)* 171
Carroll, Noël xvi, 4, 15, 90; on film's question-response structure 89n.15; on moderate moralism 111–12; on moral emotions 7–8; on suspense xvii, 67–8, 78; on villains and antipathy 120
central imagining 88n.2
Cercei Lannister *(Game of Thrones)* 134
characters: audience desires for 75; "basically good" 118n.31; construction of, flawed 162, 166; contrast 47, 48; engagement with 4, 68, 82, 87; immoral, sympathy from empathy with 102; knowledge of, through narrative mechanisms of alignment 42; liking and disliking of 13; morally complex 98
Chase, David 111, 113, 117n.1
chases, and suspense 78
Chatman, Seymour 44
chicken carcass masturbation story study 142–3, 149n.36
children, moral sensibilities of 8–9, 15–16, 36n.10
Chris Sanchez *(Damages)* 178

Christopher Moltisanti *(The Sopranos)* 39, 50, 51, 55, 62n.13
Chris *(The Wire)* 128
Claire Underwood *(House of Cards)* 170–1
class, socioeconomic, and mode of moral evaluation 142–3
classical cognitivism 18
classical suspense 67
cleaning sequence, in *Psycho* 71, 72, 75
Close, Glenn 176, 181n.31
cognitive attraction to antihero series xv
cognitive control 22. *See also* elephant fable
cognitive dissonance, avoidance of 41, 98
cognitive effects of having power 99–100
cognitive film theory xiii–xv, 4, 18, 27, 70, 71
cognitive insensitivity 113, 114
cognitive load 22, 26
cognitive miserliness 12–13, 14, 22–3, 41, 165
cognitive quarantining 28. *See also* bracketing
cognitivism, classical 18
comedy sequences, and moral inversion of suspense 78, 82, 85
complex TV: operational aesthetics of 108. *See* Quality TV
computer games 35, 60
conflict: audience, provoked by immoralism in Quality TV 117; favouritism, and avoidance of 41; and reality checks 25–6, 33–4
conflict monitor 20, 22
consequentialism, Millian 141
contrast characters 47, 48, 83, 126
conventions *vs.* moral rules 15–16
Cooke, Brandon 114
cooking sequence, in *Weeds* 181n.28
cooperation within group 17–18
core disgust 137, 138, 140
Corinne Mackey *(The Shield)* 150
The Corner: A Year in the life of an Inner-City Neighborhood (Simon and Burns) 121, 122–3
The Corner (drama mini-series) 121
cortisol 99, 118n.13
counter-cinema 93
counter-empathy 8, 9
crime drama outcomes, Raney's justice sequence study 131–2

206 *Index*

cued response xxn.5. *See also* intended response
Cuklanz, Lisa M. 123–4, 126, 129, 135, 138, 148n.29
cultural differences: in moral evaluative categories 16–17, 20, 141, 142, 148n.35 (*see also* "great narrowing"); requiring rational moral evaluation 149n.41
Currie, Gregory 18, 29–30, 31, 37n.29, 75
cycles, theory of xixn.1

Daenerys Targaryen *(Game of Thrones)* 134
Damages xix, 151, 156, 173, 174–9, 181nn.31–2
Da Mayor *(Do the Right Thing)* 93
D'Angelo Barksdale *(The Wire)* 123, 124–5, *125*, 143
Danny Rayburn *(Bloodline)* 104
Dante Aligheri 49
"dark dramas" 113
date/acquaintance rape 126–7
Days of Our Lives 133
Dead Snow 138
Deborah Ciccerone/Danielle *(The Sopranos)* 50, 51
deception and identity 180n.8. *See also* "Who are you" question
defamiliarization xvi
dehumanisation 14
Dennis 'Cutty' Shark *(The Wire)* 123, 128
deontology, Kantian 141
desire: character 75; for immoral events in fiction 76; narrative 75, 76, 103, 107; to witness revenge 130, 131
Detective Freamon *(The Wire)* 126
Detective Greggs *(The Wire)* 126
Detective McNulty *(The Wire)* 125
Detective Moreland *(The Wire)* 125
deviant sex acts 137
Dexter xi, xvi, 23–6, 138–40, 148n.32
Dexter Morgan *(Dexter)* 1, 23–6, *25*, 28, 138–40, 148n.32, 177; alien nature of 95
diegetic music, in *Breaking Bad* 81
direct suspense 69
Dirty Harry 28
disgust: connected with body and its functions 137, 140; core 137, 138, 140; moral (*see* moral disgust); triggered by antipathy 103; at violations of natural order 137, 142–3

disliking, of characters: antihero as object of xvi, 91, 92; following moral evaluation 8 (*see also* antipathy); triggered by antipathy 103
disposition, affective 8–9
distortion of consequences 14
divine nature, violations of 137, 142
DLPFC brain area 22, 26
Dr Gregory House *(House)* 40
Dr Jennifer Melfi *(The Sopranos)* 39, 48, 113, 168; offers meta-perspective on Tony 53–6, 93
Dr Kennedy *(The Sopranos)* 45–6, 46, 47
Dr Kupferberg *(The Sopranos)* 53
Dr Krakower *(The Sopranos)* 111
Donatelli, Cindy 153
Don Draper *(Mad Men)* 40, 91
Don Vito Corleone *(The Godfather)* 99
dopamine 99
Do the Right Thing 93, 113–14
double life, antiheroes' 157, 165
Douglas, Mary 137
drug addict confrontation scene *(Breaking Bad)* 83–5
dual-process model, in moral evaluation xvii, 1, 3, 18–22, 27, 74, 91, 102, 110; and dual-process model of empathy 65; and dual-process model of information processing 32–4
Du Bos, Jean-Baptiste 37n.23, 102
duck-rabbit change 163
dullness of everyday life, antihero's wife identified with 81, 157–8
Duquan *(The Wire)* 128
dynamic moral structure of antihero series 92
Dynasty 117n.1

Eaton, Annee W. 110–11, 117, 118n.26
Eden, Allison 40
electric shock experiment, Simons and Piliavin's 149n.42
elephant, Haidt's fable of 19
Ellen Parsons *(Damages)* 175–6, 178
Embodied Simulation 73
emotions: artefact *vs.* fictional 89n.14, 108, 180n.13; and attraction of antihero series xv; manipulated by narrative context 2–3; moral evaluations grounded in 143, 165 (*see also* "auto mode"); simulation of others' 36n.9 (*see also* empathy);

systemic impairment of, sufferers from 22; triggered by antipathy 103; type A 108; type F 108

empathy xvii–xviii, 8, 11, 36n.9, 36n.11; activity related to moral evaluation 9; with antihero 47, 96–103, 107; Dr Melfi's, for Tony Soprano 53; embodied 65, 72; and engagement with fiction 37n.29, 66, 79; in film theory 88n.2; and friendship 52; imaginative 65; with immoral characters 102; impairment of 114, 118n.32; judgments based on 88n.6; low-level, in *Breaking Bad* 80; and moral inversion of suspense 87 (*see also* moral inversion of suspense); overlapping with sympathy 64; parochial 42; with powerful characters 176; and simulation theory 88n.8; with Skyler (*Breaking Bad*) made difficult 161; and suspense 70, 71; *vs.* loyalty 71

endings, series: function of morality in 112, 184; importance of family in 181n.37

engagement with fiction: amoral 66, 93–4; British men's, with *The Sopranos* 96; empathic 37n.29, 66, 79; imagining and belief formation in 28–9; limits of, xiii; and moral evaluation 1–2, 3–9, 13, 22–3, 68, 107 (*see also* characters: engagement with); reliant on intuitions 75, 143, 146, 186; sympathetic 77; *vs.* non-fiction 26–35

Engaging Characters (Smith) 4

enjoyment: of antiheroes' wives 169–71; of empathy with powerful characters 176; of immorality 90 (*see also* transgressive, allure of); and moral disengagement 34, 98; of the narrative 13; of punishment of wrongdoers 24, 98; of suspense, as instant gratification 80; *vs.* appreciation 107–8. *See also* entertainment

entertainment 21, 27, 165; escapist 13, 168–9

epistemological alignment 70

escapes, and suspense 78

escapist entertainment 13, 168–9

evolutionary psychology: and moral systems 141–3; and universal condemnation of rape 135

excitation transfer 101

excuses, pleas for 24, 47, 61, 77, 90, 183. *See also* justification

experiential processing 32, 34

expressivity, of actor 89n.12

extra-textual information sources 44, 58

fabula xxn.5

fairness, moral rules about 21, 40, 62n.4, 142, 143

familiarity 42–4, 45; with antihero series genre 60, 61; increases liking 42–3, 61, 90

family: caring for, and sense of power 99; effect of antihero's behaviour on 174; as excuse for transgression 40, 104, 155, 167, 172; in hegemonic masculinity 155; inversion of antihero excuse, in *Damages* 176; loyalty to 40, 41; Mafia, betrayal of 49; negative portrayals of 81, 86, 89n.16, 153, 155–6; partiality towards own 145; separate from antihero's transgressions 179; in series endings 181n.37; as space of innocence, in melodrama 154, 179n.5; struggle with work, in *Damages* 175, 178

Fargo xi, xix, 182–5

fast thinking, intuitive 18, 21

fatherhood 155

favouritism 41, 42, 45, 141. *See also* partiality

FBI: as antagonists 39, 50–3, 62n.22; dehumanizing of 50, *51*

female antiheroes xix, 151, 171–4; husbands of 173–4

female heroine teen drama series, rapists as villains in 135

feminine sphere: cooking sequence, in *Weeds* 181n.28; and regular *vs.* Quality TV 152–6

F-emotions 89n.14, 108, 109, 180n.13

fiction: and the electric shock experiment 149n.42; engagement with (*see* engagement with fiction); exposure to, and attitude change 32; knowledge of characters, and narrative mechanisms of alignment 42; modernist 169; moral philosophy of xiii; probability, morality, and suspense in 4 (*see also* suspense); simpler moral demands of 183

208   *Index*

(*see also* cognitive miserliness); theory of 62n.9; *vs.* non-fiction 26–35, 37n.25; *vs.* real life, asymmetry between 141–6. *See also* narratives

fictional attitude (fictive stance) 29, 30–1, 34

fictional reliefs xvii, 15, 23–4, 32, 33, 34, 35, 58, 82, 86–7, 112, 114–7, 167–8, 185–6

fictional *vs.* artefact emotions 89n.14, 108, 180n.13

film noir: Flory on morally complex characters 103–4; and Spike Lee films 93

film theory: cognitive, xiii–xv, 4; embodied 18; empathy in 88n.2

Fincher, David 148n.33

Flory, Dan xiii–xiv, 93, 103–4, 113

Foot, Philippa 37n.20

footbridge problem 20–2

forensic fandom 108, 162

Frank Underwood *(House of Cards)* 170–1

Frenzy 68, 148n.32

Friend, Stacie 29

friends, loyalty to 41

friendship: characteristics of, violated by FBI 52; and morality 41–8, 55

frisson of risk xvi

Furio *(The Sopranos)* 170

Gallese, Vittorio 73

Game of Thrones 44, 134, 147n.21

gangster genre xiv, 28, 99, 118n.11, 124, xixn.1

García, Alberto N. 92

Gemma Teller *(Sons of Anarchy)* 104, 129–30, 170

general assertions, in fictional works 32, 33

General Hospital 134

genre: hybridity of, in Quality TV xvi, xixn.1, 152–3; preferences 168

genre theory, Friend's 29

Gerrig, Richard J. 31–3, 34

Gilligan, Vince 57, 117n.1

Giner-Sorolla, Roger 140

The Girl With a Dragon Tattoo (Oplev film and Fincher remake) 148n.33

Gjelsvik, Anne 148n.32

Gladiator 154

goal contagion 72, 73

The Godfather 153

The Godfather Part III 65

The Good Wife 171, 185

Grand Theft Auto: San Andreas Stories (video game) 60

Grant, Drew 174

"great narrowing" in Western moral philosophy 21, 62n.4, 141

Greene, Joshua xvii, 1, 3; and dual-process theory 27; on group cooperation 149n.41; on in-group bias 42; on moral intuitions and group cooperation 17–18; on pro-social punishment 97–8, 180n.11; on rational moral evaluation *vs.* rationalization 166; on role of moral reasoning 19–20, 180n.17; and the trolley/footbridge problem 20–2

Gripsrud, Jostein 117n.1

Grodal, Torben 71, 138

group: cooperation among 17–18, 97, 149n.41; inter-group cooperation 149n.41; loyalty to 16, 39, 42; rape within, abhorrence of 136

Guerra, Michele 73

The Guiding Light 133

Gunn, Anna 151, 161, 164, 166

Guiseppe 'Gyp' Rosetti *(Boardwalk Empire)* 105–6, *106*

Gus *(Breaking Bad)* 56, 57, 64, 85

gut responses, moral 13, 185

Haidt, Jonathan xvii, 1, 3, 15, 180n.17; on affective primacy 43; and dual-process theory 27; elephant fable 19; on "great narrowing" in Western moral philosophy 62n.4, 141; on impartiality 21; on moral disgust 137, 138, 142–3; and moral dumbfounding 165; and Moral Foundations Theory 17–18; on moral intuitions 2

handheld camera, use of in *Breaking Bad* 79

Hank *(Breaking Bad)* 81–2, 159

Hannah Horvath *(Girls)* 171

Hannibal xi, 94–5, xixn.1

Hannibal Lecter *(The Silence of the Lambs and Hannibal)* 93, 94, 94–5, 107

Happiness 133

harm, moral rules about 15–16, 21, 40, 62n.4, 142, 143

Hartmann, Tilo 35

hatred, triggered by antipathy 103

HBO xii

Heath, Stephen 4

Index 209

hegemonic masculinity xiii 155, 179n.6
Heisenberg *(Breaking Bad)* Walter White as 77, 82, 86, 89n.16
heuristics 18–19, 34, 73, 144–5
hierarchies and authorities, respect for 16, 40, 142
hierarchy of taste, Quality *vs.* regular TV 152
high-end TV. *See* Quality TV
High Plains Drifter 133
Hindsight Bias 149n.38
Hitchcock, Alfred xvii, xviii, 66, 69, 77
Hitchcockian suspense 68–74
home: and family, negative portrayals of 81, 86, 89n.16, 153, 155–6, 157; of female antihero 173
Homicide: A Year on the Killing Streets (Simon) 146n.1
Homicide: Life on the Street (TV series) 146n.1
horror/thriller genre xixn.1
House 40
House of Cards: BBC version 180n.25; U.S. version xi, xixn.1, 170–1
Howard, Douglas L. 50, 53
Howard Erickson *(Damages)* 177, 178
Hume, David 88n.6, 110, 118n.26
humiliation of the antihero, in the feminine sphere 155, 156
humour: as distancing technique 139; and suspense, enjoyable mix of 85 *(see also* comedy sequences)
hybridity, in Quality TV xvi, xixn.1, 152–3
hypocrisy, of antihero's wife 159, 165

iconography, and allegiance 6, 10
identification, psychoanalytic, and fusion model 71
illusion theory 35
imaginative resistance 36n.4
imaginative slumming 95, 96, 116
imagining: central 88n.2; and engagement with fiction 28–9; from the inside, empathy as 88n.2; primary 30, 31, 37n.29; secondary 29–30; *vs.* believing 28
imagining *vs.* believing 27
immoralism 110
immorality: enjoyment of 90; narrative importance and function of 103–7 *(see also* transgressive, allure of); and the rough hero 110; thought-provoking, in Quality TV 117

impartiality 21
incest, and moral disgust 137, 143
incest, disgust towards 135
infidelity 164, 165
in-group bias 42
in-group loyalty 49
intended response xv
intended spectator, of antihero series 91
intent, authorial/directorial 37n.25, 113
intention-response communicative theory 27, 30–1, 115
inter-group cooperation 149n.41
internal focalization, and use of handheld camera 79
Internet, as extra-textual information source 44
intuitions 2; and allegiance 11; and fast thinking 18–19; in fiction *vs.* non-fiction 26–7; manipulated by narrative context 2; and moral evaluation xvii, 3, 136, 143, 165, 166; reliability of 19; series content evoking moral preferences 185
irony, postmodern, *The Sopranos* as work of 116

Jackie Peyton *(Nurse Jackie)* xix, 100, *100*, 171
Jackson Teller *(Sons of Anarchy)* 40, 56, 99, 104
Jamie Lannister *(Game of Thrones)* 134
Jane *(Breaking Bad)* 86–7
Janicke, Sophie H. 12, 98, 102, 107
Jesse Pinkman *(Breaking Bad)* xviii, 56–7, 58, 64, 74, 78, 82, 83–5, *84*, 167–8
Jimmy-in-and-out *(Breaking Bad)* 85
Joan *(Mad Men)* 91
John Rayburn *(Bloodline)* 104
Johnson, Merri Lisa 153–4
Johnson, Michael 2
Jones, Janine 114
Judging Amy 179n.2
judgment, moral: social, and pre-reflective feelings 17 *(see also* moral evaluation)
Junior *(The Sopranos)* 39, 45, 49, 153
justice: antihero's restoration of 98, 102; of crime drama outcomes 132
justice sequence 97
justification 14; for vigilante revenge, rape as 127–8, 131. *See also* pleas for excuses
Just-World Theory 98, 144–6, 149n.38

210 *Index*

Kahneman, Daniel 18
Kai Proctor *(Banshee)* 130
Kantian deontology 141
Keisha, rape and murder of *(The Wire)* 125, 125–6
Kesebir, S. 62n.4, 141
Kevin *(Nurse Jackie)* 173–4
key-stealing scene, in *Notorious* 73
Khal Drogo *(Game of Thrones)* 134
knowledge, asymmetry of, in cognitive film theory 70
Kohlberg, Lawrence 15

Lacey, Joanne 96, 180n.20
Laura *(General Hospital)* 134
Lee, Spike 93
Lerner, Martin 144
Lester Nygaard *(Fargo)* 182–5
Levine, Elana 115–16, 133, 153, 154, 171
Life Unexpected 135
liking: of antiheroes xv, 6, 8, 91, 92; bad fan's 112–13; of characters, following moral evaluation 8; increased by exposure and familiarity 42–3, 61, 90; influenced by non-moral factors 9–15; *vs.* sympathy and allegiance 10–11, 64
Lisbeth Salander *(The Girl With a Dragon Tattoo)* 148n.33
Little Man *(The Wire)* 125
Livia *(The Sopranos)* 39, 48–9, 155–6
Loehlin, James xiv
LOP (Least Objectionable Programming) paradigm xii
Lorne Malvo *(Fargo)* 182–4, *184*
Lotz, Amanda xii; on "cable guys" and hegemonic masculinity xiii–xiv; on family as antihero's excuse 40; on male-centered serials 150, 154–5; on predominantly working women in TV series xii
Louis Toben *(Damages)* 177
Love is a Many Splendored Thing 133
low-level processing 32, 35
Low Winter Sun 185
loyalty 40; to family 40, 41, 156; to friends 41; and friendship 52; to group 16, 39, 42, 49
Lucas *(Banshee)* 130–1, 172
Luke *(General Hospital)* 134

"made guy" fantasy 180n.20
Mad Men 91–2, 180n.8

Maibom, Heidi L. 42, 88n.6
"manual mode" of moral evaluation 19–20, 34, 143. *See also* rational moral evaluation
Margaret Thompson *(Boardwalk Empire)* 170
Marie *(Breaking Bad)* 81–2, 157, 159, 160
Marion Crane *(Psycho)* 69, 71–2, 75, 89n.9
marital relationships, unstable 155
Marlo *(The Wire)* 128
masculinity: damaged, of Walter White *(Breaking Bad)* 163; and fatherhood 155; hegemonic xiii, 155, 179n.6
masturbation: with chicken carcass, moral disgust at 142–3, 149n.36; by Gyp, while being strangled *(Boardwalk Empire)* 105; unenthusiastic, by Skyler White 156
Matravers, Derek 28
Maximus *(Gladiator)* 154
McClaren *(Damages)* 178
Meadow Soprano *(The Sopranos)* 169
media violence 101, 118n.16
melodrama 158, 179n.5; avoidance of 161; home-centered 154; villains of 105–7
Michael *(The Wire)* 128
Michael Corleone *(Godfather* films) 65
Mick *(Ray Donovan)* 156
Mike Bauer *(The Guiding Light)* 133, 135
Mike *(Breaking Bad)* 57
Milch, David 117n.1
Mill, John Stuart 21, 141
Miriam Lass *(Hannibal)* 94, 94–5
mirror systems 73, 89n.11
misogyny, in *The Sopranos* 91
Mr Beneke *(Breaking Bad)* 160
Mittell, Jason xiii, 57, 108, 118n.24, 121, 132, 162–4
moderate moralism 111–12
modernist fiction 169
moral centre 92; flawed 93
moral compass, intuitive 136
moral complexity: of antihero 98; in Quality TV programmes xii–xiii
moral desirability, and suspense 67
moral disengagement xvi–xvii, 14, 23, 27–8, 34, 59, 98
moral disgust xviii, 107, 118n.22, 120; at bodily violations 140; and judgment of character *vs.* act

149n.36; at offenses against natural order 137, 142, 143; at rape 136–41; at violations of sanctity and purity 16
moral dumbfounding 19, 20, 140, 165, 166
moral evaluation: a-rational 12, 13; "auto" *vs.* "manual" settings 19–20, 34, 143; determining by, *vs.* underlying, spectator response 6; dual-process (*see* dual-process model); emotional/intuitive xvii, 2, 3, 23; and empathic activity 9; empathy-based 88n.6; and engagement with fiction 1–2, 22–3; judgments of acts *vs.* character 12
moral feelings 13; gut-reaction 17, 185. *See also* emotions; intuitions
Moral Foundations Theory 17–18, 40, 142, 148n.34
moral intuition. *See* intuitions
moral inversion of suspense xvii–xviii, 69, 74, 75, 77, 87; in *Breaking Bad* 77–80, 86, 87; in Hitchcock's snooper example 88n.8
morality: alien 36n.4; among animals 148n.27; CAD model of (*see* CAD model); conventions *vs.* moral rules 15–16; cross-cultural variations in 16–17, 20, 148n.35; embodied approach to 18; empirical explorations of 186n.4; exclusive of other culture's systems 141, 142 (*see also* "great narrowing"); and friendship 41–8; function of, in TV series endings 112; and group cooperation 17–18; Manichean 124; reliant on emotions and intuitions 17 (*see also* emotions; intuitions)
morally preferability: of antihero 24, 47, 90, 120, 127, 130, 131; of Skyler White, in *Breaking Bad* 164
moral orientation 5
moral philosophy: of fiction xiii; "great narrowing" to questions of fairness and harm 21, 62n.4, 141; Western rationalist 3, 18, 21 (*see also* rational moral evaluation)
moral psychology xiv, 3, 15, 20–4, 148n.35
moral relativism 52, 55
moral resolution 92
moral scrutiny, post-hoc 107
Morton, Adam 47

murder: arousing anger 141; disgust at 138; legitimized by narrative stage setting 139–40; perceived less gravely than rape 132, 136, 139, 140
music: and allegiance 6, 10; non-diegetic, in *Breaking Bad* 80, 81, 89n.16
mutilation of bodies, disgust at 138

Nado, Jennifer 2
Nancy Botwin *(Weeds)* xix, 171, 173
Nannicelli, Ted 152
Namond *(The Wire)* 128
narrative desires 75–6, 83, 85–6, 91, 103, 104–5, 107, 176
narrative fallacy 111
narratives: context within, and emotional moral manipulation 2–3; in empirical explorations of morality 186n.4; enjoyment of, and affective disposition 13; function of rape in 124, 127–31; importance and function of immorality in 103–7; knowledge of characters through mechanisms of alignment in 42; rhetorical force of 166; serialized 152 (*see also* antihero series; soap operas); shifted from sympathetic to ambiguous by reality checks 92; structure of, and non-moral factors 167. *See also* stories
natural order, violations of, and moral disgust 137, 142, 143
Nelson, Robin xii–xiii, xvi, 152–3
neo-Nazis *(Sons of Anarchy)* 129–30
Neron 'Nero' Padilla *(Sons of Anarchy)* 104
Newman, Michael Z. 115–16, 153, 154, 171
news stories 31, 37–8n.30
Nietzschean will to power 107
Nochimson, Martha P. 52, 53
non-diegetic music, in *Breaking Bad* 80, 81, 89n.16
non-fiction *vs.* fiction, engagement with 26–34, 37n.25
non-moral factors, influence of, on liking/disliking 9–15, 167
Norman Bates *(Psycho)* 69, 71–2, 75, 88n.8, 89n.9, 89n.12
Notorious 68, 73
'Nucky' Thompson *(Boardwalk Empire)* 99, 106, 170
Nurse Jackie xix, 151, 171, 173–4
Nussbaum, Emily 113

212 *Index*

Omar Little *(The Wire)* 126, 168
Once Upon a Time in America 133
operational aesthetics of complex TV
  108, 109
Oplev, Nils Arden 148n.33
Orange is the New Black 151, 171, 173
Overmyer, Eric 147n.2
oxyticin, favouritism experiment
  with 42

Palmer, C.T. 135
paradox of tragedy 37n.23
parochial altruism 41–2
parsimony, ethical 141
partiality xvii, 24, 45; in *Breaking Bad*
  58, 74; and the long-term TV series
  90; morality of 39, 55; towards
  own family over strangers 145; *vs.*
  relativism 52. *See also* favouritism
participatory responses 88n.3
pathos, avoidance of 161
Patty Hewes *(Damages)* xix, 151, 156,
  174–9, *177*, 181nn.31–2
Peggy *(Mad Men)* 91
Piaget, Jean 15, 36n.10
Pinker, Steven 135
Piper Chatman *(Orange is the New
  Black)* 171
Plantinga, Carl xvi, 9–12, 36n.11, 64,
  65, 92, 141, 166
playful viewing 108
pleas for excuses 24, 47, 61, 77, 90,
  183. *See also* justification
pleasure 61, 86–7, 91; in antihero's
  immoralilty 96, 101–2; in retribution
  97–8
plotlines, multiple 147n.24
Plourde, Bruce 53
Polan, Dana 53, 116, 153
police procedural genre 120, 124
political drama xixn.1
pollution, as violation of accepted
  categories 137
post-hoc moral scrutiny 107
postmodern irony, *The Sopranos* as
  work of 116
POV shots, in *Breaking Bad* 79
power: antihero's, attractive to viewer
  98–102, 107; Carmela's display
  of, in *The Sopranos* 158, 169–70;
  cognitive, behavioural, and affective
  effects of 99–100; effects of 118n.13;
  lack of, in home setting 98–102;
  Patty Hewes', in *Damages* 176; Vic

Mackey's, in *The Shield* 128; Walter's
  assertion of, to Skyler *(Breaking Bad)*
  160; will to 107, 183
preferability, moral: of antihero 24, 47,
  90, 120, 127, 130, 131; of Skyler
  White *(Breaking Bad)* 131
Prentice, Deborah A. 31–3, 34
pre-reflective feelings, and social
  judgments 17
primary imagining 30, 31, 37n.29
priming 101
Prinz, Jesse 137
Projansky, S. 147n.5
pro-morality 148n.27
pro-social punishment 90, 97–8,
  180n.11
Psycho 68–9, 71–2, 88–9nn.8–9,
  89n.12
psychopaths 22
Public Enemy xiv
punishment: of antihero at end of series
  112, 184; desire to see, and suspense
  130; gratification from witnessing
  103; of guilty expected in fiction 145;
  more severe than in real-life 102;
  pleasure in exacting 183; by private
  citizens 132 (*see also* vigilantism);
  pro-social 24, 97–8, 180n.11. *See
  also* revenge
punitiveness 132
purity and degradation, morality of
  16–17, 40, 137, 142, 143, 148n.34

Quality TV xi–xii, xvi, 185, xixn.2;
  affect towards multiple characters
  43; antiheroes on xii–xiii; and
  complex morality xii–xiii; and the
  feminine sphere 152–6, 171; genre
  hybridity in xvi, xixn.1, 152–3;
  immoralism in 117; less explicit
  exposition than in regular TV 44;
  operational aesthetics of 108
quarantining, cognitive. *See also*
  bracketing
question-response structure of film
  89n.15

Rabbit *(Banshee)* 130
racism, and the bad fan 113–14
Ralph Cifaretto *(The Sopranos)* 46, 48,
  96–7, 98, 153
Randy *(The Wire)* 123, 126, 128
Raney, Arthur R. xvi, 9, 32, 34, 165;
  on ADT 12–14; on familiarity with

the antihero series genre 58–61; on justice evaluation of crime drama outcomes 131–2; on morally complex characters 98, 102; on post-hoc moral scrutiny 107; schema theory 37n.13

rape xviii, 14, 147n.2; as disrespect towards male authorities 147n.25; of Dr Melfi *(The Sopranos)* 52, *54*, 131; and ethnic background of TV victim 146n.2; in fiction films, versatility of 147n.5; of in-group members 136; of men by men 147n.10; and moral disgust 136–41, 143, 145; narrative function of 124, 127–31; perpetrators of, as villains 126, 135, 147n.5; relative gravity of, *vs.* murder 132, 136, 139, 140; in *Rob Roy*, experimental selective showing of 132; in series with multiple plotlines 147n.24; in soap opera plots 133–4; and vigilante revenge 129, 130–1, 132, 147n.11; in *The Wire* 120–3, 120–7, 124–7

rationalism 18

"rationalist delusion", Haidt's 19

rationalist theory of morality 15, 16, 141

rationalization 20, 166

rational moral evaluation xvii; bracketing of 14; and high socioeconomic attainment 142; as "manual mode" 19–20, 34, 143, 149n.41; normative bases for 38n.31; prompted by engagement with fiction 107; of Skyler White *(Breaking Bad)* 164; *vs.* moral emotions and intuitions 1–2; *vs.* rationalization 166 *(see also* reality check)

Ray Donovan xi, 156–8, 180n.8, 185

reaction shots, in *Breaking Bad* 79

reality checks xvii, 25–6, 33–4, 112–7, 186; in *Breaking Bad* 56, 58, 82–3, 84, *84,* 86–7, 109, 114–15, 131, 164, 167–9; in *The Sopranos* 53–5; greater appeal for educated audience 169; undermining sympathy 33–4, 66, 92, 109–10, 112, 115–16

real life and fiction: asymmetry between 141–6 *(see also* fiction: *vs.* non-fiction); moral demands of 185

re-enactment, empathetic 88n.2

reflection, audience's xviii, 110, 117, 118n.24, 186. *See also* rational moral evaluation

regular TV xii, xvi, 117n.1; and the feminine sphere 152

relativism, moral 52, *55*

relaxation 21, 27

representational art, and alleviation of boredom 102

rescues, and suspense 78

response: intended xv, 27; low-level 35; participatory 88n.3

response moralism 114

retribution, pleasure in 98. *See also* punishment; revenge

revenge: desire to witness 130, 131, 183 *(see also* punishment); for rape 129, 130–1, 132, 147n.11, 148n.33; in *The Sopranos* 45

Richard LaPenna *(The Sopranos)* 53

Richard III *(Richard III)* xiv

Richie Aprile *(The Sopranos)* 48

righteous indignation 97, 103

Rights Revolution 135. *See also* fairness

risk, frisson of xvi. *See also* suspense

Robertson, Ian 99

Rob Roy experiment, Raney's 132

Robyn Sanseverino *(The Sopranos)* 50, 52

rooting for 66, 77; and comical suspense scenes 78; as sympathy 65

Rope 68

rough hero 110, 118n.26. *See also* antihero

Rozin, Paul 136–7

rules of thumb 18–19

Russell, Pascal Sophie 140

Sal *(Do the Right Thing)* 113

Sam Hess *(Fargo)* 182, 183

Sanchez *(Banshee)* 130–1

sanctity, violations of 137, 142

Saul Goodman *(Breaking Bad)* 85

Scarface xiv

schemas, for reception of fiction 34, 59

schema theory 37n.13

secondary imagining 29–30

segmentation, audience xii, 115

self-awareness, in *The Sopranos* 53–6

selfishness of antihero 98, 183

Sepinwall, Alan 150, 158

serialized narratives 152. *See also* antihero series; soap operas

Sex and the City 171

214 *Index*

sex crimes xviii; and vigilante enforcers, in *The Wire* 128. *See also* rape
Shafer, Daniel M. 12, 59
shared suspense 69
The Shield xi, 99, 128, 147n.10
Shweder, Richard 16, 136
sidekicks, antiheroes' wives as 169, 170–1
silly questions, and engagement with fiction 24
Silver, Stephen 165
Silvio Dante *(The Sopranos)* 50, 62n.22
Simon, David 121, 146n.1, 147n.2, 179n.1
simulation theory 88n.8
sinking car sequence, in *Psycho* 69, 71, 72, 75, 88n.8
sitcom format 173
situation models 29; and news stories 31
Skyler White *(Breaking Bad)* xix, 40, 58, 150; as battered wife 162–4; character not well constructed 166; and dullness of family life 81; emasculating 165; at end of series 181n.37; music associated with scenes of 81; resentful towards Walter's crimes 159; seeks divorce 159–60; talking pillow scene 81–2, *156*, 156–7
Smith, Greg M. 82
Smith, Murray xvi, 4, 5–7, 15, 36n.7, 36n.9, 90; on alignment 44–5, 46; on allegiance 10, 44–5, 55; on amoral fascination 93–4; on empathy 66; on enjoyment of the transgressive 92; on fluctuating sympathy for Tony Soprano 55, 95–6; on moral centre and resolution 92; on moral emotions 8; on "sympathy for the devil" effect 73
Smith, Susan 69, 71, 74
snooper, Hitchcock's example of 70, 88n.7
Snoop *(The Wire)* 128
soap operas 117n.1, 133–4, 152–3, 158
social judgments 17
social realism 168, 169, 186
sociopaths, and talk therapy 54
Sons of Anarchy *(Sons of Anarchy)* morally preferable to rapist 130, 147n.11
Sons of Anarchy xi, xviii, 104, 129–30, *130*, 147n.11, 170

The Sopranos xi, xvi, 65, xixn.1; and amoral fascination 93–4; bad fans of 113; British men's engagement with 96, 180n.20; Carroll and Smith on 7; ending, treatment of family in 181n.37; FBI as "bad guys" in 39, *51*, 62n.22; female characters in 153–6; loyalty and partiality in 48, 52; misogyny in 91; partiality in 39; post-hoc ethical discussions about 107; as primetime feminism 118n.6; producers' drive to copy 109–10; as Quality TV realism 180n.20; reality checks and undermining of sympathy in 93, 109; self-awareness in 53–6; and soap operas 152–3; as work of postmodern iron 116
spectator engagement. *See* engagement
splatter films 138
Stanfield, Peter xixn.1
star system, and allegiance 6, 10
stories: desired to be engaging 76 (*see also* narrative desires); expectation of justice within 8–9; literary *vs.* news 31; multiple plotlines, in series with female protagonists 147n.24; rape plots in soap operas 133–4; retaliation in 36n.10; schemas, as substitutes for moral monitoring 59–60; situational model 29
Strangers on a Train 68
Straw Dogs 133
stress, and suspense 64, 65
structure: moral, of antihero series 92; narrative, and non-moral factors 167; question-response, of film 89n.15; of suspense, in *Breaking Bad* 80–3; of sympathy 4, 36n.9, 123–4
stylistic features: corroboration of character engagement through 82–3; and dullness of family life in *Breaking Bad* 89n.16
subscription channels xii
subversion of suspense. *See* suspense, moral inversion of
Sunset Boulevard 105
suspense xvii, xix, 4, 34, 61, 64–6, 78; and antagonist's virtues 67; and audience desire for the transgressive 83, 167; classical 67–8; direct 69; fits and starts of, in *Breaking Bad* 82–3, 84–7; fostered by characters' moral complexity 103; heightened by chases and escapes 78; Hitchcockian

68–74; moral inversion of xvii–xviii, 69, 74, 75, 77–80, 86, 87, 88n.8; naturally engaging 76; of postponed revenge 130; shared 69; structure of, in *Breaking Bad* 80–3; undermining rational evaluation of antihero 90; vicarious 69
suspension of moral judgment and values 6, 55. *See also* bracketing
sympathetic allegiance 65, 74
sympathetic engagement 77
sympathy 36n.11, 90, 102; aesthetic appreciation augmented by tests of 110; creation of 66; denied to rapists 140; and engagement with fiction 77; and gangster genre 28; non-moral factors contributing to 24; overlap with empathy 64; with serial killer, evoked by burlesque and black humour 90; with Skyler White (*Breaking Bad*) prevention of 156–69; with Tony Soprano (*The Sopranos*) 7, 28, 39, 48, 54, 57; undermined by reality checks 33–4, 66, 92, 109–10, 112, 115–16; *vs.* liking and allegiance 10–11, 64; with Walter White (*Breaking Bad*) 39, 56–8, 74, 161
"sympathy for the devil" effect 73–4, 76, 101
sympathy structure 4, 36n.9, 56–8; effect of rape on, in *The Wire* 123–4
systematic processing 32, 38n.31. *See also* rational moral evaluation
syuzhet xxn.5

taboo violations 16, 19
talking pillow scene, in *Breaking Bad* 81–2, 156, 156–7
Tan, Ed S. 89n.14, 108
Taylor, Aaron 89n.12, 105
teen drama series, villainous rapists in 135
testosterone 99, 101
Thompson, Robert xi–xii
Thornhill, R. 135
thriller/horror genre xixn.1
Tony Soprano (*The Sopranos*) xvii, 1, 143; and allure of the transgressive 7; animal nature of 93, 183; antagonists to 39; beats Ralph to death 96–7, 98–9; and Dr Melfi 52–6, 93, 168; family as excuse 40; humiliates Dr Kennedy 45–6, *46*, 47; paradoxical appeal of 95; and power

99, 101; relationship with his mother 48; as rough hero 110, 118n.26; sympathy with 7, 28, 39, 48, 54, 57
Tracee (*The Sopranos*) 96–7, 153–4
tragedy: narrative desire in 75; paradox of 37n.23
transgressive, allure of 7, 87, 96, 98; as aesthetic appreciation 91; enhanced by intermittent suspense sequences 83; Murray Smith on 92; spoilsport role of antihero's wife 151, 158, 167. *See also* immorality
Treme 146–7n.2
trolley problem 20–2, 37n.20
trust 97; and friendship 52
Tuco (*Breaking Bad*) 56, 83
Turiel, Elliot 15–16
TV: antihero series (*see* antihero series); Quality (*see* Quality TV); regular (*see* regular TV)
Tversky, Amos 18
12 Years a Slave 148n.32
"two brothers" story experiment 9
"two princes" story experiment 9

uncertainty: felicitous effect of 104; and suspense 67
understanding, and friendship 52
universal principles, role of in Western moral systems 141
unnatural acts, and moral disgust 137, 142, 143

Vaage, Margrethe Bruun 42–3
values, suspension of 6. *See also* bracketing
vengeance. *See* punishment; revenge
Vernezze, Peter J. 49
Veronica Mars 135
vicarious suspense 69
Vic Mackey (*The Shield*) 99, 128
victim of rape: blaming of 144–5; lack of attention to, in TV series 123
video games 35, 60
vigilantism, and sexual assault revenge 127–8, 129, 130–1, 132
villains: aesthetic appreciation of 91, 105, 106; antipathy towards 120; fascination with 95; flamboyant grandeur of 183; melodramatic 105–7; morally worse 120; narratively desirable 103; and purity violations 148n.34; rapists as 126, 135, 147n.5 (*see also* antagonists)

216   *Index*

violence: in media 101, 118n.16; sexual, in everyday life 122 (*see also* rape); against women, rape typically seen as 148n.32

virtues, antagonist's, and suspense 67

VMPFC brain area 22, 24

Walter, Jr. *(Breaking Bad)* 81, 159–60

Walter Kendrick *(Damages)* 177

Walter White *(Breaking Bad)* xvii, xviii, 1; asserts his power to Skyler 160; attraction to 108; bad fans' reaction to 113; in comical suspense sequences 78, 79; double life 157; at end of series 181n.37; enjoyment of power 101–2; "for the family" excuse 40, 172; goes after Tuco with Jesse 83; and power 99; rooting for, encouraged by suspense sequences 82; search for drugs 64, 65; sympathy with 39, 56–8, 74; transformation of, into Heisenberg 77, 82, 86, 89n.16, 182

Walton, Kendall L. 24

Wee-Bey *(The Wire)* 123, 125, 126

Weeds xix, 151, 171, 173, 174, 181n.28, 181n.37, 185

WEIRD moralities 148n.35

White Heat xiv

"Who *are* you" question 157, *158*, 172

Williams, Linda 154, 179n.5

will to power 107, 183

The Wire xi, xviii, 147n.21; melodrama in 179n.5; rape in 120–3, 124–7; sexual abuse in 128–9; as social realism 168

wish-fulfilment 101

wives of antiheroes xix, 87, 118n.32; enjoyable 169–71; Kevin *(Nurse Jackie)* as reversal of 173–4; as objects of antipathy 150, 159; as obstacle to audience enjoyment of transgression 151, 158; transgressive 169–71

women: as antiheroes xix, 151, 171–4; misogyny in *The Sopranos* 91; and partiality, in *The Sopranos* 48–9; Quality TV and the feminine sphere 152–6; rape as typically violence against 148n.32; in series with multiple plotlines 147n.24; unhappy homemaker 157; working, predominant in TV series 179n.2. *See also* rape; wives of antiheroes; *individual female characters*

"women's film" in reverse, *Breaking Bad* as 164

Wundt, Wilhelm 43, 44

Zajonc, Roger 42, 43

Zeller-Jacques, Martin 112

Zillmann, Dolf 8, 66, 67, 73

Zwann, Rolf 31, 34, 37n.30